EDITH CRAIG

(1869–1947)

DRAMATIC LIVES

Katharine Cockin

D1339976

CASSELL
London and Washington

For a catalogue of related titles in our
Sexual Politics list
please write to us at an address below

Cassell
Wellington House
125 Strand
London WC2R 0BB

PO Box 605
Herndon, VA 20172

© Katharine Cockin 1998

All rights reserved. No part of this publication may be reproduced or transmitted in any form or
by any means, electronic or mechanical, including photocopying, recording or any information
storage or retrieval system, without prior permission in writing from the publishers.

First published 1998

British Library Cataloguing-in-Publication Data
A catalogue record for this book is available from the British Library.

Library of Congress Cataloging-in-Publication Data
Cockin, Katharine, 1963–
    Edith Craig (1869–1947): dramatic lives / Katharine Cockin.
        p.   cm.
    Includes bibliographical references and index.
    ISBN 0-304-33645-9 (hardcover). — ISBN 0-304-33644-0 (pbk.)
    1. Craig, Edith, 1869–1947.   2. Theatrical producers and
directors—Great Britain—Biography.   3. Actors—Great Britain—
Biography.   I. Title.
PN2598.C84C63   1998
792'.0233'092–dc21
    [B]   97-22464
                                                                                          CIP

ISBN 0-304-33645-9 (hardback)
        0-304-33644-0 (paperback)

Typeset by BookEns Ltd., Royston, Herts.
Printed and bound in Great Britain by Biddles Limited, Guildford and King's Lynn.

CONTENTS

ACKNOWLEDGEMENTS

My research on Edith Craig's life developed from my doctoral research on the Pioneer Players which began in 1988, funded by a British Academy Major State Studentship. Thanks are also due to the Society for Theatre Research which subsidized my research visits through a research award in 1990. I am honoured to have been appointed by the Open University to the Elizabeth Howe Memorial Research Fellowship. I am grateful to Angela V. John, Ann Riley and Steve Barlow for reading the manuscript and providing helpful comments.

I am indebted to Margaret Weare, Custodian of the Ellen Terry Memorial Museum, Smallhythe Place, Tenterden, Kent who gave me the opportunity to work on the Edith Craig Archive, and to John Chesshyre, Historic Buildings Representative, and the National Trust for employing me to continue my indexing project on the Edith Craig Archive in 1996. During this period Leicester University Library kindly agreed to house the Archive temporarily. I am grateful to the library and its staff for accommodating my work.

In the eight years of research during which this book has taken shape, I have visited numerous libraries and institutions to which I owe thanks. These include the late British Theatre Association Library, the Fawcett Library, the British Library, the Theatre Museum, the Bodleian Library, and the Mander and Mitchenson Theatre Collection. In addition to the Edith Craig Archive at the Ellen Terry Memorial Museum, I have studied the Eleanor Adlard papers at Gloucestershire Records Office and the Gilbert Murray Papers at the Bodleian Library, Oxford. I would like to thank the Shakespeare Society of Cheltenham for permitting access to the British Empire Shakespeare Society records in Gloucestershire Record Office.

At an early stage in my research I had the very great pleasure and privilege to interview Sir Donald Sinden and the late Athene Seyler. It has also been my good fortune to study one of the Pioneer Players' scrap albums thanks to the generosity of its owner, Raymond Mason. The kindness of strangers is always inspiring. I would like to thank everyone who replied to my requests for help. Lack of space prohibits naming everyone, but they include: Frances Briggs, for recollections of the British Drama League; Cynthia Carey (née Sirman) and Joan Webb for recollections of Edith Craig; Joy Dixon, Toni Wintle and Melinda Boyd Parsons for information on Pamela Colman Smith; Marij von Helmond for details of *A Pageant of Great Women* in Liverpool; Leah Leneman for information about the suffragette arboretum in Batheaston; Edward Rollinson, biographer of Sydney Valentine, for many helpful letters; Ruth Tomalin for a copy of a letter from Kate Gielgud to Christopher St John in her possession; Claire Tylee for many supportive letters and information from the Harry Ransom Humanities Research Centre, Austin, Texas; Gail Harris and the late Kathleen Barker for information from the Margaret Webster papers in the Library of Congress, Washington.

For helpful responses to my queries I would like to thank: County Records, East Sussex County Council; Gloucestershire Record Office; Hastings Reference Library; Kent County Council, Arts and Libraries; Mitchell Library, Glasgow; Nottinghamshire Archives and Southwell Diocesan Record Office; Nottinghamshire County Council, Local Studies Library; University of Bristol, Theatre Collection; Historical Association, Bristol; National Army Museum, Chelsea; Glasgow City Council Library and Archives; University of Glasgow Archives; and the British Film Institute. The Kent and East Sussex branch of the Women's Institute kindly published my request for information in their newsletter.

Many research trips were made possible by the hospitality and accommodation provided by: Mary and John Cockin; Celia and Giovanni Coltella of the Collina House Hotel, Tenterden; Ann and Mark Riley; Karen and Gary Seabourne; Adrienne and Derek Ware; and Margaret and Anthony Weare.

Photographs of documents held at the Ellen Terry Memorial Museum, Tenterden, Kent, are reproduced by permission of the National Trust, which has also kindly allowed me to quote from documents. Full publication details of quoted material are provided in the notes. However, in addition, I would like to thank the following sources for allowing me to reproduce material: the executors of the estate of Virginia Woolf; the Society of Authors on behalf of the estate of

Bernard Shaw; letters from W. B. Yeats in *The Collected Letters of W. B. Yeats Volume 3*, ed. John Kelly and Ronald Schuchard, 1994, by permission of Oxford University Press; Margaret Webster, *The Same Only Different*, Gollancz, 1969, by permission of John Johnson Ltd; *Letters of Max Beerbohm*, ed. Rupert Hart-Davis, 1989, by permission of John Murray Ltd.; Alison Roberts, *Hathor Rising: The Serpent Power of Ancient Egypt*, 1995, by permission of Northgate publishers; my thanks to Frances and Martin Pym for permission to quote from Violet Pym's speech. Every effort has been made to trace all the copyright-holders, but if any have been inadvertently overlooked the publishers will be pleased to make the necessary arrangements at the first opportunity.

INTRODUCTION

'Who put out the light?' Loss of sight before loss of life was registered in Edith Craig's last words on the morning of 27 March 1947. No more appropriate epitaph could be found. She had expected to be in control of lighting and all aspects of stage direction in her theatre career but her achievements never seemed to reach the full light of recognition. Her work as a director has been overshadowed by her more famous relatives. The shadows can sometimes appear to be a desirable place, a vantage point from which to observe and shift shape. This position was perversely sought out by Craig, as much as it was imposed upon her.[1] Obscurity has its attractions for the second generation of the famous. Any sense of freedom which this seemed to offer Craig mystifies the very real restrictions which have kept much of her work in relative obscurity. She was disheartened by the impact of what would now be called the 'glass ceiling', preventing women and other marginalized groups from reaching the top of their professions.

Edith Craig's accomplishments include many directorial firsts in British theatre. She achieved the ultimate 'first' of women's theatre history when, in London in 1914, she directed the first production of a play by Hrotsvit (c. 930–c. 990), a nun from Gandersheim (now in Germany), said to be the first female dramatist.[2] The play was translated from the Latin by Craig's lifelong partner, Christopher St John (Christabel Marshall). The celebration of women's pioneering, as Michele Barrett has shown, often subscribes to an individualism and competitiveness which otherwise prevents the majority of women from achieving basic freedoms in their daily lives.[3] The value of being the first is questionable, propagating rather than challenging hierarchies. Being the first is also a vulnerable and

1

precarious position, to which Craig became accustomed. Her talents were diverse. Apart from her chosen role as a director, she was a distinguished costumier, an accomplished actress, a trained musician, a teacher, a fencer and a dancer.

The long shadow cast by famous relatives loomed over Craig's skills and achievements. Excellent achievements are relative and hard-won when the gold standard is close to home. Siblings and offspring of the illustrious often feel perversely compelled to take an extremely different path in order to avoid risking automatic, possibly unflattering, comparisons with their relatives. Edith Craig took the risk. She was the daughter of Ellen Terry (1847–1928), one of the first women in the British acting profession to achieve star status and a salary to match. If Edith Craig has featured in theatre histories at all it has been as Ellen Terry's daughter rather than as a theatre practitioner or artist. Terry acknowledged the effect on a child of a famous parent, imagining the burden of being Mozart's son rather than the difficulty of being Mozart's daughter.[4] Since the role of the genius has customarily been solitary and masculine,[5] it seemed to fit Edith Craig's younger brother Edward Gordon Craig (1872–1966) more easily. Although insecure and uncertain about other aspects of his identity, he could feel confident in himself as an artist. Nevertheless, Edith Craig worked tirelessly to achieve her own art of the theatre with whatever came to hand, seeing the potential artist in every individual. One of the most compelling aspects about Edith Craig may prove to be her ability to disrupt preconceptions.

The fieldwork for this book began by accident. A series of questions from an entirely different research project in 1988 led me to explore the phenomenon of women in theatre. This presumed gap in my knowledge turned out to be a gap in theatre history which feminist critics had already begun to bridge. My first glimpse of Edith Craig was provided by Julie Holledge's influential study, *Innocent Flowers: Women in the Edwardian Theatre* (1981). A footnote launched the trail to the Ellen Terry Memorial Museum, which holds most of the remaining papers belonging to Edith Craig. The Edith Craig Archive, a collection of several thousand items, had been stored in a trunk in an unused room in Ellen Terry's house at Smallhythe Place, near Tenterden, Kent. The house is owned by the National Trust, which gave me the opportunity to work on these documents which were unavailable to Ellen Terry's more recent biographers, Nina Auerbach and Joy Melville.[6] This project has provided an intimate knowledge of Edith Craig's papers. Getting to know Edith Craig has been a long process: reading her archival remains against published sources generated a great deal of curiosity, sometimes indignation, which motivated me to become, albeit reluctantly, a biographer in a period when biography has become a most questionable genre.

A. S. Byatt's novel *Possession* brought some light relief along the way, as did feminist work on auto/biography. The media's criticism (and in turn exploitation) of the pitiful trade of the biographer as exploitative parasite is only the most recent addition to a long-standing critique of biography.[7] In academic discourse, boundaries between fact and fiction, autobiography and biography have been explored by poststructuralists and feminists alike. Members of the Lesbian History Group have broken new ground and challenged many prejudices in their work on the representations of lesbians in the past, in history and in biography.[8] Representing 'the other' has been the subject of a recent anthology of essays.[9] Feminist work on auto/biography has employed the slash to indicate that the writing of any self is predicated on writing others. Thus the presumed, or attempted, objectivity of the biographer is always subject to challenge.[10] In foregrounding relative perspectives, feminist auto/biographers attempt to confront competing versions of 'the truth' about their subjects.

Constructing new knowledge about Craig's life and work from these remains has exceeded the cliché of detective work. The selective destruction of documents seems to have orchestrated possible narratives of Craig's life. In addition to an assessment of the extant documents in the Edith Craig Archive, this book will assess ways in which Craig has been represented during her lifetime and subsequently. In view of the prejudices manifested in some of these representations, it was useful to explore my own values and preconceptions. This has been extremely valuable and has raised some political issues which have been widely debated, not least in the politics of 'representing the other'. My particular interest in this project has been to explore the ways in which Edith Craig's life has been represented and to analyse this in the context of my unique knowledge of the Archive. I have at times been invited to justify my view of Edith Craig as political/feminist/lesbian. The assumption that, because the subject of my research was a lesbian, I must be a lesbian as well as a feminist, has raised some important political issues about overlapping and mutually exclusive identities and categories, about appropriation and advocacy. If becoming a feminist was a major transformation for me, researching the history of sexualities produced a further shift in my perspective. Exploring the heterosexual norm, as well as what 'lesbian' means, has given me a new understanding of the positions from which my narrative is constructed. A list of identities which may be ascribed to me (white, middle-class, female, able-bodied, English, feminist, heterosexual) immediately denies, through its linearity, my simultaneous sense of belonging and desire to battle with the way in which those groupings are ordinarily (and coercively) constituted.

This self-interrogation, raising some further crucial questions for my research, enabled me to move beyond criticism towards critique. It proved that the apparently wilful misrepresentations of Craig or omissions of her work derived from complex historical circumstances. Two questions became imperative. What representations of Craig were available for those who have written about her? What was it possible for Craig to do and be? She came of age with the New Woman, and reached her middle years with the women's suffrage movement in Britain. She belonged to the generation which survived two world wars. Biography often suppresses the notion that the subject is always already framed, not once but at least twice: by the historical circumstances of her life; and by the biographer's construction of that narrative. The constituting function of different perspectives will be explored here to point up, rather than evade or efface, the ambiguities in Craig's life, to bring to the fore the machinery under the stage and behind the scenes.

Myths about Craig will be identified and traced to the anxieties which produced them. The focus will be shifted from Craig's famous relatives to her partners, Christopher St John (d. 1960), a writer, and Tony (Clare) Atwood (1866–1963), an artist, as her chosen family. This is not to suggest that they imitated the nuclear family, but that they were, apart from Ellen Terry, the closest to Craig and the ones to whom she had responsibilities. Both St John and Atwood (Atwood more so) have been written out of Craig's life as a result of writers' inability to imagine relationships beyond the couple. Unfortunately Christopher St John did not take up George Bernard Shaw's suggestion that she should write the history of the *ménage à trois*.[11] Such a book is still to be written. Atwood and St John demand biographies. Similarly, the social and cultural milieu of Smallhythe Place – of Craig, St John and Atwood and the many women who worked and socialized with them in Kent as well as London – may provide a counter-history of theatrical subcultures which anarchistically and conservatively flourished in twentieth-century Britain. That many of the plays which Craig produced were reviewed by newspapers in Spain, Belgium and France suggests an assessment of the impact of Craig's work on world theatre would usefully expand the hitherto anglocentric view.

Meanwhile, and fully aware of what Laura Marcus has called the monumentalization of death in biography,[12] this book is an act of remembrance. Its publication in the fiftieth anniversary of Craig's death is driven by the desire to celebrate Craig's life and work and to invite a reassessment of the fields in which she worked. When disciplinary boundaries and old territories are reinforced a new generation of diggers is needed to continue to question the sexual politics of cultural practices and history-making.

The shape of this biography, following a roughly chronological path, is conventional. However, in exploring Edith Craig's ambivalent relationships with the shadows and the limelight, each chapter takes one step forward and two to the side, often following Craig's footsteps. The first chapter considers Craig's relationships with her mother and her brother, and the ways in which these have been represented. In Chapter 2, Craig's education, both formal and incidental, at school and in the theatre, is compared with the development of her approach to theatre practice. Craig's relationship with Christopher St John at the dawning of the New Woman, in Chapter 3, explores crimson weeds and green carnations as well as masques and devilry, in which the artist Pamela Colman Smith and W. B. Yeats had parts to play. In Chapter 4 Craig appears as troubleshooter in the women's suffrage movement preparing her for ten years as director of the Pioneer Players, a London-based play-producing subscription society which she founded in 1911. During this period, which is discussed in Chapter 5, Tony Atwood joined Craig's and St John's household. Craig's work nationwide, and particularly in Yorkshire, in the Little Theatre movement in the 1920s and in the Barn Theatre (at Smallhythe Place) established as a memorial to Craig's mother, are visited in Chapters 6 and 7 respectively. The final chapter considers the function of the pageant in Craig's theatrical career and dramatic lives, assessing the roles of the artist and writer, the fusion of church and stage, the sacred and the profane, the possibility of anonymity as an aesthetic, the necessity and intermittent pleasures of moving from centre to margin, between the acts and between the wars.

Chapter 1

THE LONG SHADOW OR ELLEN TERRY HAD A DAUGHTER

Edith Craig was not a writer, even though she had some published articles to her name. When asked in 1923 whether she had recorded her views, developed over fifty years' work in all aspects of theatre, Craig replied: 'I never write ... the stage is too much a part of my very tissue for me to theorize about it.'[1] Her disclaimer was significant, placing writing (especially theorizing) and living in mutual opposition. The notion that writing requires distance and time inconsistent with a commitment to theatre practice has been denied by many theatre practitioners. Craig was never confident about spelling; she enlisted others to act as scribe on her behalf. Her diffidence, however, signalled more than a difficulty with the mechanics of writing. The refusal represented a need to distance and differentiate herself from her theatrical family. Her brother, Edward Gordon Craig, had already published his views on the 'art of the theatre'.[2] The anxiety which writing posed for Edith Craig was not eased by the long shadow cast by relatives who were indirectly credited for any achievement she made in the theatre. For Craig, making her own way was important; famous relatives signified an obstacle rather than the potential benefits of nepotism, as one reviewer perceived:

> Children of famous people sometimes feel it a little depressing to be continually referred to as the son (or daughter) of so-and-so. Edith Craig ... is doubly 'handicapped' in this sense, for not only is she the daughter of Ellen Terry, but she has an almost equally famous brother in Gordon Craig. She hasn't let it worry her, however. She has made her own way in the theatre as actress, designer of costumes, stage manager and producer, and has earned an honoured place for herself.[3]

Anxieties were gendered as well as generational. Both mother and daughter shared a diffidence about writing. When asked to write her autobiography on the event of her stage jubilee in 1906, Ellen Terry 'was frightened' by the prospect of exposing her 'literary sins'.[4] Terry longed for the skills of 'artists of the pen, who merely, by putting black upon white, have had the power to bring before their readers not merely themselves "as they lived", but the most homely and intimate details of their lives'.[5] Her self-doubt proved to be misplaced. The anecdotes in *The Story of My Life* demonstrate acute observation of revelatory incidents. Edy's distinctive imagination was marked for Ellen Terry by her daughter's discovery of a radish in the garden that was apparently 'as big as God!'[6] In 'Pre-Raphaelite Pets', Terry's anecdote debunks the self-importance of the artist, exposing the perversity of Dante Gabriel Rossetti's unsuccessful collection of unusual creatures. He failed not only to make them thrive but also to recognize when they had died.[7] A dead white peacock was discovered under a chair; white dormice, displayed to guests, were found to have been dead for some time.

Terry was always writing. Her letters are characterized by a range of notations – dashes, double, triple, multiple underlinings – which seductively resonate every sentence with assurances of confidence about the self. Craig refused to write. She declined to speak until the age of two, just as she refused to define herself. When she chose, she made her views known. In 1907 Craig uncharacteristically published her ideas, making her claim to be 'the first woman stage manager on record'.[8] The year of speaking out was 1932, when the airing of her views became necessary following her brother's publication of *Ellen Terry and Her Secret Self*. In this highly iconoclastic version of their mother's life (dedicated, in defiance of their separation, specifically to 'My Father'), Gordon Craig condemned his sister, particularly for her publication of Ellen Terry's letters to George Bernard Shaw, describing Shaw's preface to the volume as an 'insult [to] the dead'.[9] Gordon Craig infantilized Ellen Terry as 'that little Nelly who was my mother'.[10] The 'secret self' of Terry was not claimed as Gordon Craig's preserve: 'Nelly was someone unknown to all but her father and mother, sisters and brothers, my father and myself.'[11] Intimate knowledge of Ellen Terry is, therefore, for Gordon Craig the family faultline. He explicitly excludes both his sister and Henry Irving:

> My sister never knew her, for she always persisted in looking down on what she held to be little Nelly's 'weaknesses'. She

preferred to admire and to cling to the more solid fabric, the famous Ellen Terry, even as did Irving, Reade, Tree, Shaw and the public.[12]

In order to set the record straight, and without engaging in an unseemly tug of war, Craig officially co-edited her mother's autobiography, *The Story of My Life* (1908), as *Ellen Terry's Memoirs*. To this end she enlisted the help of one of her two lifelong partners, self-defined 'literary henchman',[13] Christopher St John. Ellen Terry's autobiography becomes the revised story of several lives. St John describes her writing partnership with Craig as 'the work of us both in council (although the actual writing is by one hand)'.[14] The singular personal pronoun was chosen in order

to allow the writer in the partnership, for whom it stands, more freedom to deal with some episodes in Ellen Terry's life than she could have if she spoke for Ellen Terry's daughter as well as for herself. What is true delicacy in a daughter may be false delicacy in a biographer.[15]

From this strange hybrid text, the narrator speaks intermittently with the authority of intimate acquaintance and the distance of objectivity conventionally attributed to the biographer.

Writing, assumed by many to be the primary means, is not the only vehicle of representation. In the many other fields in which Craig worked (directing, acting, costume design, public speaking, political activism, teaching) diffidence was not a problem. Perhaps acting was the exception. She claimed to be 'audience shy'. As a young woman she is said to have had a lisp, but this never seemed to hinder her performances.[16] Craig's theatre productions were reported in national and international newspapers during her lifetime. Her activities were at one time so much in the public eye that her pet featured in the gossip columns. Journalists reported on the melancholy of her cat, left at home while she was abroad shooting a film in 1923.[17] The praise Craig received from many of her peers went beyond the congratulatory etiquette of the acting profession. Numerous letters survive to testify to her generosity as well as her expectation of high standards and complete commitment as employer, mentor, teacher. She directed many famous actors, such as Sybil Thorndike, Edith Evans, Harcourt Williams and Miles Malleson. Sybil Thorndike regarded her performance as Synge in Paul Claudel's *The Hostage*, directed by Craig, as the best work she ever did.[18]

Many of Craig's contemporaries acknowledged that her achievements were remarkable and often insufficiently rewarded at the time. Subsequently Craig's work, like that of many women in various fields, has become 'hidden from history', to borrow Sheila Rowbotham's memorable phrase.[19] It is therefore worth assessing the process by which such achievements become written out of history, or – less dramatically – are underwritten, undervalued. Inclusion can often serve, perversely, as an instrument of disempowerment. Craig's obscurity has been thrown into relief by the prominence of Ellen Terry and Edward Gordon Craig, a triad in which Edith Craig often becomes the misplaced third term. Many of those who know of Terry are even surprised to hear that she had a daughter. Sometimes the daughterly role has subsumed Craig in Terry's identity.[20] Although feminist criticism has attempted to shed 'new light' on women such as Edith Craig,[21] metaphors of discovery and revelation do not sufficiently address the complex dynamics of exclusion and marginalization. Edith Craig was not merely overshadowed; on some occasions she was rendered forcibly invisible, disappeared. This process of concealment and loss has left Craig and many others the unmentionable subject of omissions, not only hidden from history but also outlaws to it.

The unevenness of historical exclusions becomes apparent: Edith Craig has not been consistently marginalized. Where Ellen Terry and Edward Gordon Craig are acknowledged Edith Craig is usually omitted.[22] However, Craig features in major international biographical and theatre historical sources.[23] When she is cited, her designations vary, sometimes listed as 'actress' rather than director or producer.[24] She receives only brief mention in the autobiographies of those contemporaries with whom she had worked closely. Others failed to mention her at all. Although during her lifetime, Craig found her work was inconsistently acknowledged, most of her productions were reviewed favourably in national and international newspapers. She made the papers. Her directorial approach was cited as a characteristic style or method. She made an impression on the writers of her day.

The impact Craig made on Virginia Woolf and Clemence Dane is measured by their fictional representations of her. Jane Marcus briefly cited Edith Craig as one of the 'real counterparts' of Miss La Trobe, pageant organizer in *Between the Acts*, Virginia Woolf's last novel.[25] Julie Holledge goes further and implies that she was the actual model for Woolf's Miss La Trobe.[26] The editions of *Between the Acts* currently in print do not mention this possibility, assuming, perhaps, that their readers would not recognize Ellen Terry's daughter. La Trobe is a highly ambivalent representation of a woman striving as an artist against the odds, in a form (the pageant) and at a time (on the verge of the Second World War) when disruption seems inevitable, completion impossible. Sandra Gilbert and Susan Gubar see La Trobe as 'mysterious'.[27] La Trobe in many ways signifies the impossibility of art, the limits of representation and the oppressive and profoundly disturbing deferral of meaning characteristic of postmodernity. For Quentin Bell, Miss La Trobe is 'the rather louche, emotional pageant-maker, the last of those curious artists whom Virginia places as observers in her novels'.[28]

Woolf referred to 'Pointz Hall', the narrative which became *Between the Acts*, as 'an interesting attempt in a new method'.[29] For this reason it invites exploration, but critics such as Mitchell Leaska regard it as marking a period of failure for Woolf. As the last work of a suicide, like Sylvia Plath's *Ariel, Between the Acts* poses something of an embarrassment. In such circumstances literary criticism has tended to seek in the last fictional words the 'real' author as poetic voice or protagonist. Convention requires that the disintegration of the self is textually verified in order that suicide should not appear a commonplace response to personal difficulties. Thus reduced by expressive realism, the final work becomes evidence of the state of mind of the suicide. It is possible to see a further embarrassment in *Between the Acts*. Regarded as an artist, Miss La Trobe provides an uneasy comparison with Woolf herself. The biographical reductionism implodes thus. If La Trobe is interpreted as a failed artist and as Woolf's self-portrait, then Woolf's suicide seems to be explained by such self-doubt. If La Trobe is Woolf's study of the (representatively inadequate) artist in wartime England, this entails a critical and psychological distance which would seem unlikely in the disturbed last months.

Given the involvement of Edith Craig in Woolf's social as well as imaginative world, the significance of La Trobe and the pageant demands more analysis. Reading La Trobe as Craig instead of Woolf is ultimately unhelpful. It is perhaps more fruitful to suggest that Craig represented the kind of woman, the kind of artist, with whom Woolf had little sympathy but a great deal of curiosity. Fundamental doubts concerning aesthetics, politics and sexuality coalesced for Woolf around Craig/La Trobe, symbolizing a path not taken which could have brought Woolf an understanding of anger and rage as more than bitterness, distilled from melancholy into social action. However prosaic and embedded in the closed rituals of Englishness,

La Trobe's pageant of the history of England appears at first to be, it employs a devastating closing scene which turns broken mirrors onto an audience transformed by the experience. Afterwards, frustrated by the performance which has been her only social interaction, La Trobe (known locally as 'Bossy') goes to the pub alone.

While the shadows provided La Trobe with a safe, powerful vantage point from which to observe and direct her outdoor production of the village pageant, in Clemence Dane's play, *Eighty in the Shade*, the 'shade' signifies the marginalized place where the formerly famous actress, Dame Sophia Carrell, is dominated by her daughter Blanche. The play was written to celebrate the golden wedding anniversary in 1958 of Lewis Casson and Sybil Thorndike. The scenario was modelled on Ellen Terry's relationship in later life with Edith and Edward Gordon Craig.[30] The relationship between Blanche and Sophia is represented as alternately symbiotic and mutually destructive. Sophia believes that Blanche manipulates her as if she were 'Judy in a Punch and Judy show. She will pull the strings, and then she will put me away in a box between performances',[31] and suspects that Blanche 'is longing to get me back into the theatre, but for her own ends, not mine'.[32] Blanche resents the responsibility of taking care of Sophia, whom she regards as predatory, her routine encounters with people functioning as a sinister means of replenishing her sense of self: 'You were drawing in, drawing everything to a centre, your centre. You were hypnotizing your audience into surrendering its vitality. That's why you're feeling better.'[33] Meanwhile Sophia's son Kevin is portrayed as co-conspirator against Blanche. Dane's portrayal of Blanche as hating her father and unable to distance herself from her mother corresponds to the conventional representation of lesbian as deviant and immature, consistent with Dane's novel *Regiment of Women* (1917). Dane provides Blanche with no female partners. With this exception, the mother/daughter relationship in *Eighty in the Shade* bears some similarity to that in Radclyffe Hall's novel, *The Unlit Lamp* (1924), an earlier title of which was 'The Octopi'. The octopus metaphor more acutely describes the smothering of daughter by mother, ensuring that she remains an 'unlit lamp' by thwarting her desires both for independence and for another woman.

Many of Craig's contemporaries published autobiographies in which they are ominously silent about their association with her. Clemence Dane's Blanche is recognizable in some of the fleeting references to Craig's difficult personality. Allan Wade recalls Craig as 'genial, a little brusque in speech, somewhat impatient, and certainly a very dominant personality'.[34] For Ernest Milton, the first impression of Craig was a woman who was 'disconcerting ... ruthless, but not devious'.[35] These references are difficult to interpret: doubtless her standards were high; she was prepared neither to compromise nor flatter. Craig was 'no appeaser';[36] she was notably excluded from Lilian Baylis's Old Vic Theatre because, on good authority, Baylis believed that Craig might 'upset the staff'.[37] Craig's 'disconcerting' effect on others may have been sufficient to limit the opportunities she was offered. However, at least some of the silences about Craig and the alleged difficulties in working with her emerge from a cross-current of prejudices. A woman acting the role of producer was/is sufficient to elicit resentment from misogynists. Charges of being dominating and brusque can be consistent with a lesbian stereotype. Rosemary Auchmuty suggests that since Baylis had employed other lesbians at the Old Vic, her rejection of Craig was not likely to be an instance of homophobia.[38] Another possible reason for Baylis's rejection, cited by St John, is that Baylis did not want another woman at the theatre.[39] She may have felt threatened by Craig and did not wish to share power with her. Their paths were to cross at several public theatrical events. They were both official representatives at the centenary celebration of Mrs Siddons on 8 June 1931, where Craig laid a wreath on behalf of the British Drama League. Two years later both women presented prizes at the Ambassador's Theatre for the British Empire Shakespeare Society's annual event.[40]

The perceived injustice of Craig's exclusion from commercial theatres was voiced, during Craig's lifetime, by Christopher St John. After Craig's death it prompted the publication of a commemorative anthology of essays, edited not by Christopher St John but by Eleanor Adlard. Adlard had been responsible for suggesting Florence Locke's performance of Ellen Terry's Shakespeare lectures in 1933–4.[41] Many of the essays in Adlard's anthology ring with the kind of question posed by Harcourt Williams: 'How was it that Edith Craig did not attain a more permanent place in the theatre? She had the ability to hold a position as stage-director in any theatre of high standard.'[42] This question seems to have puzzled many of her contemporaries, even shaken their faith in meritocracy. In Craig's case excellence provided no guaranteed path to rewards.

The limited opportunities of employment offered to Craig had been attributed by Christopher St John to sexual discrimination. One of Craig's successful productions,[43] allowed St John to use a review in *Time & Tide* to publicize Craig's position, aligning it with that of Labour MP, Margaret Bondfield. Institutions which are superficially open to women find ways of closing doors:

> While I was delighted at the impetuosity with which these writers let themselves go over the talents of my friend Edith Craig, I was sorry none of them commented on the irony of her not being in control of a single one of London's many stages. Does Lady Astor's theory of 'sub-conscious jealousy' explain this as well as Miss Margaret Bondfield's not being in the Cabinet? If it does, the more reason for the women of England who are in the majority among playgoers to bestir themselves and give Edith Craig an opportunity before it is too late, of showing how many plays can reach and delight audiences, when handled by a genuine artist of the theatre. ... It is conceivable that the whole history of the English stage might be changed if Edith Craig could hand on to some young people working under her in a theatre the secret of her power to make a play alive as well as the less mysterious one of her technical efficiency.[44]

In Bondfield's case, the door was to be opened when she became the first female cabinet minister. Although St John's view was shared by John Gielgud, Craig's second cousin, who argued that Craig was resented as one of the few female directors,[45] Craig denied that this was the case: 'If you know your job there is no actor who will resent you because you are a woman.'[46] She even argued that the relationship between female director and female performer cut across gender stereotypes and possibly the flirtations of heterosexual encounters:

> A woman producer was better than a man where actresses were concerned because a man was often frightened of offending them, and thought they would burst into tears. With a man producer an actress was always trying to make the best of herself, but with a woman she was keen to get on with the job.[47]

For Craig the theatre was a different 'country' where women could achieve an equality not to be found outside.[48] She believed that theatre was the realm of meritocracy. Such views were inevitable, given Craig's position as daughter of one of the first female stars of the British theatre. Since Craig's role model was exceptional, it was harder for her to accept that gender was a divisive system; her mother, after all, seemed to soar over potential obstacles with the formulaic regularity of a fairy-tale.

Ellen Terry's first marriage in 1864 at the age of sixteen to artist G. F. Watts (1817–1904) was short-lived. Other differences besides some thirty years in age contributed to the ensuing difficulties. Terry referred to herself as 'the girl-wife of a famous painter'.[49] Her perception of the role of wife to Watts seems to have been limited to that of artist's model. The marriage came to its end. Terry recollects that their separation deed stated 'differences of temper', whereas 'difference of occupation' would have been more accurate.[50] She recalls her first marriage as if it were a dream, a time of enchantment, during which she was mesmerized as Beauty to Watts's Beast.

Once released from the spell, Terry was drawn into a second, other-worldly romance, which offered another opportunity to broaden her cultural experience beyond the stage. She regretted that she had had merely a passing interest in the famous writers and artists of the day with whom Watts brought her into contact. With Edward William Godwin (1833–86), Terry was able to explore and experiment. Godwin, unlike Watts, was able to move productively as an artist beyond one discipline. Godwin's work as an architect and designer led him to develop views on historically accurate scenery, staging and costume in theatrical production.[51] Perhaps encouraged by these new experiences and possibilities, Terry's love for Godwin was sufficient to risk everything, to transgress the mores of the time. She eloped with Godwin on 10 October 1868. They lived outside marriage and the metropolis, in Hertfordshire, where their two children were born.

After the seven-year relationship came to an end, Godwin seems to have attempted to kidnap his daughter. Joy Melville has identified the failed attempt, which was described by Terry thus: 'He tried by unfair means to get my little girl from me (I had offered to let him have the boy) and I now distinctly refuse to hold any communication whatever with him.'[52] Extraordinarily, Terry's response to such possessiveness was to bargain, and her preference was for Edy over Teddy.[53] Such pragmatism derived from the precarious position of a married woman estranged from her husband and the mother of illegitimate children. The uncertainty of these times must have weighed heavily. Ellen Terry faced social stigma as a 'fallen' woman. Nevertheless her characteristic optimism, as well as economic necessity, saw her return to the theatre and to achieve more than financial independence. A chance meeting with dramatist Charles Reade (fellow transgressor in a longstanding cohabitation, with actress Laura Seymour) brought Terry an offer of work and marked her return to the stage.

Terry's work at the Lyceum Theatre brought her into contact with Henry Irving, who was in many ways to represent the primary masculine role for Terry's children. Their biological father and their mother's legal husbands (G. F. Watts, m. 1864; Charles Wardell (Kelly), m. 1877; James Carew, m. 1907) could at best understudy the part which Henry Irving realized. Irving's masculinity was impossibly excessive, committed to exert control, determined to achieve. No surprise, perhaps, that Henry Irving's stage-manager, Bram Stoker, wrote *Dracula* in the image of Irving.[54] Ellen Terry's claim that her children 'were exceptional, and they had an exceptional bringing up'[55] is accurate and not merely a parent's customary boast. Dracula was a father-figure. Their mother was the most successful British actress of the day.

Terry claimed that her children prevented her from missing the stage during her 'six-year vacation'.[56] At a time when illegitimacy meant exile from respectability, she managed, extraordinarily, to raise both of her children relatively unscathed. This owed much to the power of storytelling, demonstrated in her autobiography *The Story of My Life*. An unlikely but fortuitous event in her own childhood typified events in her charmed life. She seems to construct her narrative as a talisman, a means of coming to terms with her own exceptional life. Terry and her siblings owed their survival to their mother, Sarah, who saved them from a fire in their lodgings. The fact that Sarah still managed to return to the stage proves the adage that 'the show must go on', but also signifies the economics of acting. A child saved, however much a blessing, must also be fed. Jack's beanstalk was after all produced from a very spare handful of beans. A jarring blend of the exceptional gift and the grindingly necessitous chore was to characterize Terry's life and to leave its impression on her children. If they seemed unmarked by illegitimacy they were deeply imbued with an expectation of hard work to do and the promise of dreams to be realized.[57]

As one of eleven children in a family of travelling actors, Ellen Terry acted professionally on the stage from an early age, accustomed to a childhood of self-reliance. Edith Craig shared her mother's belief in the benefits of childhood training on the stage and was sufficiently determined in this belief to be outspoken on the issue at a time when it was the subject of protective legislation.[58] Similarly Italia Conti, whose school trained the young Noël Coward, Gertrude Lawrence and Hermione Gingold, was concerned that the Education Act 1944 would restrict children's theatrical training.[59] Terry's earliest memory, seemingly not an unpleasant one, was of being locked in an attic room while her entire family was at work. This she seems to have accepted as unavoidable, regretting not that she was alone but that she could not join her family in the theatre. The Victorian travelling theatrical family, living and working together, differed from the middle-class norm. Children were seen, heard and expected to project their voices on the stage from an early age. Terry's own success and wealth meant that she was able to provide her two children with materially better conditions than she had enjoyed as a child. They were accustomed to a household with a servant. They were privately educated. Ellen Terry was later able to support more than one home, or 'bolt hole' as the artist Graham-Robertson called them: the Audrey Arms at Uxbridge, Vine Cottage at Kingston Vale and Tower Cottage at Winchelsea.[60] It was the fourteenth-century, former port officer's house at Smallhythe Place on the Romney Marshes near Tenterden which became the home, and subsequent memorial museum, of Ellen Terry.

Ellen Terry's children lived under unconventional conditions. They were sometimes overwhelmed by their mother's letters. She was determined that they should not only thrive but also prosper – in precisely the way she advised. At times Terry's multiple underlinings and dashes were less than seductive, more coercive. Terry wrote to Shaw that she despaired of her daughter and what she would become.[61] Consequently Craig suffered from the weight of her mother's exhortations: 'Re-reading these letters after the lapse of years, Edith Craig said: "If I could have done all Mother advised me to do, been all she wanted me to be, I should now be a very splendid and wise woman"'.[62] They were expected to achieve, and seemed to accept, self-reliance and independence. In their mother's absence the children were entrusted to the care of housekeeper Boo Rumball (d. 1913).

The combined effects of a mother who was exceptionally talented, successful, but frequently absent, and who detailed her wishes regarding the children's every move, were to instil in both children an extraordinary belief in the possibilities of their lives. This was confirmed at the children's christening when they were reinvented, defying the patronymic and aligning them with other relationships. Edith became Edith Ailsa Geraldine Craig. Like the young Jane Eyre who felt affinity with sea birds, Craig was affiliated to the dramatic, but isolated Scottish rocky island Ailsa Craig. Her human guardian was her godmother, Geraldine Coleridge. Edward became Edward Henry Gordon Craig, associated with Henry Irving and Lady Gordon, his godparents, and through her new name, with his sister.[63] As a child Edward Gordon Craig believed that the declaration 'I am Ellen Terry's little boy' would ensure that a missed train would be halted. Margaret Webster attributed this story to Edith Craig,[64] for whom being Ellen Terry's little girl must have been a different and more precarious claim to make. Both children were made aware of their place in the theatrical world as Ellen Terry's children and of the extremely high expectations which their mother held for them. In many respects the theatrical dynasty into which Craig was born entailed privileges. Later in life she attended a Forum Club dinner in honour of 'The Clans of the Theatre', although she seems to have disagreed with the ethos of the event.[65] A wealthy, as well as resourceful, mother brought Craig numerous opportunities. This sometimes incited professional jealousies and detracted from the value of Craig's success.

Nevertheless, Craig had a life beyond her work and beyond her biological family. The antipathy which she sometimes met was attributable to homophobia as well as sexism. The designation of a 'difficult' personality to Craig, even bearing in mind her abrasiveness and insistence on high standards, provided a convenient mask for homophobia. The following article typifies the understated antipathy often directed towards Craig, but unusually refers to her mesmerizing effect on women:

> Edith Craig has not the famous Terry charm; indeed, at first glance she seems almost hard and forbidding. But that she possesses a charm of her own is undeniable; it lies deeper and is more sweeping in its effect upon those it captivates. I know quite a number of women who would unhesitatingly lay down their lives for Edith Craig. She is not only their friend and teacher, but their very goddess. Edith Craig's influence upon many of the younger artists of the stage is more far-reaching than the public would suppose. Like her celebrated brother, however, she seems fated to do the greater and more important part of her life's work away from the searching limelight.[66]

Craig's lifelong partners Christopher St John and Tony Atwood have rarely been considered as influential on Craig's work or life. If at all, they have featured obliquely as 'friends' or in references to Craig's inability to form 'normal' relationships.[67]

In many ways Craig defies the conventions of biography. Her life and work awkwardly challenge the orthodoxies of current thinking about the period in which she lived. She resists attempts to perceive her work in terms of the solitary genius whose achievements are concentrated in one field. Contrary to Julie Holledge's assertion, Craig's career was not a linear process of elimination, proceeding from musician to actress, costumier to director.[68] Each transition entailed an accumulation and expansion of her skills, rather than a shift from one discarded enterprise to another. Craig was a polymath. Her life was one of squirreldom, collecting talents as often as the clippings from newspapers for her scrapbooks, as Florence Locke recalled:

> Her critical faculties were enriched by her prodigious antiquarian knowledge. It was her delight to know everything down to the minutest detail of all the costumes, furnishing and customs of man through the ages. She collected pictures and clippings by the thousand bearing on this engrossing study ... Her collecting was by no means an end in itself.[69]

She collected pictures of theatres and stage sets, of renowned as well as obscure actors and performers, artists, politicians: Mathea Merryfield, a 6-foot tall American 'Fan dancer with many fans'; Signor Mussolini's daughter, Countess Edda Ciano with Douglas Fairbanks and the American actress, Laura la Plante 'Impersonating a boy' during a visit to Warner Brothers' film studios, Teddington; Hitler and Goering at a memorial service at the State Opera House, Berlin. It was a lifelong collection, begun when she was eight years old.[70] Craig's scrapbooks, described by Marguerite Steen in terms of Victorian convention,[71] constituted an artist's resource book of ideas. Some aspects of the collection give it the appearance of an informal research project. Craig's approach was visionary; it crossed disciplinary and other boundaries. It was hard to define, but Craig seems to have felt that definitions are not always desirable. During the most productive phase of her directorial career, she was associated in 1915 with an anti-theoretical stance.[72]

Craig's position was not, however, so evasive as to be unidentifiable. In many respects, like her brother, she was interested in developing a role for the director as single authority in the pictorial aspect of a production, but unlike Edward Gordon Craig, she did not see the director's authoritative position entailing a proportionate diminution of the actor. She brought to such an innovative role extensive professional experience of all areas of theatrical work, including the hard graft of set building and rigging up lights. She was artisan as well as artist. She gained the respect of her colleagues by knowing every job in the theatre. Like Bertolt Brecht, Edith Craig was concerned to rouse the audience, but the intended direction of the audience's transformed selves was for Craig never harnessed to one socio-political movement. At one moment, the issue might be the need to transform the law to grant equality to women in marriage. On another occasion, it was women's position in divorce which was the subject for critique. Craig subscribed to a fundamental humanism, a belief in the progress of the spirit. It was theatre, more than poetry or literature, which provided the possibility of consolidating communities after the First World War. The theatre, like English literature, was burdened with the quest for individual and national salvation. Nationwide involvement in the theatre at a local level promised to guarantee peace by fostering humanist values otherwise only accessible through the writings of the best minds.[73] Such values seemed to be more readily instilled through a communal experience. Amateur dramatics and folk song and dance were ideal.

As Cicely Hamilton claimed, Edith Craig's concern was with issues of justice.[74] She was not a single-issue politician; she would most likely have disdained the label of politician. When she took up an issue, her commitment was complete. Craig was well known for her dedication to hard and unglamorous work; she gave her time generously but in return expected commitment from others. She not only directed plays in support of women's suffrage but she also took part in street processions, sold suffrage newspapers in the streets, contributed to political funds and attended branch meetings.

Hamilton described Craig as 'a good feminist', mainly attributable to the example set by Ellen Terry. While feminism has always represented diverse positions, it was, for Hamilton, a movement to change society at every level – economic, cultural, psychological – to ensure that women and men enjoyed full equality, in their participation as citizens in a democracy and in their creative lives as dreamers, in an imagination not limited by gender. A commitment to women's suffrage and a denial of feminism (understood as a movement to change the lives of all women) was possible.[75] The urgency for women's enfranchisement on the same basis as that already granted to men was felt most keenly by those women who would benefit: middle-class, propertied women who regarded their enfranchisement as enabling them to represent working-class women. The enfranchisement of the 'angel in the house', Coventry Patmore's epitomy of Victorian femininity, could be considered as extending the moral duties of woman's concern with the domestic to housekeeping for the state.[76] Thus the social function and value of motherhood, and attempts to define and represent women as a group, frequently surfaced as troubling arguments in women's suffrage debates.

Some female suffragists were not feminists. On occasions, even those women who identified with feminist ideals were tempted to work with other women in a competitive and exploitative manner. Many suffragists were concerned only with the enfranchisement of women, not the total transformation of women's lives. Others engaged in controversial areas such as freedom from domestic work and child care, the exercise of choice regarding conception and childbirth, and the economic and ideological freedom to decide not to marry, to live a celibate life, or to choose same-sex relationships. This is most evident in the post-enfranchisement backlash which, as Sheila Jeffreys has shown, saw both the reinforcement of the social status of the family, marriage and motherhood and the condemnation of celibacy, the unmarried woman (or 'spinster') and the lesbian.[77] Ironically, Craig was to regret what she perceived as the limitations in her political activity, in that she had never been imprisoned as a result of her participation in the women's suffrage movement. However, regardless, or in defiance of, the normative pressures, Craig was continuing to live a new life with women which had begun in 1899.

Craig's party-political affiliations post-enfranchisement were ambivalent. She did not have Margaret Bondfield's staying power in the face of the glass ceiling. Ellen Terry indicated Craig's socialist leanings: 'Edy will plump for Labour.'[78] Margaret Webster, May Whitty's daughter, described Edy and Chris as 'the Bolshies' wearing red scarves,[79] reminiscent of the Russian communist youth movement, the Pioneers. The diversity of Craig's work and, seemingly, her political affiliations, are exemplified by two notable productions. In 1930, at Harold Scott's invitation, Edith Craig directed Upton Sinclair's *Singing Jailbirds* for the Independent Labour Party, the historic London debut of the Masses' Stage and Film Guild. In 1936 local Tory MP, Edward Percy Smith, asked her to direct a play (*The Merry Wives of Windsor*) for the local Conservative Party.

Did Edith Craig's political views swing to the Right in later life? Many women found party politics disenchanting even after enfranchisement.[80] Such anomalies typify Craig's life story and indicate her inconsistency, her non-partisan stance and commitment to the production/event over and above its political implications. The political attractions of these productions may have been secondary to the opportunity for helping friends. Edward Percy Smith was one of seventeen friends to contribute memories of Craig to Eleanor Adlard's anthology of 1949. He also published his own elegy for Craig.[81]

Such events in Craig's life point to the contradictions and

conflicts which are customarily effaced by biographers producing the inexorable teleology which is 'The Life Of' – what Liz Stanley calls 'an unseamed, uncontradictory whole'.[82] These anomalies, however, deserve exploring since they point up some of the ways in which terms such as 'political', 'feminist' and 'woman' become problematized by the lesbian subject. Party politics or single-issue affiliations failed to represent women who were designated 'abnormal' by pseudo-scientific discourses. More recently, lesbian critics such as Monique Wittig have explored the notion that the category woman does not represent the lesbian.[83] When homophobic discourse associates homosexuality with a reversal of gender roles, the lesbian is regarded as a deviant, an imitation of a man; her lover defies definition. Thus, Elizabeth Meese contends that a lesbian identity which rejects this homophobic translation of heterosexual roles onto homosexuality is shadowy.[84] Martha Vicinus has identified the question of the 'privileging of the visible as a sexual sign', the restriction of debate to public/published declarations in extant auto/biographies and a 'fetishization of difference visibly inscribed on the physical appearance of the woman'.[85] Vicinus points out the inadequacy of the two dominant categories of same-sex love: romantic friendship or butch/femme role-playing. In challenging debates about anachronism and what constitutes 'valid' historical evidence, she states, 'Indeed, I want to caution against focusing on what is said – either by others or by a woman herself.'[86] In considering what is not said, not visible, the uncertainty of the lesbian subject, the metaphors of shadowy or ghostly existence may be contextualized.

Not only is this version of Craig's life, as Stanley commends, 'a self refracted through others', avoiding the 'spotlight' approach to biography,[87] it also explores a number of deeply fraught and differently marginalized positions: the woman in theatre; the female artist; the feminist; the lesbian.

The inconsistent refusal of self-representation and a diffidence regarding identification extended beyond Craig's relationship with her formidably talented, famous relatives, and beyond the difficulties she may have had as a woman. Chadwick and de Courtivron have argued that the influence and creative interaction between partners in a relationship is a matter of 'reading between the lives and between the lines'.[88] Creative influences may traffic beyond the couple, towards the triad. Thus, describing the extent of the influence on Craig of those closest to her puts pressure on existing language, demands new terms.

Group identity in the *ménage à trois* – and beyond – was forged around a variety of names suggestive of different kinds of relationship. As St John recalled, 'in our circle ... everyone who joined it was sooner or later awarded a nickname'.[89] Vera Holme was Jacko. Gabrielle Enthoven was Gabriellino. Craig's and St John's first home together at 7 Smith Square generated the nickname 'The Squares'.[90] Their adversarial role was reinforced by the name the 'Bolshies', while Chris and Tony were known in relation to Edy as the 'Boys', the 'Serfs' or the 'Djinns'.[91] They were accustomed to playing – and playing with – a relatively subordinate role, suggested by Tony's ironically insubordinate allusion, which remained a lasting memory for Vita Sackville-West: 'Edy has bitten off more than we can chew.'[92] Chris and Tony as the Boys to Edy's 'Master Baby' or the 'Matka' were playing with gender as well as generational roles.[93] The transposition of power relationships within the triad through racial or class differences (the feudalism of the Serfs and the colonialism of the Djinns) indicates the pressure on language to represent their relationships. This imperial narrative is apparent in an eloquent account of the three women as a colony of trouts.[94] A signifier of eccentricity and age, the trout – a slippery fish to catch – also locates the difference of the triad at the extreme level of the species in their natural habitat. Many of those who knew Edith Craig, Christopher St John and Tony Atwood found some difficulty in describing their relationship and in representing the (different kinds of) difference which they symbolized. Perhaps most significantly, while others were often confounded by the difficulty of describing their lives together, they were living it.

In many instances, the difference was articulated in non-secular terms. May Whitty's description of 'Edy the Magician' attributes to Craig almost shamanistic powers of creation, while Margaret Webster claimed that 'Edy made herself a channel for the age-old "life-force" of the theatre.'[95] Edy talking was a captivating, Promethean event:

> Edy sitting by a gas-fire wrapped in an old (but colourful) dressing-gown, just talking – telling stories, discussing, recalling, planning, prophesying, throwing out splinters of ideas with every sentence, sparks flying from her words as if she worked over an anvil with a hammer and red-hot iron.[96]

Extraordinary sources provided reference points for Craig. Margaret Webster recalled a conversation between Craig and St John during a rehearsal of Susan Glaspell's *The Verge* at 31 Bedford Street, the

London flat where St John, Craig and later Atwood lived together, when Craig made the inscrutable claim that 'most rules for acting' were to be found in the Apostle's Creed.[97] Craig's reluctance to represent herself ebbed and flowed. She apparently dictated her memoirs to (an unnamed) friend before her death, but these are not extant.[98] This seemed to me to make the task of biography harder, certainly more imperative. Craig may have followed her mother's example in sorting and destroying her personal correspondence,[99] and Christopher St John (a historian as well as translator and writer) is said to have destroyed Craig's papers (and presumably the memoirs) after Craig's death. The papers that remain form St John's and Craig's archaeology of an acceptable past.

Craig's memoirs may not have survived but a life of Craig has already been orchestrated; other lives are to be found in the gaps. Occasional trails of intrigue flair up in the correspondence: complaints over noises on the roof from a neighbour; disputes over directorial rights. For some theatre productions a wealth of documents — tickets for plays, copies of accounts and lighting plots — seem to survive self-consciously as evidence. The historian's hand is at work, selectively recording significant events. Other productions are represented by a single playscript or programme fragment. Some evidence survives of possible factors which contributed to the unevenness of the records of Craig's work. Craig on occasion had acted as dramatist's advocate. W. F. Casey wrote to Craig demoralized by hissing audiences and scathing critics.[100] H. F. Rubinstein thanked her for supporting his play, which had eventually been staged after some acrimonious dispute.[101] The absence of papers relating to Craig's relationships and social life invites interpretation. Protective hands have been at work in shaping what can be known about Edith Craig's life.[102]

St John and Atwood compensated for Craig's reluctance for self-representation during her lifetime. Tony Atwood's portraits of Craig show her at work.[103] St John not only wrote about her relationship after Craig's death but also during her lifetime published a *roman-à-clef* in which Craig appears thinly disguised as Sally. *Hungerheart* has been read directly as autobiography by Joy Melville, Roger Manvell and Marguerite Steen.[104] It was, however, published anonymously in 1915 and while many of its events correspond to St John's life, its fictionalized form should be considered. The protagonist in *Hungerheart* is the victim of 'sexological' theorizing, a self-diagnosed invert.[105] Sally is presented as the detached, almost unattainable love-object, perceived as much in Petrarchan mode as in a guilty denial only rendered tolerable through Roman Catholicism, ritualizing and sanctioning internalized self-hatred. In her 1949 essay, 'Close-Up', St John writes of Craig as a saint, and her intimacy with Craig is represented in conventional terms as 'heavenly love'.[106] Craig is depicted in Franciscan mode, talking to animals and delighting in nature.[107] In St John's unpublished love journal to Craig, 'The Golden Book', she refers more intimately to their relationship. In *Ellen Terry's Memoirs* (1932), which St John and Craig co-edited, St John refers to herself as Craig's 'most intimate friend',[108] a term she uses elsewhere for Ethel Smyth's many female lovers. In 'Close-Up', she reiterates the story from *Hungerheart* of her prophetic first meeting with Craig, who 'did not put [her needle] down before shaking hands, with the result that I was pricked by her needle. Cupid's dart, for I loved Edy from that moment'.[109] The pain which instigated their relationship is essential to St John's narrative of martyrdom and, indeed, to her interpretation of her sexual identity through the lens of Catholicism.[110]

In the absence of Craig's memoirs or any other personal papers, any attempt to establish how she identified herself or described her relationships with St John and Atwood can only be speculative. St John gives the impression that Craig did not discuss her feelings, a portrait which is consistent with Ellen Terry's frustration with an undemonstrative daughter: 'She loathes emotional people, yet adores me. I scarcely ever dare kiss her, and I'm always dying to, but she hates it from anyone. It "cuts both ways" I assure you, the having an impersonal person for a daughter.'[111] George Bernard Shaw reported that during rehearsal he had no idea what Edith Craig was thinking.[112] Even St John concluded: 'I often felt that I had not the faintest notion of what was going on in her mind and heart and soul. She seldom talked about herself; she was as reticent on that subject as she was frank and explicit on others.'[113]

St John's narrative dominates and it largely omits Atwood. It was Craig's concern for St John's tendency to jealous feelings which prompted her to warn Atwood when she joined their household that she must leave should Chris object.[114] Although this seems to suggest that the relationship between Craig and St John at first took precedence, St John's representation of their life together emphasizes that it was founded on community and solitude, balancing their communal life together with separate spaces in which they could each work. Above all, she foregrounds the pleasure of their camaraderie, their differences from each other as well as their similarities:

Such discords as there were in our communal life were always quickly resolved. As we all had another life, apart, in our work, we did not really see much of one another. The fine point of our pleasure in being together was not blunted by excess of it. It always had the flavour of a treat, whatever its source, a meal in common, going to the theatre, cinema, concerts or picture-galleries, playing Mahjong, or Bezique, listening in, discussing books we had read, talking about all sorts of people and things, exchanging reminiscences, chaffing, teasing, joking, quarrelling. Different as were our antecedents, our characters, our tempera-ments, our talents, we belonged to the same world, the artist's world. That established a camaraderie which was perfectly easy, unguarded and spontaneous.[115]

The common centre of their relationship was membership of 'the artist's world'. The Smallhythe Place *ménage à trois* conformed to dominant representations of lesbians by identifying itself in relation to art.[116] In this context, the ways in which they individually identified with modes of representation seem to have been intimately bound up with their sense of their sexual identities. While writing and painting were recognized as arts, drama took longer to acquire such a status.

Unlike Ellen Terry and Edward Gordon Craig, Edith Craig achieved a lifelong emotional relationship. Craig's life partners were also inspiring to her work. Although Tony Atwood's self-effacing description of herself as 'lodger' suggests a temporary and peripheral role,[117] it is ironically her commemorative essay in Adlard's anthology which is most perceptive on the issue of Craig's relationship with representation, with music and art. She reveals that Craig drew her ideas rather than wrote them down:

Edy always had a pencil and it always had a point. ... This pointed pencil of Edy's was always in action. Her little thumb-nail sketches were much easier to work from and simpler to understand than written directions or long explanations, for Edy was a draughtsman whose sense of construction gave, in a few strokes, exactly what she wanted to convey.[118]

Craig's artwork was, according to Atwood, functional and technically adequate. The choice of the sketch rather than narrative may have signified provisionality and control. Writing and the proper use of its tools had a symbolic function for both Edith and Edward Gordon Craig beyond the straightforwardly phallic.[119] Two particular encounters illustrate the different anxieties which this represented for the siblings.

Edward Gordon Craig's relationship with Isadora Duncan was thwarted by his inability to tolerate sharing the role of artist, particularly with a woman. As Duncan reports, it was

> the waging of the fiercest battle that was ever known, between the genius of Gordon Craig and the inspiration of my Art. 'Why don't you stop this?' he used to say. 'Why do you want to go on the stage and wave your arms about? Why don't you stay at home and sharpen my lead pencils?'[120]

Edward Gordon Craig believed in the concept of genius but found it hard to acknowledge female genius as a possibility. His contribution to Eleanor Adlard's anthology, entitled 'Edy Playing', closes with a cursory claim for Edith Craig's genius attributable to family heritage.[121] Although the essay was written after brother and sister had been reconciled, it is sad to read. The intimate memory he recalls in tribute to his sister is transformed into a self-congratulatory piece, pointedly ignoring her theatre productions. As an onlooker, he describes Edith Craig and Ellen Terry playing a duet, reducing Craig's musical talent to petulant rivalry.

Edith Craig did not regard the servicing of pencils as the job for a woman. Vita Sackville-West wrote angrily about an encounter in which her attempts to sharpen a pencil met with an extraordinary rebuke. Craig's response challenged Vita's competence and her femininity: 'Seeing me trying to sharpen a pencil, she came up and took it away. "Here, give me that," she said, "no woman knows how to sharpen a pencil." You may imagine Orlando's indignation.'[122] This aligned Sackville-West with 'woman' but displaced Craig, described vigorously in the same letter as 'the most tearing old Lesbian – not unlike your friend Radclyffe Hall – but without any charms for me, I hasten to add'. Such indignation represents a clash of identities.[123] Vita saw Edy, but not herself, as a lesbian. Other differences were apparent. She appeared as one of the local landed gentry, guests of honour at a garden party organized by Craig. In addition to the likely distinction between theatrefolk and writers, Vita was also married.

If, as Marguerite Steen's book, A Pride of Terrys suggests, Edith Craig and Edward Gordon Craig were leonine members of a new aristocracy in the theatre, they were, like Edward VIII, holding court in exile. Roger Manvell represents them as rivals. Nina Auerbach sees them as Romantic and Modernist.[124] They shared many views on theatre but did not represent opposing sides in the Battle of the Books. They disagreed on where to place the emphasis, on the implementation and social function of their aesthetic. Their conceptualizations of modernity differed. So did the status of their ideas. In 1922 Edith Craig judged her brother's two models for *Hamlet* in the Victoria and Albert Museum's International Theatre Exhibition as 'the best'. This judgement is expressed in her own copy of the exhibition catalogue in pencilled marginalia, the most provisional of forms. By contrast, Edward Gordon Craig's views got into print, published in the foreword to the catalogue under the classic, formalist title, 'A New Way of Looking at an Old Thing'. The following chapters will contend that Edith Craig found a different way of doing just that.

Chapter 2

LIFELONG LESSONS

That Edith Craig's education could be different from her mother's was a benefit of Ellen Terry's professional success as well as improvements in education. Edith Craig was educated at a co-educational school and privately in England and Germany. Ellen Terry's education was in the theatre. She observed, learned by heart and performed the works of William Shakespeare, with whom her relationship was organic. At the Shakespeare tercentenary celebration in 1916, Terry paid respects to 'My friend, my sorrow's cure, my teacher,/My companion, the very eyes of me.'[1] She regretted her lack of formal education but had no need to. Her lectures on women in Shakespeare's drama and her performance notes testify to a detailed knowledge of the plays and the significance of the roles. Francis Turner Palgrave, whose anthology of poetry became well known to generations of students, was surprised by Terry's wide reading: 'she was familiar with much less well known poets as Arthur O'Shaugnessy, Richard Wilton and William Barnes; and that she knew and loved the poems of Blake, Newman's writings in poetry and prose, and the poems of Dante and Christina Rossetti'.[2] The collection of books in Ellen Terry's library, reflecting an enduring interest in the theatre and in literature, would have provided a rich resource for her children's home tuition. This was impossible. Her work demanded unsocial hours. However, the decision to send the children to school was more than practical; she was determined that they should receive better educational opportunities than she had experienced herself.

Terry's professional success and financial independence meant that the education of her two children could be very different from her own. Ellen Terry's was a life in the theatre from earliest childhood. Like that of other children in a travelling theatrical family of the 1850s, Terry's was an *ad hoc* education gathered from family members and gleaned from colleagues at the theatre. Private education by a governess or tutor, followed by public school for boys, was customary for a middle-class child of the same period. Twenty years later male actors were more likely to have attended school or even university.[3] For Edith Craig, a child of the 1870s, an adolescent of the 1880s, reaching the age of twenty-one in 1890, possibilities and expectations were very different. During her formative years Craig was instilled with a tremendous sense of the possibilities of a woman's life. In Terry's female household the abilities of women were taken for granted. The absence of men in this primal scene seems to have been accepted. It has been suggested that the household benefited materially from Terry's financial success, making illegitimacy and the absence of men seem less problematic for her children.[4]

Craig's unique environment gave rise to some high expectations. These were endorsed by the development of progressive education for women. During Craig's youth the content and purpose of women's education was the subject of debate and experiment. The advisability of vocational or university education for women and the implications of single-sex education as opposed to co-education were all live, controversial issues. By the year of Craig's death women were finally allowed to graduate officially from Cambridge University.

Terry sent both children to a co-educational school run by a Mrs Cole in Foxton Road, Earls Court, London. Some of Mrs Cole's students were to have distinguished careers. (Sir) Walter Raleigh became Oxford University's first Professor of English Literature,[5] and H. F. Rubinstein, later a prominent dramatist and solicitor, was notable for his defence of Radclyffe Hall's novel *The Well of Loneliness* (1928).[6] In 1883 Edith Craig became a boarder at the school while Ellen Terry was away on the first Lyceum Theatre tour of America.

Ellen Terry's accounts of Edith Craig's early years suggest she was an unconventional, independent, even other-worldly, spirit. When visiting France, she became absorbed in the atmosphere of a cathedral, claiming: 'Miss Edy has seen the angels!'[7] The customary use of the third person has been cited as evidence of Edy's oddness,[8] but the fact that Teddy shared this habit seems to detract from the interpretation. The ability to perceive the self as other, to stand aside and provide startlingly unconventional judgements and perceptions, may have been something peculiar to Edy. Perhaps more character-istic was her association of bravery with femininity, demonstrated by her response to her brother's fear of the dark: 'She used to hit him on the head with a wooden spoon for crying, and exhort him, when he said, "Master Teddy afraid of the dark", to be a *woman!*'[9] Edward Gordon Craig understandably bemoaned this abuse at the hands of his sister. At a very early age, Edith Craig did not associate being a woman with the passivity of conventional Victorian femininity; being a woman entailed a courage to which fear of the dark was unintelligible. This incident remained a powerful memory for Craig, surfacing again in 1937 in her public speech in Glasgow at a commemorative dinner of the Representation of the People's Act.[10]

Craig was to revise her views on what being a woman entailed. Acting like a Woman was something to be done on stage, but not by Craig. Her acting roles were 'character' parts, often for women synonymous with an unattractive appearance. Craig differentiated between acting the impossible part of the conventionally feminine woman (later vilified by suffragists as the 'Womanly Woman') and being the woman of one's choice. The feminine landscape of choice was a reality in Craig's early years. The possibility that all women might share in this pleasure was something towards which the women's suffrage movement was later to strive.

The extent of Edith Craig's pleasure in such female possibilities was matched by that of her brother's fear of its implications for masculinity. Edward Gordon Craig seems to have been dogged by feelings of insecurity and anger. After attending Mrs Cole's school, he went to school in Tunbridge Wells and then public school at Bradfield College, resenting this exclusion from the theatre, which he felt was the proper place for his education. Ellen Terry temporarily succumbed to his demands, allowing him time off school to visit her in America.[11] Edith Craig had accompanied her mother on a regional tour in 1880 with Charles Kelly (Wardell)'s company, but she was not allowed to join the American tour. Gordon Craig's trip to America did not mark the end of his schooling; in 1887 he spent some time at a small college in Heidelberg.[12] By contrast the sons of Henry Irving, Ellen Terry's colleague and manager of the Lyceum Theatre, were positively discouraged from entertaining ideas of a theatrical career. A theatrical dynasty was an unattractive prospect for an ambitious parent. After Marlborough Harry Irving went up to New College in 1888.[13] Even this did not insure him against the stage, however, as he became involved in the Oxford University Dramatic Society

(OUDS). He eventually became a barrister. Laurence Irving was educated privately in Paris and Russia. Only when their father's financial situation had deteriorated were both sons invited to join the Lyceum company.[14] Their reluctance was partly informed by the need to protect their jealous mother whose dismissive attitude to her husband's work in the theatre had apparently led to their estrangement. Florence's jealousy sanctioned the Irving boys' private reference to Terry as 'the Wench', a designation confirming their perception of Terry's precarious position in the minefield of Victorian sexual mores. Socializing with actors (especially female actors) was part of the repertoire of warnings dispensed by a middle-class parent, as Bram Stoker was to discover when he wrote to his father about a Parisian encounter with a Miss Henry.[15]

Although Ellen Terry's attitude towards her children's education was generally progressive, there were differences in her expectations for their futures. In a patriarchal society, the education of boys symbolizes the family's social status, whereas the education of girls becomes burdened with the expectations of women's role in society, imbricated in dominant gender roles. Education deemed appropriate for girls had long been associated with the prospective domestic duties of a married woman. Edith Craig's education brought her into contact with women who were deeply involved in the contemporary debates about educational changes demanded by women and working-class people.

After her co-educational schooling with Mrs Cole, Edith Craig was educated privately for a time at Dixton Manor Hall, Winchcombe, Gloucestershire. In *Ellen Terry's Memoirs* it states that Craig's 'education was continued in Gloucestershire at the home of Mrs Cole's sister, Mrs Malleson'.[16] It has therefore been assumed that Elizabeth Malleson (1828–1916) ran a school at Dixton Manor.[17] Malleson's husband Frank and daughter Mabel were managers of the nearby Alderton School for local villagers. Malleson was co-opted by Dorothea Beale to help found a Working Men's College and a Young Women's Institute in Cheltenham in 1883.[18] No record of a school at Dixton Manor survives. The family's move to Dixton Manor in June 1882 was made at a time when both Elizabeth and Frank Malleson were approaching retirement, seeking a respite from ill-health and a retreat from the activities of London. It is therefore unlikely that Elizabeth Malleson ran even a small school at Dixton Manor. Edith Craig's stay was temporary, described by Elizabeth Malleson's daughter, Hope, in terms of a place of safety. Terry's 'daughter was an inmate of Dixton for several years off and on during a time of home difficulty'.[19] The dates of Craig's sporadic visits seem to have spanned the period 1885/6 to 1890. The 'home difficulty' in question had begun with the separation of Terry and Godwin in November 1875. In 1881 Terry separated from her second husband, Charles Kelly (Wardell) after four years of marriage. The impact of the deaths of Charles Kelly and Edward Godwin in 1885–6 prompted Terry's letter of thanks to Elizabeth Malleson: 'For can I ever repay the "debt immense of endless gratitude", for all your good services to me in a time of real perplexity of mind and pain of body? ... You are always in my heart of hearts among the best of the best.'[20]

Terry's gratitude was longstanding, as Hope Malleson acknowledges: 'The bond with Ellen Terry so made never slackened though she and Elizabeth Malleson did not meet often or write for long intervals ... She used to descend upon Dixton for brief flying visits – a whirlwind of gaiety charm and affection.'[21] The unconventional aspects of Ellen Terry's life would have been accepted by Malleson, for whom supporting women suffering the unjust pressure of convention was a lifelong commitment. She had publicly supported George Eliot in her election to the Albemarle Club in London and privately made known her sympathy by taking her flowers every Christmas until Eliot's death in 1880.[22]

Elizabeth Malleson was an influential role model for Craig: she challenged convention and questioned authority. She was brought up as a Unitarian, but took an unconventional line even for a nonconformist.[23] Malleson's disregard for restrictive convention was a family trait. Her parents were involved in anti-corn law agitations and Malleson had attended meetings at Drury Lane Theatre in her youth. When she moved to Dixton Manor, a friend warned that her unorthodox views would not be welcomed by the local clergy. Malleson's response was emphatic. She replied that if she 'could not work with them she would fight them'.[24] Malleson's confidence had developed from early self-reliance. As a result of her parents' commitment to various social, religious and political movements, her upbringing had been delegated to her grandmother. By the time she moved to Gloucestershire, her confidence was backed by impressive credentials.

As early as 1854 Malleson had been involved in the movement for women's enfranchisement (a founder member of the London Committee for Women's Suffrage, of which John Stuart Mill was President), campaigns against the Contagious Diseases (CD) Act and the movement to provide education for working-class and female students. With Barbara Leigh Smith (Bodichon) she worked at the People's Elementary School in North London. In 1864 Malleson founded and acted in the role of Principal (although named only as Honorary Secretary) of the Working Women's College in 29 Queen Street, Bloomsbury, London. Unusually, as June Purvis states, it had an open-door policy, enforcing no minimum requirements of literacy, unlike its male counterpart.[25] Its evening classes provided for working-class women a broad general education. Class distinctions were minimized. An emphasis was placed on socializing between teachers and students as a means of education based on the principle of making learning enjoyable. Malleson in particular was committed to the college tradition and its 'pursuit of knowledge for its own sake, unrelated to any vocational purpose'.[26] Lectures at the college were given by distinguished women such as Elizabeth Blackwell and the classical scholar, Jane Harrison.

The issue of single-sex versus co-education split the college in 1874. Elizabeth Malleson took the less fashionable line, arguing for co-educational principles. She ran the Working Men and Women's College (incorporating the former Working Women's College), later continued at Queen Street. The single-sex faction founded a separate college (the College for Working Women run by Frances Martin and located in Fitzroy Street, London) which was supported by individuals such as Elizabeth Garrett Anderson and Lady Paget. It outlived the co-educational college, which was to close in 1901.

Malleson would have appreciated the performance of tableaux from the *Iliad* and Greek myth designed by Arthur Blunt,[27] but some developments in the Working Men and Women's College were not consistent with her principles. The college had been committed to the principles of the non-vocational motivation for learning (therefore no prizes) and no examination preparation for its students. Both of these ideals were brought into question, possibly, as June Purvis suggests, in the face of pressure from students. In 1876 vocational classes sponsored by the Froebel Society were given on kindergarten occupations and in 1878 students were prepared for Cambridge higher local examinations.[28]

Malleson's education at a 'Dame' school in Northfleet and the rote-learning at the Unitarian school of the Misses Woods at Clapton were less influential than the model of her spirited grandparents. Malleson recalled that her grandfather, Francis Macguire, a Surgeon General with the army, wanted his 'children to be educated after the method of Rousseau's "Emile" – the "nature study" which is now flaunted in the face of the teachers as a surprising new discovery'.[29] Malleson was determined to make learning 'pleasurable',[30] unsectarian and 'open to all comers'. Early in her teaching career at Portman Hall School, opened by Barbara Leigh Smith, she worked with the ethos of co-education and teaching all social classes together. Malleson sponsored 'habits of goodness' rather than a system of rewards and punishments, foreshadowing Maria Montessori in her commitment to 'self development in a suitable environment'.[31] Malleson published a monograph, *Notes on the Early Training of Children* (1854), on the subject.

An educationalist as well as a teacher, Malleson argued strongly for improving the standard of education for women and the working classes. She used a legacy to build the village hall at Gotherington so that villagers had a space other than the public house in which to socialize. At nearby Alstone and Alderton, she set up reading rooms and lending libraries and promoted 'technical education' such as needlework, hygiene, carving, laundry and veterinary work.[32] In 1889 and without the backing of Florence Nightingale, which she had solicited, Malleson founded and successfully organized the Rural Nursing Association (affiliated to the Queen Victoria's Jubilee Institute of Nurses) to ensure that trained district nurses were available in remote rural areas.

The story of Malleson's grandmother, Elizabeth Macguire (1775–1857), may have influenced Malleson's interest in the importance of health care for all, particularly the need for nursing during childbirth. Elizabeth Macguire travelled with her husband's regiment, and, while imprisoned with him and other soldiers for a year in France, had given birth to her eldest daughter. Malleson advocated encouraging middle-class women to take up district nursing. Although Craig was not attracted to this career, the stories of Malleson's grandparents were ones she would have remembered.

Stories were vital at Dixton Manor. The ability to entertain oneself becomes more acutely valuable in remote places. Dixton Manor was sufficiently remote to have been owned by the Lunacy Commission. It was not for sale, and had therefore been taken by the Mallesons on a long lease. A sixteenth-century stone house, overlooking Prescott Hill and acres of countryside, it is represented in two oil paintings (anon, c. 1730) on display at Cheltenham Art Gallery. The house is still recognizable and remains strikingly remote today. In Malleson's day, the shops and railway station were seven miles away, the post office five miles away and the nearest village a couple of miles away.[33] Edith Craig kept photographs, showing the outside of the house, her bedroom and the sitting room. None of these include people; they are empty scenes, formally recording the location, a sense of place without any faces. Yet the house and its extensive grounds promised adventure. Edward Gordon Craig recalled sitting on the roof. Dixton Manor seems to have provided Craig with a safe haven during a time of crisis. It also reinforced her belief in the abilities of women. Malleson provided a working model of social change.

While Edith Craig was under Elizabeth Malleson's instruction, Ellen Terry wrote that prizes might elicit some 'careful drawings' from her daughter.[34] Given Elizabeth Malleson's views on the detrimental role of prize-giving and her belief in education for life, this seems extraordinary. The enthusiasm for training young women for Girton College attributed by Nina Auerbach to Malleson seems misplaced. Both Mabel and Hope Malleson were educated at Cambridge University, and it may be that Terry was referring to this fact when she wrote to Edward Gordon Craig that 'all Mrs Malleson's girls are Girton girls'.[35] Terry was determined that her daughter should pass the examination. University entrance may have been intended to distract Craig from the theatre and, following Malleson's example, to take her into other fields of endeavour, such as teaching or district nursing.

Malleson did not believe, as Auerbach suggests, that self-abnegation was required from women in exchange for education. A much more pleasurable relationship to learning was a founding principle for Malleson. Her egalitarian ethos cut across class and gender conflicts and was characterized by a non-conformist scepticism, principles that are manifested in Malleson's work and in her publications.

Since Elizabeth Malleson set little store by qualifications, it seems unlikely that she would have shared Terry's disappointment when Craig failed the entrance examination. Edith's response to this failure is hard to judge. Perhaps by way of an alternative rite of passage, she was christened and confirmed at Exeter Cathedral on 11 January 1887 at age seventeen. She shared with Gordon Craig her geographical rather than family name and a godfather in Henry Irving.[36] For Ellen Terry, Craig's private christening in Exeter by the Bishop, Dr Bickersteth, signified the improved fortunes of the family. She recorded the contrast in her diary: how in her youth, when family funds were short, she had had to walk to Exeter from Bristol.[37] For Terry these different circumstances were determined by 'God's blessing' rather than economics.

Ellen Terry's insecurity may have made her more determined that her children's different opportunities might compensate for her own lack of formal education. A conflict arose, however, between the kind of education she made available for her children and the fields of employment this opened up for them. This conflict was perhaps more intense for Terry where her daughter was concerned; her daughter must be different from herself. A university education may have placed Craig outside, or differently within, the theatre. (Lilian Baylis used her academic title.[38]) The desire for Craig to be different was not fulfilled in the way that her mother may have wished: she was 'odd'.[39] Terry became determined that Craig should be an actress. She named her daughter for the stage, but as Ailsa Craig, after the remote rocky island, hard and cold – fixing for Edy the sense of her detachment and isolation. After some years of acting, the stage name was rejected by Craig – apparently to distinguish herself from another actress of the same name. In resuming her original first name, she confirmed her decision to be the same as her off-stage self, being the same as her mother but in a different way. The fields of directing and costume design attracted Craig more than acting. She claimed to be 'audience shy',[40] fearing exposure, judgement, comparison. She was a dweller in the shadows, backstage by choice as long as she could still be powerful in a limited but directed way.

Co-educational schooling and the prominent female role models of Mrs Cole and Elizabeth Malleson reinforced for Edith Craig the possibility, even the likelihood, of professional success and financial independence for women, for herself. Ellen Terry's belief that environment and training in observation were most important in a child's education must have influenced Craig. Terry's scholarship was acquired outside academic institutions; learning through experience, practice and involvement in work was Terry's pragmatic ethos and became Craig's also. In a letter of 1885 Terry made clear her educational ideals: 'Oh, work, work until one drops from fatigue – anything better than theorize – Talk – & not do = It's bad in a woman, but terrible in a man = .'[41]

Gordon Craig, by contrast, exhibited a fear of involvement and a sense of detachment from the theatre, about which he was keen to theorize but within which he found it hard to work. Ben Webster recounts the story of the spear-carriers' revenge on Gordon Craig who put little store by learning from others working on or behind the stage.[42] Webster found himself jostled and prodded by the extras who apologized for having mistaken him for Gordon Craig. Perhaps this fear of involvement attached to itself a fear of being compared and judged, a fear of losing control. C. B. Cochran, for instance, offered Gordon Craig a theatre for his work but was refused.[43] As George Bernard Shaw remarked, he cultivated a public performance in the role of 'Thwarted Genius'.[44] For Edith Craig a fear of not working was a primary driving force. Even while in conversation, she was constantly doing something else; if she ceased her activity she might cease to exist. This habit greatly annoyed Christopher St John,[45] while Atwood captured it in one of her portraits.[46] Craig's involvement in work combined an extreme concentration on the quality of the work achieved, and consequent selflessness, with a commitment to accomplishing complete control in the orchestration of the production; she was both autocratic and enabling. She had a fear of succeeding, more than a fear of failure. Failures had impinged on her youthful consciousness and brought out the pragmatism of the survivor, the optimism of a traveller.

After rejection from university, Craig was to be promised, and then deprived of, another possible career. This time she was limited not by academic ability or commitment to study, but by her health. Craig studied music in Germany with Alexis Hollander and in London at the Royal Academy. The sources have provided uncertain dates for these periods of study. Christopher St John states that Craig went from the Royal Academy of Music to Germany where she had studied music until 1887.[47] Her time in Germany in 1887 was spent in the company of Mabel Malleson, whom Ellen Terry seems to have felt the need to protect, warning Craig to 'guard against being selfish in regard to her'.[48] However, Ellen Terry wrote to Sir Alexander Mackenzie asking him to take Craig as a student at the Royal Academy of Music in spring 1890, after her return from Germany. Fellow student, Lena Pocock (later Ashwell) caught the attention of Ellen Terry, invited as prize-giver by Mackenzie to the end-of-term elocution competition.[49] Although Craig's musical career was thwarted by rheumatism,[50] she had added another skill to the broad repertoire that would be of use later in her career. In March 1890 her success in a piano exam to the tune of 76 per cent proved that this failure was relative.[51] By most standards her musical skills were excellent. Together with Violet Gordon Woodhouse, Princess de Polignac, Maurice Baring and Ronald Storrs, Edith Craig was named by the composer, Dame Ethel Smyth, as one of her most musical friends.[52]

Craig's time in Berlin was one of many opportunities for foreign travel she was to enjoy. In 1895, Terry was accompanied on the

Lyceum tour to America by her daughter, who had been a regular member of the company for five years. On Saturday 31 August they sailed on board the US mail steamer, *New York*, under Captain C. H. Grant's leadership. Even on board ship Craig's customary note-taking, more commonly practised in judgement of theatre performances, was at work. Her souvenir copy of the list of passengers is annotated with her critical opinion of fellow travellers.[53] Mr and Mrs Bendall, Mr Stanford and Mrs White, Miss Bessie Daly and Miss Margaret S. Gibson were all deemed to be 'nice' or 'very nice'. At the other extreme were Mr C. J. Abud and valet, who were stigmatized concisely with the inscription 'Oh No!', while '*Master White*' was treated with asterisks and designated 'Too sweet for words'. A case of mistaken identity provided a story which whiled away some of the hours at sea. While her mother was married to the actor Charles Kelly (Wardell), Edith Craig took the name of Wardell. Recorded next to the name of a fellow passenger on board the *New York*, Mr Wardell, was the explanation, 'who got my letter it not being addressed Craig'.

This was a time of experiment for Craig. During the 1895 American tour she began, or at least contemplated, a relationship with fellow actor, Sydney Valentine. He was already married and thus, in Ellen Terry's opinion, he was out of bounds for her daughter. During the trip Craig's friendships with two American women, Satty Fairchild and the artist Pamela Colman Smith, were cemented. Smith recorded, in the form of caricatures, something of the tensions within the company, representing herself and Craig as the 'devils' on the periphery of each scene. Published in *The Story of My Life* is a silhouette drawing by Smith, 'Our Adventures: Sir Henry Irving and Miss Ellen Terry on One of Their Provincial Tours'.[54] This depicts a disrupted train journey, capturing the moment of travelling actors off-duty, off-stage. The phenomenon intrigued journalists. One stowed away on a specially chartered train just to observe anticipated nocturnal visits.

For Craig the trip to America consolidated her place in the Lyceum company. At twenty-six years old and not before time, she was beginning to think about how her life and career, so far associated with her mother, might develop independently. The Lyceum Theatre had been Craig's school and she was ready to leave. For her stage debut, Craig had not been introduced to the theatre gently. Both of Terry's children made their first appearance on stage as walk-on parts in *Olivia* at the Court Theatre, a play which was to achieve a family significance. At nine years old, Craig made her debut a couple of years later than her mother. Craig showed a certain aptitude, providing precocious but influential advice on Irving's portrayal of the Vicar and an irreverent response to Tennyson's reading of *The Cup*, sitting on Irving's knee and laughing over his shoulder.[55] Perhaps more than many parents, Ellen Terry was concerned to help both of her children. She had a great deal invested in their success, regarding it as a chance to rewrite her own uneven opportunities in, and out of, the theatre.

Ellen Terry had sought openings for both of her children in commercial and amateur theatre. Possibly Craig's first exploration of the private theatre society was in 1888, while living at 22 Barkston Gardens. She was a member of The Mummers which, in 1889, gave a performance of music, drama and recitations at a Harley Street address in aid of the London Throat Hospital.[56] Ellen Terry was President, but the stage-manager was Jocelyn Brandon, not Edith Craig. Craig was one of the ordinary members, together with Terry's friends and neighbours, Dr Kalisch, Ella and Nelia Casella.[57] The private theatre society offered an opportunity for training in the theatre, elsewhere available only in the form of apprenticeships to older actors or as members of theatre companies, such as Sarah Thorne's at Margate, recommended by Ellen Terry to Gertrude Kingston. There was some concern to establish an accessible and regulated system of training for actors, but it was not to materialize for many years. Meanwhile, learning the ropes was very much a haphazard affair, dependent on securing the appropriate range of roles, sufficiently regularly to provide financial support, and performing well enough to reach the notice of critics and managers whose favourable opinion might secure a long run.

At the Lyceum, Craig was extremely fortunate in these respects. She had acted in many minor roles in a wide range of plays. Her Shakespearean roles included Ursula, *Much Ado About Nothing*; Jessica, *The Merchant of Venice*; Donalbain, *Macbeth*; and the King's Page, *Richard III*. The leading roles were invariably performed by Henry Irving and Ellen Terry. In *The Merchant of Venice* and *Richard III* she acted alongside her brother. Christopher St John dates Craig's permanent membership of the Lyceum company from 1887 to 1899. It was during the last seven years or so of that period that Craig worked independently with other prominent actors such as George Alexander and Stella (Mrs Patrick) Campbell. Craig's minor roles made an impact on some major theatrical critics. George Bernard Shaw's notice of Craig's performance as 'a rather sinister maid-servant' in A. W. Pinero's one-act play, *Bygones* (1895), was good but did not, for Harcourt Williams, pay sufficient credit to Craig's achievement: 'To me she projected a strange and intriguing personality across the footlights. Her voice had an individual timbre, not at all like her mother's.'[58] Eleanora Duse praised Craig's performance in the unpromising role of Niece to the Postmaster in Charles Reade's *The Lyons Mail* (1895), distinguishing her as 'the best actress in the company'.[59] In Leopold Lewis's melodrama, *The Bells*, Craig acted as Sozel to Irving's Mathias (1895–6). It was during 1896 that she chose Edith over Ailsa as her on-stage name.

Working in the theatre could be dangerous as well as exhilarating. Later in her life Craig recalled the use of unprotected gas jets precariously near to hanging draperies, which on many occasions caused fires. According to Michael Baker, during the period 1866–92, ten theatres in London were destroyed by fire and many female performers suffered accidents in fire-related incidents.[60] Craig remembered seeing stagehands, who had fallen asleep on the great canvas gas containers, being abruptly woken up as the gas ran out and their improvised beds, deflating, brought them sharply to the floor. The mishaps she recalls evoke the pressures a young actor faced in trying to find her feet amongst the company of actors and stagehands and in conforming (or not) to rigorous stage discipline. She negotiated what may have been a dangerous initiation ceremony after the advent of electric lighting. When acting in *King Arthur* she recalled, 'It was considered great fun to make the current spark up and down the metal parts' of her chain-mail costume.[61] However, the need for self-discipline as an actor was brought home to her when she was sacked from the Adelphi Theatre for laughing on stage. William Terris was so incensed by this news that he threatened to punch the manager of the theatre on the nose. In Craig's own categorization of actresses (great geniuses, beautiful actresses and useful actresses) she would have placed herself in the latter category.

Craig's experience of acting small roles while observing the most distinguished performances of major roles spanned a broad range of plays – Shakespearean comedy, tragedy and history, the naturalist drama of Pinero, Sardou and Reade, the melodrama of Lewis, the symbolist drama of Maurice Maeterlinck. By 1895 Edith Craig was already the subject of an unsigned biographical portrait. Her acting career to date listed her roles thus: Gentlewoman, *Henry VIII*; Clarissant, *King Arthur*; Jessica, *Merchant of Venice*; Ursula, *Much Ado About Nothing*; Bella, *Bygones*; Gypsy, *Olivia*; and Donalbain,

Macbeth. The latter marked a shift in theatrical tradition: 'In *Macbeth*, revived for a brief period last July, Sir Henry Irving reverted to the tradition which assigns Donalbain to a lady. In 1888–9 the part was played by Mr Martin Harvey.'[62] Harcourt Williams judged two of Craig's performances first rate: Saart in Christopher St John's translation of Herman Heijermans's *The Good Hope*; and the bishop's wife in George Bernard Shaw's *Getting Married*.[63]

The Lyceum Theatre production of Victorien Sardou's *Robespierre* (1899) was a turning point in Craig's career, as Joy Melville has suggested.[64] Craig's involvement went beyond her performance in the role of Madame de Lavergne. Irving asked her to make all of the costumes and they were judged to be a success. Craig had long been involved in arranging her mother's costumes. She made her own costume as Jessica in *The Merchant of Venice* with an ingenious arrangement of scarves that it defied May Whitty to reproduce when she acted as understudy.[65] Craig had already gained Irving's trust, producing some inspirational touches in costume design, such as the wreath of oak leaves for Coriolanus and a scarf for Shylock. In 1898 she had been trusted with a mission to Paris to make a prompt book of *Cyrano de Bergerac*.[66] From 1900 to 1906 her involvement in London theatre was more frequently in the capacity of costumier than as actor. Craig believed that costumes should be designed and made by the same person, and on many occasions she is acknowledged for both tasks. She had experience of working to someone else's designs when she supervised the making of costumes to Walter Crane's design for *The Snow Man* at the Lyceum in December 1899.[67] Her work on Laurence Irving's *Bonnie Dundee* at the Adelphi Theatre in March 1900 was the first occasion on which she designed and supervised the making of all of the costumes.[68]

Edith Craig's interest in theatre costume gave her rare confidence to write on the subject, and the articles she published in *The Kensington* and *Fortnightly Review* reflect her commitment to historical accuracy.[69] It was essential for her that every detail should be historically accurate and the costumes should appear to have been well worn. Although she was critical of the anachronistic costumes of Lillie Langtry and Janette Steer in *A Royal Necklace*, she particularly regretted the shiny appearance of Louis XVI: 'What an effect might have been gained had he been dressed in the sombre and shabby clothes of history.'[70] However, Steer's cross-dressing costume compensated for the anachronistic errors: 'Miss Steer, who (I dare say from playing Hamlet) has gained a freedom of movement in masculine garb which many actresses might covet, wears a long Directoire coat (in 1787!) with admirable style!'[71] Craig argued that costumes should be correct for the period and social class of the character portrayed and she deplored the lazy practice of ignoring the design details of the back of a garment.

Craig's London work in costume production while Ellen Terry was working at the Lyceum Theatre has been characterized very much as a family affair. Atwood referred to Craig's approach to costume design as characteristic of her father, Edward Godwin, who had designed costumes for the production of John Fletcher's pastoral play, *The Faithfull Shepherdess*, in 1885. When she established her own costumier business, Edith Craig & Co., in Henrietta Street, Covent Garden, she was strongly supported by Ellen Terry who financially subsidized it, drumming up business. The credits for the business's work in London seem to begin in 1901. After Terry left the Lyceum and had taken the lease of the Imperial Theatre she gave Edward Gordon Craig 'a free hand' in the field of stage design.[72] Edith Craig's department was costume design. She also supervised voice; W. B. Yeats complained about the results.[73] Terry's lease of the Imperial was short-lived. The losses incurred by the extravagant production of Ibsen's *The Vikings* forced her to go on tour to recover financially. The play she chose was Christopher St John's translation from the Dutch of Herman Heijermans's *The Good Hope*. This naturalist play represents the tragedy of a fishing village exploited but struggling against the grip of poverty. As Terry noted, the play was modern and with the role of Kniertje gave her the first opportunity to play an older woman.[74]

Craig was subject to other influences beyond her immediate family at this time. In addition to the review article for *The Kensington*, she developed her talent in the third of her categories – the useful actress – and learned a great deal about a fourth category which she failed to mention: the unruly actress.

Towards the end of Craig's nine years of apprenticeship with the Lyceum Theatre she acted as servant to Stella (Mrs Patrick) Campbell's Melisande in Maeterlinck's *Pelleas and Melisande* in 1898–9. The play shows love to be overpowering, proprietorial and deadly. Woman is beautiful, driven, uncontrollable, initiating a deadly chain of events which fundamentally disrupts all relationships: within marriage, within biological family relationships, within the kingdom. A *femme fatale* on stage might serve a warning that a well-ordered society expects to contain disruptive forces, of which women are taken to be representative. Playing a female character who has such a profound social effect (albeit deadly and self-destructive) might be more attractive than the docile cyphers whose function is to represent women's ineffectiveness. Unfortunately the satisfaction of playing the *femme fatale* could only be short-lived: the cost of even temporary disruption is the inevitable death or destruction of the female character.

Some aspects of Maeterlinck's drama attracted Craig: the critique of a proprietorial love which masks the trade in women; the representation of woman as dangerous and disruptive; the technically challenging, allusive aspects of the play, which tentatively explored a disruptive female sexual desire as well as fixing that desire in a deadly androcentric vortex.

Although Edith Craig acted in *Candida* at George Bernard Shaw's suggestion, she was never one of his New Women. It was her friend Satty Fairchild who was to relieve Shaw's tension.[75] Craig refused to flatter him and was even dismissive when he read *You Never Can Tell* to her.[76] In the Independent Theatre's tour led by Janet Achurch and Charles Charrington, Craig played Prossy in *Candida* and Mrs Linden in *A Doll's House*. Ellen wanted Edy back. She wrote to Shaw, 'It is so bad for her to be far from me for a long time.'[77] Terry and Shaw had arranged Craig's engagement between them.[78] The plays were shown in Aberdeen and elsewhere on tour and in London in July 1900 for the Stage Society. Since Craig had seen Janet Achurch's performance as Nora in the premiere of Ibsen's *A Doll's House* in June 1889, Achurch had toured in Australia and New Zealand, returning to Britain in 1892. Shaw's attempt to have *Candida* staged in New York with Richard Mansfield had failed. Achurch's unsalubrious habits (Charrington was imprudent with money; Achurch had added a morphia addiction to alcoholism) did not deter Shaw, but Mansfield had rejected Achurch and the play.[79]

Edith Craig's involvement in the play featured in Shaw's flirtatious correspondence with Terry. Terry had flippantly suggested that Shaw marry her daughter: 'Nobody else will. The ninnies are frightened at her!'[80] Shaw was to be disappointed in both this regard and in the production of *Candida*. Apart from work experience independent of her mother, the tour provided Craig with some worldly experience, dealing with Achurch's attempts to borrow money. Terry felt that her daughter had acquired a 'moth-eaten' appearance and worried that her involvement with the Independent Theatre would not bring the publicity much needed by a developing actor.[81]

The tour led to Craig's membership of another subscription

society. The Stage Society became associated with producing drama by George Bernard Shaw. Edith Craig was invited to join its council of management and acted in several plays for the society,[82] although her work during this period tended to be in the field of costume design. The Stage Society acknowledged her work as Mistress of the Robes.[83]

Craig's childhood familiarity with Walter Crane's artwork, from which she learned to discriminate between acceptable and 'vulgar' toys with alarming precision, was revived. At the Lyceum Theatre in *The Snow Man* in 1899 she 'supervised the preparation of the children's dresses after [Walter] Crane's models and no pains have been spared to secure absolute fidelity'[84] in the production. Fidelity and authenticity were keynotes of her costumes. She designed costumes for children's plays and period costume drama. In May 1900 she designed costumes for her aunt, Miss Terry, in the role of Rosalind for the Stratford Festival. The leather tabard was modelled on a picture by the artist Perugino.[85]

Craig's expertise in historically accurate costume was enlisted by the committee organizing the Kendal celebrations on the event of the coronation of Edward VII. There were to be illuminations, a historical fancy-dress cycle parade, a children's procession, sports and a gala. Craig provided costumes and wigs for the 'historical procession' of thirty characters consisting of a chronological display of English monarchs.[86] The inclusion of Milton's daughters, Katharine Parr and Elizabeth I, and the conclusion with Queen Victoria (represented by a Miss Lyttelton) disturbed the patriarchal line-up. In 1901 she designed 'remarkably effective and thoroughly correct Breton peasant costumes'[87] for *The Sacrament of Judas* by Louis N. Parker, later an expert in pageant production. Such Edwardian pageantry was characteristically enacted to confirm, with the authority of public spectacle, the right and proper place in history – and in the present – of each of the monarch's subjects.[88] It was in this context that Craig, described by Terry as a 'born archaeologist',[89] exercised her skills at Kendal. Although successful, the procession through the streets was reported as transient and inconclusive. It seems Craig was not on hand to supervise. This was rarely the case in her later open-air productions. While Irving would study a play for three months before rehearsals, Craig made a long-term study of pageants, adding to her collection of cuttings and sketches of costumes an extensive collection of pageant books and programmes.[90] This study was to come to fruition in the 1930s and achieve for Craig a nationwide reputation as a pageant organizer.

Another strand in Craig's varied career was founded in the early days, when another valuable role model in unruliness presented herself. Craig had been invited by Cora Brown-Potter (1857–1936) to join a tour of Africa. Ellen Terry, desperately worried about the distance, wrote to George Bernard Shaw in April 1898: 'If she is in any real difficulty she always sends to me, or comes to me, and we pick up her ends together. But when she is in Africa! Oh Lord, whom will she go to?'[91] The Boer War may have thwarted Craig's plans.[92] The Mallesons had visited their two children in Africa in the winters of 1894–5 and 1896–7, the latter visit cut short as a result of impending military action. If Craig did tour Africa at such a time it is an unusual omission in both St John's and Atwood's listing of Craig's travels.[93]

The unruly woman was a familiar role to Brown-Potter. After her performance as Charlotte Corday, the assassin of Marat during the French Revolution, she became another classic monstrous woman: Nicandra the snake-woman. Russell Vaun's play *Nicandra* rewrites Egyptian mythology, in particular Hathor, the serpent-eye goddess. Hathor embodies female power manifested through desire and anger; as Alison Roberts argues, the metamorphosis of Hathor serves to 'transform violent, uncontrolled female rage into a radiant, beneficent force'.[94] Since female power is ultimately a creative force in Egyptian mythology, and an essential counterpart to male power, its transformation does not signify the subjection of the female principle. The interest in Egyptian myth, culture and archaeological remains coincided at the turn of the nineteenth century with an exploration of women's relationship to power and sexual desire, which, in Western cultures, have been represented as dangerous and entirely destructive phenomena.[95] Thus the 'beneficent' value of female power which, as Roberts has shown, was a central feature of Hathor has been minimized in travesties such as Nicandra, and emphatically devalued in Bram Stoker's *The Jewel of the Seven Stars* (1903) and *The Lair of the White Worm* (1911). In the latter, the destruction of the snake-woman distastefully contributes to the male narrator's intense satisfaction.

Vaun's *Nicandra*, staged at the Avenue Theatre and billed as 'a mystic farce', was presumably a parody of an earlier version of the play.[96] The play was a comedy, as one review states, 'provocative of much laughter'.[97] The transformations of Nicandra, the snake-woman, unlike those of Hathor in Egyptian myth, are crucially brought about by external forces for the purpose of punishment:

Nicandra was a wicked priestess who was punished by the goddess Isis. She was transformed into a serpent and Professor T. secures the reptile and introduces it at his home in Lowndes Square. By an accident Nicandra is restored to her original form and she at once begins to work as much mischief as she can on all and sundry. The whole household is upset and the trouble would go on forever but the Professor presents her with a black pigeon which has the remarkable effect of transforming her once more into a serpent.[98]

An extant play programme records the involvement of Edith Craig and Madame Fouilloux in producing the 'ladies' costumes'.[99] The dress worn by Nicandra as the snake-woman was technically difficult and reminiscent of Ellen Terry's Lady Macbeth dress:[100]

> [The] gown is so cleverly designed and made as to carry out the serpentine idea to perfection for every curve of her supple figure is followed by a sheath-like robe of emerald-green tissue, shot with gleams of vivid violet, and now and again with a shimmer of silver. Over this comes a transparent and trailing drapery of black net wrought with a scale-like device in jet paillettes, while scarves of violet and green chiffon are draped at the decollete, and caught together here and there on the white arms by jewelled clasps. Two great square-cut emeralds fall low down on her forehead from strings of pearls wound in her ruddy hair. Altogether, Nicandra is a veritable enchantress.[101]

The use of contrasting colours, appropriately textured materials and ingeniously appliqued beading to represent scales made the dress remarkable. It was also perceived to be indiscreet. The *Illustrated Sporting and Dramatic News* published a satirical cartoon of Brown-Potter and a scathing description of her immodest costume: 'She is seen in but one dress or what would be one dress were it cut more liberally where the sleeves should be.'[102] Craig's sole involvement in the design of Brown-Potter's snake dress is now brought into question by an extant costume sketch by Pamela Colman Smith found in one of Craig's scrapbooks, and it may be that Colman Smith collaborated on the design with Craig.[103]

The power of the snake goddess in Egyptian myth resided in her self-transformation, not in being transformed by others. The widespread and deeply rooted fears of women's power and creativity and their effect on society had been rumbling for several decades. The unmarried-woman phenomenon had been identified as a social problem in Britain from mid-century, arising from demographic anomalies and leading to the categorization of 'surplus women'.[104] Suggestions for a remedy ranged from the outrageous to the economically expedient: redistribution of 'surplus' women by deportation to the outposts of empire to make up a shortfall in the stocks of white women in colonized countries; alleviation of the financial burden incurred by male relatives by the employment of unmarried relatives in roles new to middle-class women such as the governess.

The dilemmas concerning the idea of marriage and what it might entail – a redefinition of femininity – were more directly explored in Frederick Fenn's *A Married Woman*, performed at the Metropole Theatre, Camberwell, in 1902. Craig's role as Lady Muriel in the subplot seems to be peripheral but it works its way through the contradictions of the play, which, at a formal level, exposes the problematics of marriage and gender identity. The marriage of Cicely Kent, the female protagonist, to an alcoholic is portrayed as imprisonment, a view of marriage that was selfish and frivolous according to the *News of the World*: 'the woman in question is one of the modern neurotic type, who is by no means satisfied to take married life for better or worse, but sighs for liberty and ideals'.[105] Escape is, in fact, engineered by something more substantial than sighing. Craig's remark about Janette Steer's freedom of movement as Hamlet surfaces; Cicely Kent becomes Mr Holroyd by cross-dressing. Clothes take on a symbolic force. The rejection of gendered clothing – corsets and stays, skirts and dresses – symbolizes a more generalized breaking out. Wearing the trousers has been caricatured as usurping male power and as a means of achieving the intimacy of friendship with a man. Ironically, like Rosalind in *As You Like It*, it is only dressed as a man that Cicely Kent can learn that Richard Strake is attracted to her, forcing the woman to dispense with the disguise.

The play centres on the fear of struggle or conflict in relationships. The subplot brings out the conflict in a more explicitly sinister way in a wager between men on their power over a woman. The perception of women, especially conventionally unattractive women, as powerless, unworthy of serious exchange, is undermined by the play. The negative value of the Lady Muriel, the plain (and 'surplus') woman, is shown to be of surface value in a patriarchal economy. She makes herself more conventionally attractive deliberately to subvert the male wager, making Gilbert Dexter fall in love with her in order to refuse him. Her refusal of marriage forms a revenge plot.

The title belies the centrality of the unmarried woman in the play. What the play is unable to explore is the similarity between the two women: the married woman implausibly remains married and even returns to her alcoholic husband.

The reviews were favourable, and Craig's performance promised even to 'advance her reputation as an actress'.[106] Several reviewers failed to mention the subplot, confounded by Lady Muriel's appearance. Described as 'an ugly duckling',[107] she was 'a woman who cannot always show herself to the best advantage',[108] and who 'does not know how to make the best of herself'.[109] These descriptions emulate Gilbert Dexter's perspective; Muriel is perceived as a disappointing object of the male gaze. The entire point of Muriel's revenge is misunderstood by these reviewers. As a woman, Muriel disempowers the male gaze by refusing the role of object. Several reviewers did acknowledge, for instance, 'incongruous elements',[110] but only Max Beerbohm perceived the potentially threatening significance of cross-dressing and the play's requirement that Cicely Kent should, when cross-dressed, be credible as a man:

[Although there have been] in modern history several well-known instances of a woman palming herself off as a man for many years ... these deceivers have been, invariably, women of a peculiar kind – women whose nature was more masculine than feminine, and who chose a masculine life, not by caprice, but because a feminine life dissatisfied them. But Mrs Kent is quite an ordinary woman, and she falls duly in love with the baronet who harbours her. Being an ordinary woman, she is bound to look more than ever womanly in masculine attire, and could not for a moment impose on anyone except on a blind man; ... She could not possibly (unless she were one of the irrelevant monsters whom I have mentioned) look like anyone but Miss Tilley.[111]

Beerbohm argues that even Vesta Tilley, a professional male impersonator, still looked like a woman in drag; hence her 'success'. In these terms, a woman's ability to pass as a man signifies lesbian, or as Beerbohm categorizes, an 'irrelevant monster'. What confuses Beerbohm is his necessary connection of sexuality with gender. The play denies this: providing a critique of gender, it leaves conventional notions of sexuality merely disturbed. Thus a woman choosing a masculine role by more than 'caprice' cannot be 'an ordinary woman' and thus attracted to a man. The rigidity of 'separate spheres', the regulatory force of gender, is played out here, and emphatically defied by both female characters. The confusion which arises from exceeding such boundaries is registered by Beerbohm's location of the play 'in a suburb' and his description of Craig's performance as a hybrid, unbefitting her membership of the Terry family: 'Miss Edith Craig, in a lesser part, grafted the Terry charm on a brusque and un-Terryish realism, all her own.' [112] Edward Gordon Craig was concerned above all to protect his mother from an 'un-Terryish' environment. [113]

The role of character actress in a supporting role was peripheral, and not sufficiently satisfying for Craig. Although she claims to have given up performance because she was 'audience shy', it seems likely that she also found the kinds of female supporting roles available rarely matched that of Lady Muriel. In a later interview she referred to the prudence of choosing the appropriate role in the theatre, and having the capacity to look beyond acting. [114] Edith Craig had the opportunity to do just this at the Lyceum Theatre. Her work has been perceived in terms of apprenticeship to Henry Irving or in relation to working within the family firm. In terms of Craig's family narrative perhaps the most intriguing Lyceum production may have been merely a play-reading rather than a performance. In May 1897, in Bram Stoker's *Dracula or The Undead*, a Miss Craig played Mina Harker. Stoker's play was written and staged as a security measure, to prevent others from bootlegging the novel and profiting from its dramatization. [115] Daniel Farson provides brief information about the performance at the Lyceum Theatre on Tuesday 18 May 1897 of the five-act play. [116] Farson argues that extant play programmes suggest that the production may have been a commercial venture rather than a read-through to secure copyright over the dramatization. The Lyceum Theatre, where Stoker had been manager since 1878, seemed a convenient venue to stage his insurance-policy performance, but he found harsh critics at home. Henry Irving was not pleased with the result. He did not, as one might expect, play the role of Dracula and Ellen Terry was absent from the cast.

A further anomaly arises when considering Edith Craig's role in this play. Stoker's biographers, Daniel Farson and Barbara Belford, state unequivocally that Ellen Terry's daughter took part. However, the play programme ambiguously omits first names and the year 1896 appears to be the year that Craig took up Edith as her stage name in place of Ailsa to differentiate herself from another actor of the same name. [117] Edith Craig had good reason to become involved in the production of *Dracula*: in many ways it was timely, and spoke to her at a crucial moment of transition.

Stoker's *Dracula* has been read as a Gothic novel antagonistic to realism, constructing an alternative story to repress rather than answer the questions which realism ultimately resolves. *Dracula* exhibits the formal conventions of the Gothic novel: multiple narrators; the juxtaposition of different discourses manifested by documents such as diaries and letters which peddle competing versions of the truth. At a thematic level, characters are driven, clashing and rumbling through the novel with a sense of inevitability. The disinherited male meets the single economically independent woman. The 'foreigner' is brought into the family. Institutions are threatened, their hold on society's confidence appearing relative and contingent. Thus religion is challenged by individual moral choice, marriage is threatened by desire (outside marriage or otherwise forbidden). Social mobility breaks the boundaries of class. At the same time the blustering territorial claims of these categories, unaccustomed to justifying themselves, become questionable. Boundaries are transgressed, familiar values and institutions are rendered uncertain.

By contrast, travelling abroad and failing to regulate the family and marriage have devastating effects in *Dracula*. The Count is the ultimate xenophobic representation, posing a fundamental threat to the English family and society, disrupting Harker's marriage, destroying Lucy Westenra. The temptation he offers is represented in terms of desire rather than mere immortality. Submission to Dracula's consumption proves to be destructive. Dracula's family is perverse. The taboo boundary between daughters and wives is broken. Blasphemous to the Christian religion, he appropriates the roles of the Father and the Son, the father and the husband to his 'brides'.

Occupying the shadows is represented in *Dracula* as dangerous, deadly and pleasurable, associating sexual desire with the forbidden not the permissible. The Gothic novel is determined to keep these oppositions apart and to plot the inexorable and devastating effects of transgressing boundaries. Interpretations of the Gothic novel have ranged from promoting transgression by representing it, to championing conservatism by illustrating the devastating effects of the transgression. Thus in *Dracula* it is Mina Harker, not Lucy Westenra the New Woman, who speaks at the centre and the end of the narrative.[118] It is the need to save Mina which motivates the final destruction of Dracula and it is her role as mother which is ultimately emphasized. Harker's final note picks up the tale seven years later, referring to Mina's child whose birthday is the same day as that on which Quincey Morris died. His mother holds, I know, the secret belief that some of our brave friend's spirit has passed into him. His bundle of names links all our little band of men together; but we call him Quincey.[119]

Ellen Terry's children had been given a bundle of names, transgressing the patronymic or even the familial.

The Gothic novel impinged on Craig's adolescence through Stoker's novel. In many ways the tensions between the Gothic and realist modes dominated Craig's childhood. In *Wuthering Heights* Heathcliff is given a single name, obscuring origins which are never revealed. Craig's change of name signifies the obscurity of origins necessary for the mysterious character who will later be claimed and whose true identity will ultimately be revealed. Edith and Edward were given multiple names, accumulating 'Wardell' when their mother married for a second time, but never their father's name, Godwin. Edward Gordon Craig felt this discrepancy poignantly. The fictional identities constructed for them by their mother did not prevent the children from feeling uncertainty regarding their father. Ellen Terry's storytelling provided an emotional blanket to catch the children, but it also mystified their origins, turning the staple elements of Gothic fiction into rational links in the realist narrative. What Ellen Terry, like Nellie Dean, omits proves to be the most significant. She cannot – would not wish to – name sexual relationships outside marriage or illegitimacy directly in *The Story of My Life*.

Ellen Terry's own youth had its Gothic moments. She regretted her parents' distress regarding her liaison with Godwin. During a period of estrangement from her parents, they mistakenly identified the body of a drowned woman as their daughter. The subsequent reunion with their estranged Ellen bridged an awkward gap in the narrative. Terry's guilt became uncannily embodied. She had transgressed the sexual mores of her time and lived to tell the tale; extraordinarily her actions did not forfeit her place in the public eye, although she was occasionally made to feel the disapproval.

Nina Auerbach associates Edith Craig with Henry Irving as a purveyor of Romanticism, pointing out that Irving's Lyceum Theatre was characterized by the theatrical practices of the nineteenth century rather than the dawning modern age. In some ways, however, Irving's vision was realist. His attitude to the difficulties of his life conformed to the selective vision and the determination to control, repressing that which cannot be answered or countenanced. *Dracula* challenged the limits of realism, dissolving certainty and authority. It would have undermined Irving's faith. No wonder that his response to the play was 'Dreadful!'[120] While Irving is said to have influenced Stoker's Dracula, Ellen Terry features explicitly in the novel. She is named in one of the *Westminster Gazette* newspaper articles cited in the novel which report on the abduction of children in Hampstead by a 'bloofer lady'. The games of local children incorporate these events, acting out the roles of the 'bloofer lady' in such a manner that the correspondent suggests, 'even Ellen Terry could not be so winningly attractive as some of these grubby-faced little children pretend – and even imagine themselves – to be'.[121] Stoker therefore explicitly incorporated Terry into the novel, albeit in an understated manner. Ellen Terry's appearance had in fact taken on for her new neighbours a mysterious significance as 'the Greek lady' when they noticed her unconventionally dressed figure at the window of her house.[122]

Ellen Terry was accustomed to the freedom of the night. She was criticized by Irving for visiting the Minories (East End) on her own one evening; the purpose of her excursion was to visit a man who had written her a begging letter.[123] As regards personal safety, she was fearless. On another occasion swift self-defence successfully ejected a drunken man from the carriage which she was driving alone.[124] The darkness held attractions rather than fears for Terry, as for her daughter. W. Graham-Robertson, recounting stories of Terry's nocturnal ventures, inadvertently borrows Stoker's metaphor: 'Ellen Terry was a daughter of the night, happy in its shadow and mystery and loving the moon with a strange ecstasy which I have never met with in another.'[125]

If Ellen Terry's was a life in theatre, the dominant aesthetic modes of Edith Craig's adolescence were the Gothic and the fairytale. Craig read in reverse the Gothic novel's opposition between nuclear family and alternative (apparently disruptive) social formations. Identification with the disruptive non-familial other, with the uncanny, became for Craig common-sense. While for Stoker, *Dracula* seems to have articulated a number of deeply troubling issues with which he could not personally come to terms, for Craig *Dracula* was another familiar story, a family romance.

In a moment of resentment, Craig had identified Godwin with the devil.[126] During the period of Stoker's *Dracula*, she risked a devil's-eye view of the Lyceum with 'Ellen Peg's Book of Merry Joys', written by Edith Craig and Pamela Colman Smith, 'the 2 little devils Pixie & Puck, authors of the Peggy Picture Book 1900'. Smith represented Craig in her caricatures as Puck or one of the 'devils', marginal but mischievously observing the antics of the Lyceum company: Edward Gordon Craig as 'the Tedpecker'; and Bram Stoker as the 'Bramy Joker' in evening dress and bat-winged cape. In many ways Smith's representation of herself and Craig as 'the devils' subverts both the solemnity of Stoker's *Dracula* and the security of Irving's autocracy.

Craig's education emphasized the new opportunities available to women. She served an apprenticeship at the Lyceum, but an autocratic Irving was not the only role model for Craig and her costume design work was not limited to Lyceum productions. Above all, if there were lessons for Craig to learn during this period they formed distinct elements which were to exert varying and long-standing pressures on the direction she was to take. She was provided with role models, all of whom were excellent, gaining valuable lessons from Cora Brown-Potter, Stella Campbell, Janet Achurch and Charles Charrington. High expectations of her were held and publicly expressed in many quarters. She was not completely dependent on either her mother or Irving. She did not have to wait for her work in the women's suffrage movement to receive public recognition independently from her illustrious family. Newspapers were beginning to cater specifically for women, identified as a new market in a turbulent economy. In 1901 in a women's column in the *Free Lance* newspaper, Craig's work as a costumier is reported by 'Frou Frou':

> I wonder when an era will dawn upon stage dressing, and we shall value the sublime artistic genius of women like Miss Ailsa Craig, the daughter of Miss Ellen Terry, as it deserves to be valued? ... She looked like some stately lady of rich old Holland, who had stepped out of the shadows of a Rubens to look at our vulgarities with grave, grey eyes, and who would bye-and-bye go back again to her grander world of bygones. I think one of the nicest things one can tell of her is that her workwomen, who are mostly poor and sad, love her intensely, with a love that is as personal as it is reverential.[127]

Overtly complimentary in its attribution to Craig of the values of a benevolent and aristocratic patron, whose apprentices are personally committed as well as gratefully indebted to her, this review's citation of Rubens provides a shortform for Craig's class, status and aesthetic. As John Berger acutely observed, European oil painting saw the world in terms of commodities, recording the wealth and power of the patron, emphasized by formality and distance.[128] Craig breaks the rules by making visible a relationship between artist and workwomen, denying individualism which such a 'lady' in such a painting signifies. Ironically, the reviewer places Craig in a subversive role in relation to this tradition; she is stepping out of the shadows, out of the frame, a time-travelling visitor from the seventeenth century who emerges to present a gaze critical of modern 'vulgarities'. By doing so she has been transformed from object to subject; deprived of the artist/Rubens role, she could only be represented as the aristocratic or patronal model in his painting.

Three issues emerge in this 1901 article which were to be recurrent features of Craig's career: the perceived marginalization of Craig's work; the association of Craig with an earlier age and alternative social order; Craig's identification with women. She was made aware of her limitations, intellectually and bodily, but the extent of her talents were confirmed. She was never to be an academic or concert pianist. Instead she learned the subversive power of parody and of the obscurity of the margins.

In 1902, the end of Irving's management of the Lyceum altered the direction of Terry's career. Craig was thirty-three years old. She had already taken steps to establish herself independently. If, as Nina Auerbach has suggested, Henry Irving was Edith Craig's role model, it was as an innovator not as an autocratic conservative. However, if Craig needed a role model in unruliness (besides her mother), she had several to choose from: Janet Achurch, Cora Brown-Potter and Stella Campbell. Theatre was not the only field open to Craig. If social reform had attracted Craig, she had the opportunity of being involved in district nursing or teaching. Craig's work had already received recognition and critical approval from critics and contemporaries such as George Bernard Shaw and Eleanora Duse. Even at the earliest stages of her career the influences on Craig came from beyond that of her immediate family. Henry Irving proclaimed the theatre as a temple. It was uncertain what beliefs and values Craig would attempt to foster in the theatre. If she were to reinvent herself as anyone's daughter, would it be Nicandra's or Dracula's?

Chapter 3

COMING OF AGE WITH THE NEW WOMAN:
Experiments and Alternatives
1899–1907

In 1899, her thirtieth year, Edith Craig set up house with Christopher St John. In 1907 both women accompanied Ellen Terry on tour in America, which proved to be a major event in each of their lives. St John produced her biography of Terry. Craig published an article, staking her claim to be the first woman stage-manager. Ellen Terry married for the third time. The turn of the century gave rise to anxieties as well as celebrations. The phenomenon of the 'New Woman', propagated through journalism, poetry, novels and drama, registered the level of widespread fear about the changing social role of the middle-class woman. Although the New Woman was rarely a means of self-identification, it brought into public debate the limits of gender. It served to regulate fears concerning the changing roles and expectations of women. The new century was exhibiting some strange symptoms. A common diagnosis was an unstable femininity in the ascendancy.[1]

Edith Craig had grown up with the New Woman, in literature and in life. She and her mother had been closely involved in the imaginative landscapes of Bram Stoker's *Dracula* and in Shaw's dramatic New Women. Although Terry has been described as the Victorian ideal woman,[2] she was sometimes appropriated as representative of oppositional femininity. Terry was aware of the range of her public images. In 1911, the first edition of *The Freewoman*, a controversial newspaper, cited Ellen Terry as its model:

Where are the women of whom and for whom you write who are free? Can they be pointed out, or named by name? There must be, say, ten in the British Isles. The question is pertinent enough, but it is difficult to answer, because its answer must of necessity become personal. We might, perhaps, hazard the name of one Freewoman who has become a sufficiently national figure to make her mention impersonal – Ellen Terry. There at least is one, and for the rest the inquisitors must be content with being enabled to arrive at the conception of Freewomen by way of a description of Bond-women.[3]

Although no debate ensued on the validity of the far from 'impersonal' attribution of Freewoman to Ellen Terry, the newspaper elicited some strong responses. Critical of the perceived narrow focus of the women's suffrage movement, *The Freewoman* claimed to have opened debates on wider issues, such as homosexuality and (hetero)sexual relationships outside marriage. Although the image of an Ellen Terry completely independent of convention was exaggerated, *The Freewoman* had, like George Bernard Shaw, recognized Terry's modernity. According to Shaw, Ellen Terry 'had not had to break Mrs Alving's chains, never having worn them'.[4] In this respect she was indeed an exceptional woman.

The boundaries of the feminine role were negotiated by women involved in organizations and in specific campaigns. The interventions of individual women to improve conditions for other women beyond the exercise of generosity had their revolutionary potential. Ellen Terry was always extremely generous. On several occasions she looked beyond the distressing circumstances of an individual to the need for longer-term support. She wrote to George Bernard Shaw of her intention to make use of her new cottage in Kingston Vale to provide respite for impoverished actresses.[5] Increasingly, women like Terry, empowered to bring about change through economic independence or social class, were becoming involved in organizations.[6] Religious, charitable and educational institutions provided the necessary infrastructure for middle-class women slowly to establish wider social changes. Many of these women did not classify themselves as 'New Women'. They regarded their individual interventions for change in the context of social justice, religious duty or professional pedagogy rather than politics. Even though Ellen Terry was claimed as a revolutionary figure, she did not take the initiative in political organizations. When enfranchisement came she was not sure what to do with it and in this respect she was not alone.

The New Woman was represented, particularly by male authors and those contemptuous of the innovations associated with such women, as a new species. In rejecting the confines of Victorian femininity, casting off restrictive conventions like clothing, the New Woman was striving for the naked truth of a prelapsarian state.[7] In another secular context, this threatened an unveiling which was profoundly disruptive, a demystifying of femininity. The liberatory discourse of the New Woman shocked and threatened, and was symptomatic of the limits of a social structure under stress. Women had been burdened with the responsibility of the moral centre of the family. If women were evolving into new and unruly forms, this was cited as a function of either the evolution or degeneration of society. Charlotte Perkins Gilman envisaged a self-sufficient, self-propagating community of women in *Herland*. Frances Swiney argued for the superiority of women as 'creatrix of the [white] race' through long periods of celibacy, an ideal matriarchy aspiring to female parthenogenesis.[8] In addition to the racist ideology of Social Darwinism and the elision of women with reproduction and motherhood, Swiney's theories were grounded in religious association (with theosophy). However, Sheila Jeffreys has argued that Swiney allowed a rare oppositional stance for women to emerge: the possibility of women taking control of their sexual relationships with men. Any alternatives were hard to define within the prevailing limited and dualistic terms. As banisher of beasts, the New Woman did not acquire the status of St George.[9] She was widely regarded as monstrous, stepping out of line to invade men's proper sphere, a transgression of conventional boundaries threatening more than localized problems in the bedroom. The wholesale breaking-out represented by the New Woman drew attention to the extent to which many women had been quietly contained and separated.

For a middle-class woman, walking in the streets unaccompanied was sufficient to incur public censure and ridicule, to engender privately expressed panic. Thus Max Beerbohm, who had found the cross-dressing of *A Married Woman* so disturbing, wrote to Ada Leverson (a woman subsequently designated a New Woman writer) about the 'fear of this so-called New Woman', reportedly a 'well-dressed woman, wearing a black costume and a thick veil' alleged to have stabbed two people in Kensington in December 1894.[10] Fear of female violence runs deep, embedded in the expectation of women's routine subordination. In the same letter Beerbohm describes his impression of Elizabeth Robins, actress and author, most famous in her performance as Hedda Gabler: 'She is fearfully Ibsenish and talks of souls that are involved in a nerve turmoil and are seeking a common platform. This is literally what she said. Her very words. I kept peeping under the table to see if she really wore a skirt.'[11] Robins's interest in spirituality was charged with a sexual politics trivialized by Beerbohm's parody. The perceived intellectual inferiority of women was demonstrated by a susceptibility to the fake, the inauthentic, the sentimental.

The expression by women of unusual or, in some cases, any ideas at all, defied belief. More than a signifier of eccentricity, 'spirituality' alluded to an alternative belief system, the existence of which denied the singularity of dominant discourse. The New Woman had to be hysterical; her claims to rational powers of thought and her disregard for the maternal/familial were in direct contradiction of current medical knowledge. The proposition of women's intellectual inferiority was given a biological basis by scientists. Anatomically, the brain of a white woman (like those of other 'races') was considered to be less developed than that of the white male. Similarly, the association of women with inconsistent, emotional, even irrational or 'mad' thinking and behaviour was determined by the systematic 'hysterization of women',[12] reducing women to the reproductive function. When Beerbohm seeks confirmation that such alarming ideas are emanating from a skirt-wearer, his act of 'peeping' exposes the level of fear inspired by defiance of gender boundaries and markers which ordinarily were perceived to regulate and contain dangerous ideas. Speaking out of turn might lead women to other deviant behaviour: involvement in politics; socializing independently; riding bicycles and engaging in other sports; smoking openly; preferring reading and studying to the company of men. An interest in Ibsen became a shortform for, or a sign of sympathy with, the New Woman. All manner of activities which, at the end of the twentieth century may appear to be commonplace, were weighted with social significance at the end of the nineteenth century. Thus a friend wrote to Elizabeth Malleson:

> How we poor pioneers were reviled and ridiculed. Our successors don't know at what a cost to some of us their comparative emancipation has been attained. But the bicycle has been a greater emancipation than anything. It is nothing short of a social revolution for women.[13]

For all their transgressions and involvement in social reforms, the riding of a bicycle had appeared to bring about the most freedom for women. The ability to move from A to B unaccompanied symbolized more than independent movement: it indicated an independence of thought and intention which might lead women to follow alternative routes. Edith Craig and Christopher St John cycled from London to Kent, staying overnight at the Saracen Inn, Ashford.[14] Ellen Terry had sent them to look at the property near Tenterden which she had longed to buy. She had spotted the house by chance and asked to be notified when it came up for sale. While the concepts of women travelling alone, riding bicycles or buying property were forming the topics for debate and for fiction, they were already realities for Craig, St John and Terry.

Edith Craig frequently exceeded the conventions of even the New Woman in dress, deed and thought. Her favourite clothes had always been unconventional. As a small child she had been brought up on aesthetic values, trained to eliminate anything 'vulgar'. She was photographed wearing her kimono, a gift from Whistler,[15] but as an adult Craig's interest in unorthodox clothing was to shift from aesthetic dress to more symbolic clothing. Craig shared St John's taste. Craig's first impression of St John was of her 'red coat, and a small three-cornered hat'.[16] Both women enjoyed wearing unconventional clothing not confined to the stereotypical masculine dress routinely associated with the New Woman. Early photographic portraits show both in conventional attire,[17] and a publicity photograph from the 1920s presents Craig in a glamorous beaded dress. Her use of colour was distinctive, catching the eye of the press. Spotted in the street, she was 'a dignified sandalled figure in black ... with a vivid orange scarf'.[18] More characteristic of Craig, as recalled by both Vita Sackville-West and Violet Pym, was a rustic smock and sandals. The insistence on comfort signified a sense of self-determination. However, it also reflected the changing cultural meanings of clothing. The movements for Rational Dress or dress reform developed in the context of utopian social movements concerned with political change. Particular items of clothing (such as sandals, shorts and bloomers) or styles (the utilitarian rather than decorative) were attributed to unconventional value systems. George Bernard Shaw's commitment to Jaegerism led him to claim great benefits from wearing woollen fabrics next to the skin. As Elizabeth Wilson notes, the twentieth century brought a shift in the cultural meaning of clothes, so that clothing could signify identity.[19] Descriptions of Craig's appearance are significantly contradictory. St John recalls Craig's graceful stature, but others, in spite of photographic evidence to the contrary, have described her as 'an ugly duckling'.[20]

In autumn 1899 Edith Craig and Christopher St John were living together at 7 Smith Square, Westminster. The significance of their cohabitation at this time is not straightforward. Craig had previously shared a house with Satty Fairchild at 15 Barton Street, Westminster.[21] Unmarried women who were economically independent were demonstrating a new independence in other aspects of their life by living apart from their biological families.[22] Such a break was difficult to make. It radically altered the middle-class family structure dominating nineteenth-century Britain in which the unmarried woman was inseparable from the family, perceived alternately as a financial burden or as an unpaid supernumary domestic servant or governess. Jerome K. Jerome recalled a way of life which was becoming available to middle-class women: 'Amy Hogg was also a pioneer. She lived by herself in diggings opposite the British Museum, frequented restaurants and Aerated Bread Shops, and had many men friends: all of which was considered very shocking in those days.'[23]

The fact of living alone or with others outside marriage appeared to deny the necessity of marriage. Experiments in communal living had been developing on a small scale within the utopian socialist movement in Britain. The settlement movement in the 1880s brought middle-class social workers and working class together in residential homes, motivated by the belief in the transforming effect of close contact, friendship and examples in living rather than impersonal economic interventions. The Toynbee Hall Settlement and the Fellowship of the New Life were examples of new social formations which signified a reassessment of the political dimension of culture as a whole way of life. Martha Vicinus has traced the developing independence which middle-class women were finding in such settlements. The ways many women were living in these new institutions, outside the bounds of marriage and family, provided, as Vicinus states, a history of 'paradox of power and marginality, of enormous strength within narrow limits, of unity and support linked with division and doubt'.[24] Around the same time as Craig and St John set up house, Edward Carpenter and George Merrill started life together at Millthorpe.[25] Carpenter's principles in unorthodox living were put into practice, attracting many visitors. This unconventional way of living became known as 'the simple life', and featured vegetarianism, making and wearing sandals, and rational dress. For Carpenter this included same-sex relationships. The 'simple life' was practised by individuals with very different views who shared a basic commitment to a broad-based egalitarianism, determined to combine their political beliefs with their entire way of life. The move towards holistic thinking was beginning to break down received ideas about the separate spheres of gender and other compartmentalized aspects of life: 'Carpenter, with his sandals, his cottage and his conscience quietly following the heart and suggesting that others might do so to advantage struck at the delicate division of emotional labour which helped to keep class and sex domination in its place.'[26]

In exploring the limits of gender, other boundaries were reassessed, tested, broken down or reinforced. The reassessment of the political and the extension of the political into the so-called 'private' gave rise to an awareness of cultural and sexual politics. The experiments in (hetero)sexual relationships outside marriage in this period have been characterized by individuals such as H. G. Wells and George Bernard Shaw. For women such as Rebecca West, of course, the risks were great; methods of contraception were unpredictable. Even within politically radical groups gender was often the last orthodoxy to be questioned. 'Free love' signified an alternative to marriage in promising a more equal union. However, experiments in 'free love' often distributed such 'freedom' unequally between women and men. Sheila Jeffreys has demonstrated how this has been disempowering for women.[27]

Edith Craig lived with Christopher St John from 1899 until Craig's death in 1947. In 1916 Tony (Clare) Atwood joined their household. St John was a writer and she chose to write about her relationships (with Craig and others). Her essay, 'Close-Up' (1949), provides a brief account of Craig's career, foregrounding in its title the authority of St John's intimacy in her representation of Craig. St John published two novels, *The Crimson Weed* (1900) and the anonymously published *Hungerheart* (1915). Her representation of life with Craig dispels any suspicion that Craig, St John and Atwood were just good friends who shared a house. However, St John's representation decentres Atwood. St John does not suggest that living with Craig was a matter of convenience, an economic decision based on a recognition that three could live more cheaply together than one. Indeed the house at Smith Square, the first of their shared homes, was, according to St John, 'recklessly beyond [their] means'.[28] Their social life was shared. Smith Square was located in a prime spot, close to Westminster. It was not a transitory place, convenient lodgings. They took time to cultivate a garden. Neither was it clandestine. Their social life was shared. Smith Square was one of the three addresses they were to share which became vibrant cultural centres. Others came to stay.[29] Harcourt Williams recalls living there:

Once a Twelfth Night Party was held there. They mulled ale in my bedroom after a recipe by Nigel Playfair, fumigating the chamber with a pungent, lingering aroma. Eventually we made a circle round the fire bent on telling ghost stories one to another – W. B. Yeats was one of us, his raven black hair and pale, bird-like features caught in the firelight. It was he who set the ball rolling, but his stories were so enthralling that none of us wanted to interrupt him, nor did we.[30]

St John and Craig also lived for a while in a flat in Adelphi Terrace House, near to Bernard and Charlotte Shaw,[31] a coincidence which led to Craig being cast as the bishop's wife, Mrs Bridgnorth, in Shaw's *Getting Married*. Shaw reputedly recognized the ideal voice for Mrs Bridgnorth when he heard Craig shouting for St John to throw down the front-door key.[32]

The cohabitation of St John and Craig signified a decision to make a commitment to each other. Craig's relationships with two men were experimental. This became particularly apparent in her involvement with Martin Shaw. A musician and friend of Edward Gordon Craig since 1899, Shaw had worked on the performances of *Dido and Aeneas* for the Purcell Operatic Society, Hampstead, founded by Shaw, and *The Masque of Love*. Shaw proposed marriage to Edith Craig.[33] When St John learned of this, she attempted suicide.[34] Craig's relationship with Shaw was also discouraged by Ellen Terry who, it is claimed, disliked Shaw's appearance; the relationship ended. Edward Gordon Craig seems to have been sympathetic to Shaw and wrote to advise his sister, claiming more insight into such matters than their mother. The specific details are omitted, but the episode is consigned by St John to Gothic terms, an interment of powerful and taboo emotions:

> This first phase in my long friendship with Edy cannot be epitomized as an idyll. It came near to being a tragedy. Of that Edy never spoke in after years. I think our life together subsequently was all the happier, because we did not break open the grave of a thing past which had threatened to separate us.[35]

To St John, Craig's brush with marriage was something of an aberration, 'a thing past'. It seems that it was taboo for what it signified about their own relationship as much as Craig's relationship with Martin Shaw. The 'tragedy' may refer, as Roger Manvell has assumed, to St John's suicide attempt.[36] It could equally apply to Craig's temptation to marriage. This would have been tragic if

Craig's feelings for Martin Shaw were insincere or uncertain, subject to the pressure to marry and to deny her feelings for St John. Although Terry had elsewhere expressed her wish that her daughter should marry, it was important that she marry someone suitable. Christopher St John was to gain Ellen Terry's approval.

St John's representation of this episode emphasizes how traumatic it was, revealing her sense of guilt, and acknowledging her role in emotionally blackmailing Craig. St John also seems to give the impression that Shaw disappeared from Craig's life completely once the possibility of marriage was dispelled. This is inaccurate, probably because St John needed to dramatize Craig's decision. The language of rites of passage or 'coming out' were unavailable. Shaw and Craig worked together later, in the League of Arts.[37] By this time Shaw had been married to Jean Cobbold for several years. Like many of Edith Craig's colleagues, he does not mention her, even in a professional capacity, in his autobiography.

St John felt the need to write about this difficult episode in her relationship with Craig. Her interpretation of the 'tragedy' risks depoliticizing Craig's choice by implying that it was a sacrifice. It is crucial to contextualize this in St John's Catholicism, which can only represent same-sex desire obliquely through the discourse of martyrdom, in terms of pain and suffering.[38]

The few relationships with men which Edith Craig formed were, it seems, non-starters. More attention has been given to the ending of these relationships (even by St John) than to Craig's decision to continue her relationship with St John and their mutual decision, after seventeen years together, to form a relationship with Tony (Clare) Atwood. Roger Manvell glosses Christopher St John's description of the Martin Shaw episode thus:

> This was a reference to one of Edy's unhappy attempts to achieve a normal love affair. [Ellen Terry's] opposition, whether well- or ill-considered, only served to increase Edy's sense of frustration, and force her to find consolation in the devotion of the friend whose torturing jealousy was raised by this threat of marriage.[39]

Manvell's interpretation involves some questionable chronology (Craig's relationship with St John predated her relationship with, and ultimate rejection of, Shaw) and the wrong man.[40] The coincidence that both of the men with whom Craig was involved were facially disfigured was remarked upon rather than their compatibility with Craig, considering their professional excellence in cultural fields. Thus, Craig's relationships with women have been explicitly identified as compensatory and abnormal. Steen takes a more explicitly partisan approach than Manvell: 'It was Ellen who interfered with Edy's love affair, and diverted the normal pattern of her daughter's life into the channel it followed from 1899 onwards.'[41] A more impartial view is taken by Webster, who, unlike Steen or Manvell, does not abuse the differential positions of power involved in representing the 'other' (assuming that the undisclosed sexuality of these writers signifies their heterosexuality). St John's role as writer is inconsistently represented by Steen, who exposes her claim to illegitimacy as fictional, her involvement with Ellen Terry's publications as an act of interference.

The ascription of difference to St John by many of those who have written about Terry serves several purposes. It drives a wedge between the biographer and subject,[42] attributing Craig's sexuality to the bad influence of St John. The intimacy of Edith Craig and Ellen Terry, particularly in later life, provoked intense feelings. That Ellen Terry did not take steps to exclude her daughter or her partners, and that a rift, albeit short-lived, opened up between Terry and Craig over Terry's marriage to James Carew, confounded some of Craig's critics. The intensity of Marguerite Steen's narrative is a product of the difference of opinion which split Terry's friends over Craig's treatment of her mother. There were those who felt that Craig exploited her mother's fame and wealth, controlled her social and working life, sometimes neglecting her. Claims were made that Craig increasingly resembled Terry. This was expressed uneasily, especially where much had been invested in emphasizing the differences between mother and daughter. Steen suggested that Olive Terry, Ellen Terry's niece who became custodian of the Ellen Terry Memorial Museum, also acquired Terry's looks. Craig's resemblance to Terry was no longer unique, but a product of Terry's spiritual immortality manifested through the devotion she inspired in others.

An unevenness has been produced by St John's representation of Craig and Terry, and by Craig's comparative silence. It has been suggested that St John used her role as writer to exploit her position in her relationship with Terry and Craig, reflecting in the glory of the famous actress, and that in destroying their personal papers after their deaths she exerted control over them. In styling herself as 'literary henchman', St John claims the authority of collaborator, if not conspirator, in producing Terry's published life. The covert register of the term signifies the discreet service which St John regarded herself as providing. She took on the burden of dutiful service to the woman whom she had adored even before she met Edith Craig.

Martin Shaw seems to have been the second man with whom Craig was involved. When on tour with the Lyceum company in America in 1895, Craig had fallen 'deeply and passionately in love' with the actor Sydney Valentine.[43] Valentine became famous for his work in developing the Actors' Association as a trade union. His name marks a landmark in actors' working rights: the Valentine Standard Contract. The relationship between Craig and Valentine was terminated by Ellen Terry. Valentine was married and therefore, according to Terry's morality (conventional when it applied to her daughter), forbidden fruit. The ultimatum for Craig was to desist or be sent home. It seems unlikely that this interference, considerable though it was, thwarted relationships which would otherwise have flourished. Craig was a forthright woman; that she did not defy these prohibitions suggests that she was unsure of her feelings for these men rather than submitting to pressures, parental, peer or otherwise.

Christopher St John was unambiguous about her sexuality. In *Hungerheart* she describes her relationship with Craig and with other women in a way which conformed to prevalent, conventional representations of lesbianism. In a way, St John was ahead of her time in making visible (albeit through an anonymously published book) her sexual preference for women, more so in her way of life:

> It is ironic that in 'real life' during the first half of this century, writers such as Michael Field and Gertrude Stein could combine what was not yet 'granted' in writing of lesbians from the period: creativity and relationality. What could be written about was clearly behind what could be lived.[44]

The way in which St John represented same-sex relationships in her writings was constrained. The keynote of *Hungerheart* is the unfulfilled desire of the wandering protagonist who shifts from one agonizing relationship to another. Illegitimacy is an essential ingredient of the alienating environment required by dominant discourses to explain the abnormality of homosexuality. The 'hunger' driving the protagonist is fulfilled partly by her relationship with 'Sally' (assumed to represent a thinly disguised Craig) and by her conversion to Catholicism.[45]

The ways of understanding same-sex relationships available to Craig and St John (in St John's case reflected in her writings) were extremely disempowering. It was not until the end of the nineteenth century that same-sex encounters, hitherto perceived in terms of specific acts or practices, coalesced in the modern sense of an identity. Once homosexuality was constructed as a category in scientific discourse, same-sex relationships became pathologized, attributed to a biological, congenital defect. This positioned the subject as helpless victim of a medical condition to be managed through appropriate self-control, and eliciting tolerance and sympathy from others. In the process of defining homosexuality in (pseudo)scientific terms, writers such as Havelock Ellis, Edward Carpenter and Krafft-Ebing fixed the meaning of homosexuality on the body and overshadowed the accompanying social formations and cultural meanings which contributed to a homosexual or a heterosexual identity. It has been argued that a homosexual identity was unintelligible prior to the late nineteenth century.[46] Thus to avoid the anachronistic use of terms which originate from later frames of reference, critics have employed terms such as 'same-sex passion'.[47] The problematic is not merely one of chronology. As Eve Sedgwick has argued, multiple identities are equally available now; the problematizing of same-sex relationships in the past tends to presume a stable present from which to argue.[48]

Representations are fraught and debatable at any moment. Sheila Jeffreys emphasizes that lesbian history is contingent upon an understanding of the connections between women's passionate relationships before and after the construction of a homosexual identity.[49] It is possible that Craig, St John and Atwood had different senses of their relationship, but the significance of their life together, as represented by St John and by their contemporaries, places them within Jeffreys's usefully broad scope for lesbianism:

> lesbianism as understood by lesbian feminists is a passionate commitment to women, a culture, a political alternative to the basic institution of male supremacy, a means through which women have always gained self-respect and pursued their own goals and achievements with the support of other women. It is more than likely to include a sensual component, which may or may not take a genital form.[50]

Heterosexism places undue emphasis on specific sexual acts or practices,[51] while playing down the political, institutional challenge constituted by a passionate commitment between women. Edith Craig's relatives and some of her contemporaries registered their antipathy to her woman-centred life. This is apparent explicitly and implicitly in criticisms of her personality: her 'aggressive traits' and her status as a 'troublemaker'.[52] Edward Gordon Craig excludes Christopher St John and Tony Atwood completely from his narrative.[53]

In some of Ellen Terry's more unguarded and frivolous letters to George Bernard Shaw she puzzled over her daughter's unmarried status, where its undecidability is frequently an issue of power and self-determination:

> Edy says she'd never marry because she would not stay anywhere where she was not entirely happy. I heard she said once: 'Not one minute would I stop with Mother, but that I do just as I like.' (She thinks she does, but really she does as I like.) To my mind she never wants to be naughty in any way. One thing I desire. That she shall never be frightened at me. She's such a baby – and yet so clever.[54]

Edward Gordon Craig makes the conventional attribution of his sister's rejection of marriage and preference for women to a hatred of men, initiated by her hatred of their father. She was 'somehow or other, prejudiced in some odd way against the male sex, though always kind to me'.[55] Roger Manvell contends that 'Edy always excited different reactions; she was whatever you saw her to be.'[56] This should not be used to mystify her. Internal contradictions suggest that the marginalization of Craig's work often resulted from prejudice. Steen, for instance, claims that Craig, unlike her brother, never contributed anything original to theatre,[57] but elsewhere refers to the accolades which her work received from contemporaries.

While passionate relationships between women had been socially acceptable, even encouraged, it was in the 1890s that the antipathy towards spinster feminists and their push for social change created a climate in which love between women became the subject of condemnation. The Labouchere amendment to the Criminal Law Amendment Act 1885 had legislated against specific sexual acts between men. However, a homosexual identity was not reducible to any 'sexual act'. What came to be defined as lesbianism was invisible, widely unintelligible. The heterosexist lens produces a necessary connection between sexuality and gender; the lesbian stereotype (the masculine woman) and the gay stereotype (the effeminate man) are produced through the association of same-sex passion with gender reversal. As Esther Newton has argued, the 'mannish lesbian' was 'mythic'.[58] Lesbian women who were not masculine were invisible, unrepresentable. They therefore exposed the inadequacy of available discourse: 'The notion of a feminine lesbian contradicted the congenital theory [of homosexuality].'[59] The attempt to move beyond the limits of the binary categories which language imposes (female/male, feminine/masculine, homosexual/heterosexual) produces a 'strategic undecidability' which defies decorum.[60] Thus the cumulative effect of Edith Craig's rudeness, her defiant reticence, as well as her failure to comply consistently with the stereotype of the masculine lesbian is to defy categorization.

Craig's reticence is significant and characteristic. Margaret Webster, for instance, comments on Craig's treatment of her mother's relationship with Irving thus: 'Edy on this, as on other issues, opposed a public silence to her brother's written views.'[61] Christopher St John, by contrast, rarely chose silence. It is St John's representations of Craig which dominate, and she was used as a spokesperson by Craig as well as Terry. Later she functioned as Craig's intermediary with the world, practically a medium, even while Craig lived.[62] St John had an investment in reading her own sexual orientation in terms of the dominant, as productive of a 'hungerheart', a burden of suffering to be overcome. The means whereby St John transforms this into a tolerable self-image is, bizarrely, through Catholicism. Her conversion to Catholicism led to the acquisition of a new name from John the Baptist. John was the evangelist, baptizer of Christ, witness of the crucifixion, scholar, voice in the wilderness. The story of John's naming prioritizes writing over speech: Zacharias, struck dumb at John's birth, names him through writing, not speaking. John's moral purity attracts the destructive desire of Salome, who demands from King Herod John's head in payment for her dance. The story of John the Baptist held a special significance for both Christopher St John and for Edith Craig.

Religions, and spirituality more generally, have often been invoked as an endorsement of radical or controversial ideas. The incongruous nexus of Catholicism and lesbianism explored in detail by Joanne Glasgow[63] suggests that Christopher St John's religious faith ironically enabled her to assume that since it did not (could not) mention her sexuality it 'was seen as innocent by the church. Lesbian sexuality did not exist as a Catholic reality.'[64] This omission was read as permission. The prevailing invisibility of lesbianism became internalized as a challenge or test to be overcome; more explicitly than for André Gide, it was the strait gate through which she passed. The institutional endorsement of suffering, ritualized guilt and confession of sins provided a context for such internalized self-disgust. Confession has a place in ritual, sanctioning its expression as dramatic performance. Ritual, sin and performance dominate the cultural forms associated with decadence, aestheticism and *fin de siècle*. The morbidity characteristic of European writing of this period functions as a displacement of desires which cannot directly be represented. The cost of fulfilling that desire is perceived to be death, defied only by an elite whose power and status permits their transgression to avoid (or perhaps only postpone) punishment. Thus, in the figure of the Romantic artist, the lone struggle to explore forbidden values may be represented. The separation of art and life, if not the substitution of art for life claimed in Oscar Wilde's *The Picture of Dorian Gray* (1891) or Huysmans's *Against Nature* (1884), provides a separate space for the pursuit, and representation, of forbidden desires. It can also function as an exclusionary space, not real, unavoidably different, excluded from the familiarity of daily life, condemned never to be ordinary. Thus Alan Sinfield has explored the implications of Wilde having been charged with a 'pose', not a reality.[65]

Passion, manifested as obsessive love or as revenge, is symbolized for St John as a destructive 'crimson weed' which feeds upon the 'siren voices of the flesh'. A year after she moved to Smith Square with Edith Craig, St John's novel, *The Crimson Weed*, was published by Duckworth.[66] A lurid tale of revenge, it deploys irregular liaisons, enforced marriage, class prejudice and destructive passion. The male protagonist Luke (rather than Dorian) Gray discovers that he is illegitimate, and that his 'father' is adoptive. This disclosure of obscured origins sets into motion a devastating chain of events, leading ultimately to Gray's decline into mental illness. Gray is driven by a need to exact revenge upon his biological father who deceived and then abandoned his mother. His mother concentrated on her own survival rather than revenge, achieving a successful career as an opera singer. Thus abused mothers and irresponsible fathers, illegitimacy, exile and performance (some of the powerful cross-currents of Craig's life) are brought together in a Gothic exploration of same-sex desires. This is obliquely symbolized through the title of the novel and embodied in the relationship between Luke Gray (characterized as 'hyacinth') and his male friend, Richard Savile. St John's novel explores sexual anguish with some sympathy, but it offers little resistance to the moral condemnation of sexual desire.

By the time St John's novel was published, the red rose, which for Aubrey Beardsley and Oscar Wilde symbolized forbidden passion,[67] had officially been turned into a crimson weed. The language of flowers provides a discreet signifying system. Wilde's favourite buttonhole, a carnation made green by standing it in ink, gave the title to Robert Hichens's novel. *The Green Carnation*, published in September 1894, was a 'skit' on Wilde's relationship with Lord Alfred Douglas, whose analogues are respectively Esme Amarinth and Lord Reggie Hastings.[68] Wilde is one of several 'real' individuals directly named (like Ellen Terry in *Dracula*) to constitute the realistic 'connective tissue' (to borrow St John's term) of the novel. In Hichens's novel the title refers to the signifier linking Hastings and Amarinth: when Hastings offers Lady Locke's son a green carnation, she reads the flower and quietly intercedes to prohibit it. The novel counterpoints nature and art, manliness and effeminacy, foregrounding (but refraining from explicitly defining) 'sin', which features in most of the dialogues. Although Hichens is said to have withdrawn the novel from publication (not to be reprinted until 1949), since it helped to fuel arguments concerning Wilde's 'true' sexuality in the trials,[69] the novel was in fact reprinted at least twice after the trials, in 1896 and 1901.[70] William Heinemann published Hichens's novel in The Pioneer Series, locating it with twenty-one other novels.[71]

In *The Crimson Weed* passion is destructive. Luke Gray becomes mentally unstable, exiled, defeated in his desire for revenge or reconciliation, unable to acknowledge the relationship with his friend Savile. The point of view shifts towards the end of the third-person narrative, forcing the reader to regard Gray from a distance. This device forces the reader to regard Gray from a distance. An uncomfortable wrench stylistically, this serves to challenge the reader to sympathize with Gray, to overcome the objectification built up by the narrative effects and the social pressures which condemned him to exile and instability.

St John's representation of male characters' forbidden desires risks reinforcing the dominant view of specifically *male* same-sex desire as productive only of a bleak, self-destructive outcome. Although my reading of the novel foregrounds the destabilizing point of view at the end of the narrative and the thematic treatment of irregular family structures and relationships, it could be argued that St John's religious belief attributed the fate of the characters to their status as unbelievers. In *The Crimson Weed*, the female characters are represented as demonic or manipulative: Cecilia Rabucca (Luke's cousin) is Medusa, Maria (Luke's mother) is Ariadne with 'slim hips like a boy's'.

St John's representation of significant relationships between women was never realized directly in the novel genre. Her experiment in *The Crimson Weed* preceded her journal, 'The Golden Book', apparently given to Craig in 1911, and the anonymously published hybrid, *Hungerheart*. In formal terms, *Hungerheart* is a *Bildungsroman*, or novel of development. It has been interpreted as a *roman à clef*, in which the characters are thinly disguised as identifiable individuals. If, as has been suggested, it is 'an anonymous autobiography',[72] it remains to be seen which aspects of the narrative are 'true' and which are 'fictional'. Marguerite Steen dismissed St John's claim to illegitimacy in this narrative as evidence of her untrustworthiness. According to Steen, St John was the daughter of novelist Emma Marshall.[73] The rewriting of origins is, nevertheless, a significant project for the lesbian writer in the era of inversion.

In 'The Golden Book', the unpublished journal addressed to Craig as beloved, St John expresses her desire and Craig's reticence, alluding to what she regarded as troubling aspects of their relationship, even as she attempted to rationalize them.[74] The reticence seems to have been mutual, St John using her writing as a confessional space, a means of disclosure. The expected readership of the journal is uncertain. The narrative voice of the journal shifts from addressing Craig directly to speaking of her. Saying and doing are, in many ways, displaced by St John's writing. The journal may have functioned in their relationship as a testimony of their commitment to each other which could not otherwise be expressed. St John's account does not indicate to me, as it does to Laurie Wolf, the obscurity of Craig's sexual orientation.[75] It does, however, demonstrate the diversity of same-sex relationships and St John's growing acknowledgement of this in the beloved.

Hungerheart deploys the factual and fictional, the famous and the anonymous, interweaving a life which contains a representation of Craig. Some major shifts in attitudes to lesbianism in Britain occurred during St John's lifelong relationship with Craig (to be discussed at length later), but these were not met with an immediate written response from St John. Her need to bear witness took other forms. George Bernard Shaw's suggestion that St John should write the history of the *ménage à trois* was dismissed by Steen: 'Pretending to some degree of intimacy, he must well have known that such a history was unwriteable.'[76] For Manvell, Shaw's notion was 'ironic', for Steen it was 'naievete or mischief'.[77] Such unsubstantiated interpretations ignore Shaw's fearless attitude to the unorthodox and his longstanding respect for Craig and St John, apparent both in his involvement in the publication of the *Terry–Shaw Correspondence* and his defence of Craig in the light of her brother's public condemnation of her in *Ellen Terry and Her Secret Self*.

If 1900 was the year of *The Crimson Weed*, it was for Craig the year of the Stage Society. She repeated her Independent Theatre performances as Prossy in *Candida* on its London debut for the Stage Society. George Bernard Shaw met Edy before Ellen. He read his play, *You Never Can Tell*, to an unimpressed Edith Craig and Satty Fairchild.[78] In the 1903 regional tour of plays which Ellen Terry ran to make up the financial losses of the Imperial Theatre productions, Edith Craig developed some useful managerial skills. Gordon Craig's criticism of his mother's judgement seems to deny this: '[Terry] never found any first class manager to organize her affairs for her, and her theatrical course, during and after "The Vikings" was zigzag, for she was rudderless.'[79] He was keen to distinguish between the commercial management of a production and its artistic direction: 'I have never confused the two marked divisions of theatrical work – the stage work and the business work.'[80] His sister's attempts to develop her expertise in artistic direction through work experience were thus dismissed. Her experiments always involved a struggle with the facts of the theatre as a workplace, as a business, even though at times she deeply resented the economic restrictions this imposed on her. For her brother, such 'facts' were always split off, someone else's department. The demarcation was one in which he firmly believed. He tried to dematerialize the theatre. In order to train as a director, rather than an actor or even a costumier, Edith Craig was not given the financial support of a patron. Although she was subsidized by her mother, she needed to find the space to develop her skills by relentless, and often disappointing, toil, launching one-off productions for charities or the so-called independent theatre.

The spaces in which the 'new drama' was fostered were temporary and peripheral, often ill-defined but pitched in opposition to the commercial theatre, against tradition.[81] These new formations emerged unexpectedly, dissolving just as quickly, each one leaving its impression. In the European metropolis the cultural dynamic of numerous one-off incursions into experiments with form and representation formed a stalactite bridge of innovations across the two centuries. The conditions in which these experiments could take hold can be appreciated by plotting the tensions and conflicts of a failure.

Edith Craig's membership of a society called The Mummers in 1888 gave her some sense of the opportunities which play-producing subscription societies could offer. Subsequently she was a founder member of a new theatre society (ultimately called The Masquers at Walter Crane's suggestion). It was formed on 28 March 1903 during a meeting held at Edith Craig's costumier in 13 Henrietta Street, Covent Garden; the offices of the society were run from her flat at 7 Smith Square.[82] Like many organizations of its kind it established a management group and drafted a statement around which its work promised to coalesce. It was common for such statements to be fairly vague and often to fail to represent the actual principles of the organization which could be discerned in retrospect through its practices. The Masquers was formed to produce various types of performance, including ballets and ceremonies, which conveyed 'a sentiment of beauty'. A leaflet advertised the society, listing its plans as well as those who were to put them into effect.[83] Edith Craig's role in the society has been considered to be peripheral compared with that of the more famous members of the committee such as W. B. Yeats, Gilbert Murray and Walter Crane.

Edith Craig had already worked with several members of the committee. She had made costumes for a play by Walter Crane and in 1902 had met Yeats when she, together with Pamela Colman Smith, designed scenery for his play, *Where There Is Nothing*. They collaborated also on designs for Synge's *The Well of the Saints*. *Where There Is Nothing* was produced by the Stage Society in June 1904, largely thanks to Edith Craig's influence and resourcefulness. Yeats had provided some verses and advice on their performance for *The Vikings*, and had attended Edward Gordon Craig's production of Laurence Housman's nativity play, *Bethlehem*. Edith Craig heard Yeats read his work on several occasions towards the end of 1902. Edith Craig proved to be useful to Yeats. She gave him an insight into the costume designs and lighting arrangements for *Bethlehem*, which amused Yeats but annoyed her brother.[84] On another occasion, earlier in December 1902, Yeats perceived some competition: 'Pixie' Smith and 'Edie' Craig were using Edward Gordon Craig's 'stage dodges ... rather to his annoyance'.[85] Their designs for the monastery scene and garden topiary described in this letter have survived in Edith Craig's papers. Smith's caricatures had represented Edy in the mischievous role of 'The Puck', while Teddy was single-mindedly 'The Ted Pecker' industriously tapping at a woodcut.[86] Yeats shared with Smith membership of the Order of the Golden Dawn, and he valued the creativity of both women. All three were brought together in The

Masquers, where Smith was inexplicably designated librarian, rather than artist or costumier. The participation of Gilbert Murray on the committee and the membership of Jane Harrison may be explained by the society's intention to produce Murray's translation of *Hippolytus*. For Yeats, The Masquers promised to become the 'theatre of beauty' which he longed for.[87]

Extant correspondence from members of the committee and ordinary members demonstrates Craig's role as prime mover in the society. When it collapsed Yeats wrote her a consoling letter, referring to the society as her idea: 'I am sorry, however, that a plan of yours should have gone astray.'[88] This could be interpreted as flattery and appeasement, but she clearly put a lot of work into the society. This is substantiated by the range of letters she received which related to subscriptions, suggestions for performances and the opening ceremony.[89] It should be noted that Yeats knew that he had much to learn about the mechanics of the theatre and on the event of Edith Craig showing him backstage at *Bethlehem*, he later wrote to Lady Gregory, 'I have learned a great deal about the staging of plays from "the Nativity".'[90]

The problems facing the society were many and difficult to resolve. Members of the committee had different ideas about the aims of the society. It was suggested that The Masquers offer to produce D'Annunzio's *La città morta* for Eleanora Duse if the Lord Chamberlain were to refuse the play a licence for public performance.[91] The private performance of plays to members-only circumvented the licence required for public performances considered by many to constitute stage censorship. The Masquers was not to exploit this legal loophole. Stella Campbell's unusual ideas for make-up and performance in Gilbert Murray's translation of *Hippolytus* did not secure Murray's confidence.[92] There were concerns about the financial stability of the society and the need to operate on a secure footing. Perhaps more critical were worries about the direction the society seemed to be taking. The function of acting members of the society, perhaps as advisers, was perceived by some members to challenge the power of the committee. The anticipated roles of Smith and Craig is debatable. The correspondence shows that Craig's involvement was in an authoritative rather than merely administrative role, probably with responsibility for stage design. The plays which the society planned to produce were difficult to stage and likely to appeal to a small audience, ranging as they did from Greek tragedy to symbolist and poetic drama and translated plays.

Several members of The Masquers had work published in Pamela Colman Smith's little magazine, *The Green Sheaf*.[93] This magazine was hand-coloured and, like Jack B. Yeats's *Broad Sheet*, to which Smith had contributed, executed in a manner which challenged modern printing processes. Christopher St John and Lady Alix Egerton contributed short stories. The magazine published all manner of dream poems, mystical and quirky stories and illustrations.

The collapse of The Masquers was a reminder of the difficulties facing any newly forming theatre society. It did not have the complete agreement or support of its committee. Innovative ideas need to secure confidence. Resistance emerged amongst the writers, who were voicing their doubts about the relative status of theatre practitioners in the society. Played out across these conflicts were suspicions and insecurities based on gender. In particular it exemplifies the difficulties facing women in organizations attempting to implement changes. Stella Campbell may well have enjoyed unnerving Gilbert Murray with her ideas for performance,[94] and in some quarters there was underlying mistrust of Craig and those who might have influence over her.[95] Control of the society was unclear; the power base was shifting from author to actor. The gaps created by this transition embraced the newly developing roles of stage designer and director. As far as Craig was concerned, The Masquers gave her the opportunity to develop her work in costume design and probably in directing several significant productions. Her commitment to the society's success was therefore probably the greatest. That The Masquers was a separate space from her mother and her brother meant that Craig could begin to forge an independent professional profile. She saw her career developing in the control of production, but getting her experiments off the ground would involve women changing relationships in the theatre.

In 1905 on Henry Irving's death, Christopher St John published an elegaic monograph, in which she objected to inaccurate and hackneyed obituaries, to criticisms of Irving's diction, his unconventional approach to Shakespeare, the dominance of his personality in every role. Her tribute claims for Irving a modernist role: 'Henry Irving, the poetic actor, was as impersonal as the poet.'[96] As a director, Irving's powers of observation were put into effect in the detail of his preparation: 'He had every move clear in his head. There was no faltering, fumbling, or bungling. "We'll try that" was a phrase that he scorned. With him it was always, "Here it is. Now do it."'[97] In perfecting a character, Irving continued to be receptive to improvements to the detail of his performance. For his costume as

Shylock in *The Merchant of Venice*, he enlisted Edith Craig to make a scarf, ' "a rich, flaunting scarf . . . a scarf covered with all my jewels . . . a scarf that looks as if I were wearing my whole fortune on my head". And afterwards in that scene Shylock's shabby old clothes were always surmounted by a glowing, jewelled scarf – a touch of imagination all as bright'.[98] Thus Irving used costume as an element in the interpretation of a character, the smallest detail symbolizing the character's values and outlook.

St John's tribute concludes with a call for an appropriate memorial to Henry Irving. Rejecting the proposed endowment of beds for sick actors in London hospitals, she demanded instead 'a theatre to carry on his work'.[99] It is likely that she envisaged Edith Craig as the inheritor of Irving's memorial theatre. Her monograph was dedicated to Craig and published by the Green Sheaf. The front cover illustration seems to have been designed by Pamela Colman Smith. Above the motto 'Mors mihi lucrum' is a sketch of a smoking lantern on the point of being extinguished, the two plumes of smoke perhaps symbolizing spiritual inspiration leaving the body of Irving and the Lyceum.[100] The light which had burned brightly at the Lyceum Theatre had indeed been extinguished with Henry Irving's death.

For Craig and St John the death of Irving, first knight in 1895 of the acting profession, had meant very definitely the end of something. St John's tribute gestures towards a route by which a continuity could be sustained. In suggesting a memorial theatre to Irving she was thinking about Craig. By 1905 Craig had lost the Lyceum and the Imperial Theatre as spaces in which to cultivate and develop her experiments. Not only having access to a theatrical space but also controlling it became a crucial factor in the development of directors in theatre at this time. One way of gaining a temporary space was to work unofficially, setting up *ad hoc* performances to which invited guests or subscription-paying members constituted the audience. Such practices were widespread in Britain and Europe.

The high status of experimentation was one attraction to Craig in organizing theatre rather than being one of many organized within it. Another attraction was the means it presented of establishing herself in various ways – in a career and as an adult. The statement made famous by Matthew Arnold ('the theatre is irresistible, organize the theatre') was for women like Craig a compelling next step. Craig's experiments in theatre included acting in some of the most remarkable productions of Ibsen in Britain. While the Imperial

Theatre was Edward Gordon Craig's chance of establishing his reputation, the small experimental theatre society of The Masquers became Edith Craig's opportunity. Although The Masquers failed, it provided experience which was useful later for Craig in the Pioneer Players and the Barn Theatre, both of which were run on members' subscriptions.

The transition from working in the Lyceum and commercial theatres to the avant-garde theatre societies like the Independent Theatre or the Stage Society was for Craig more of a continuity than for many others. Ellen Terry regarded it as a retrograde step, moving from centre stage to the wings. Craig disagreed with the view that Irving's work was rooted in tradition. Stefan Hock, who had worked with Max Reinhardt for many years, compared Irving with Beerbohm Tree in that they 'never intended to be anything else but the custodians of time-honoured traditions, even though laying stress on the outward accoutrements of the stage'.[101] Hock asserts that Reinhardt, by contrast, was an interpreter of the play, a leader and teacher of actors, conducting fastidious research on the play before producing it. In the margins of Craig's copy of Hock's article an exclamation mark of surprise suggests that, for Craig, Henry Irving had been on the front line, revolutionizing the staging of plays in his own way. Ellen Terry had experimented with Ibsen's drama and regarded her short-lived stint in management as an incursion into modernity. In more ways than this, Terry felt the transition of the new age.

In 1906 Ellen Terry's stage jubilee was marked by a commemorative performance at Drury Lane Theatre. The unofficial story of the jubilee is told by Christopher St John. Terry was astonished to discover that the all-male executive committee of the jubilee performance had restricted the participation of actresses to a tableau: 'An actress-less programme in honour of an actress! what a joke!' [102] She wrote to Arthur Pinero, chairperson of the committee, promising to appear, like the other actresses, only in the tableau. Terry responded emphatically to the implications for women of being placed in the tableau compared to a speaking part. Her intervention, to ensure that her colleagues would not be compromised by their desire to honour her and by enduring an affront to their professional status, was successful. The jubilee event served to galvanize Terry to write her memoirs, and gave her an opportunity to assess her achievements. For St John, collaboration on Terry's autobiography was the ultimate achievement; St John had loved Terry even before she met Craig. It was to become a deeply painful rejection. Terry's unexpected marriage to the young actor James Carew while in America left St John a 'deserted collaborator'.[103] For Craig, it was a time to reassess her career.

During Terry's tour of America in 1907, Edith Craig's role changed. For Craig and St John it was a working trip. St John saved the day, understudying for Craig as Saart in *The Good Hope* when Craig fell ill in Chicago.[104] Formerly the unofficial assistant, adviser and designer of costume, Craig was officially designated stage-manager/director. This new direction was formalized by the publication of Craig's article in *Munsey's Magazine* entitled 'Producing a Play'. Craig refers to journalists' claims for her: the revolutionary role of first female stage-manager, pioneer of a new departure in theatre, a new profession for women. Revolution was something which came naturally to Craig. She cites Henry Irving as the ideal stage-manager: an autocrat only in his control of every minute detail. Otherwise his demands on each individual involved in the production were democratic; everyone was expected to think and contribute to the play. By contrast, Edward Gordon Craig is described by Craig as 'a root and branch reformer' intent on sweeping out the old for the new, even playing the role of hypnotist, controlling (the presumed) blank minds of the actors.[105] Edith Craig's position was thus closer to Irving's but not straightforwardly as autocrat. She argues for the need to adapt existing material to ensure that it is properly used. The mechanical effect of technology on the thinking of theatre personnel was deplored, since 'everyone ought to contribute a little bit of life to the performance'.[106] She therefore condemned the dogmatic adherence to the same routine effects (to create a stage sunset, for instance) whereby theatre staff knew which switches to throw but, in the event of mechanical failure, were unable to improvise.[107]

Craig's use of lighting was characterized by 'subdued footlights', a technique developed not, as had been claimed, to flatter her mother, but as a matter of principle, 'as a means of helping the acting'.[108] She condemned 'the mania for lighting a scene like a saloon bar'.[109] For instance, at the Empire Theatre, New York, she lit Herman Heijermans's *The Good Hope* so that the cottage interior, where the women talk about their lives in the fishing village, is sombre, shadowy in its corners and gloomy ceiling, but the actors are lit subtly to signify lamplight. Craig's priority was to represent both the 'pictorial effect' and 'dramatic situation', contending that every play has 'certain pictorial moments' which need to be enhanced.[110]

Craig explicitly disagreed with her brother, claiming that 'The play is in the hands of the actors', but she emphasized the significance of appropriate stage setting, costume, music and the pictorial use of small, representative groups of 'supers' rather than the distracting, counter-productive crowds of extras.[111] Inappropriate costume could, she believed, hamper the actor and 'kill his efforts' if the colours 'are working against him'.[112] The effect of stage lighting on costume is ignored at peril. She alludes to 'a high authority on archaeological costumes in London' who arranged, at great expense, to have fabric dyed purple, only to find that the final effect on stage was a dull brown.[113]

The slippage of terms in the article reflects on the changing role which Craig is claiming, even helping to develop, in the theatre. The title of the article refers to 'producing' a play. The subtitle cites Craig as 'the "first woman stage-manager on record" ', while Craig, in the first sentence, refers to her work on the American tour as 'stage-director'. The relationships between these different roles – producer, stage-manager, director – were becoming differentiated. Craig later claimed to loathe the term 'producer', more commonly choosing the title 'stage director'.[114] In this article she notes that whereas the stage-manager often acts merely as a prompter, the role she has in mind is a person 'who has control of the stage'.[115] In this respect, she is defining the role which elsewhere was filled by men, such as Max Reinhardt, working with a greater degree of financial support. The difficulty for a woman pursuing this role in the theatre frames the article. It begins with a careful distancing from the attribution to her of the pioneering role and closes with a flattering comparison of American with British men. In America, she found that politeness ensured that her wishes were executed, whereas 'In England men create another objection by resenting a woman "bossing" them in a professional capacity'.[116] However, one Brooklyn newspaper proved this generalization to be mistaken.

Edith Craig and St John returned to Britain elated with their successes.[117] They had ridden the storm. In America Craig's work and integrity had been challenged in a Brooklyn newspaper story with the headline: 'Ellen Terry Bossed by Autocratic Daughter: Miss Craig Real Ruler Behind the Scenes'.[118] Opening with the line, 'The woman stage manager has at last appeared in the person of Edith Craig', this article consisted of a number of misogynistic representations of professional women, still recognizable today. The introduction by Craig of a fine for actors who forgot their lines was interpreted, not as a disciplinary measure, but as 'a joke or a deep laid plot to get the rest of poor Ellen Terry's money away from her?' [119] It attributes to women a tendency towards vindictiveness, a competitiveness which prevents even mother and daughter from working together effectively. The emotive storyline ignores the substance of Craig's work, failing even to name the play or theatre in question. Craig was to meet such a response later. Gordon Craig fails to mention the significant theatre work (with the Pioneer Players, the Leeds Art Theatre or the Everyman Theatre) which Edith Craig achieved to national, and often international acclaim, after her years with Ellen Terry at the Imperial Theatre and on regional tours.

Edith Craig was involved in new directions, new forms of organization in her relationships at home and at work. The experimental relationships which she had were with men. Her relationship with Christopher St John was a specific choice, her primary relationship, however she may have understood it. In her career, Craig had participated in the alternative theatres of her day. In her role in The Masquers, hitherto overshadowed by that of the more famous participants such as W. B. Yeats and Gilbert Murray, she emerges as prime mover. Craig had been transformed by Pamela Colman Smith into 'The Puck'. It was time for Craig to begin to represent herself, to organize herself as well as the theatre.

Chapter 4

WOMEN'S SUFFRAGE:
Desires to Vote

In many ways Edith Craig already enjoyed some of the freedoms
which other women were hoping enfranchisement would provide for
them. In 1907, the year of Elizabeth Robins's play *Votes for Women*,
Craig's work as producer had been used to claim a role for women in
theatre. In 1909, four months after her release from prison, Emmeline
Pethick Lawrence, the Honorary Treasurer of the Women's Social
and Political Union (WSPU), visited Craig and St John at their third-
floor flat at 31 Bedford Street, in Covent Garden. Emmeline Pethick
Lawrence sent a congratulatory letter: 'It was a real joy to me to see
you yesterday in your home which is like a happy dream fulfilled.'[1]
The women's suffrage movement brought women together; it dealt in
dreams and realities, promising to transform women's lives. Winning
the vote symbolized for many women more than the powers of
citizenship. As a political movement, it had several founding
moments before the famous interruption of the Liberal Party's
meeting at the Free Trade Hall in Manchester in October 1905 by
Annie Kenney and Christabel Pankhurst.[2] Christopher St John's
former employer, Winston Churchill, was present and, for a short
time, even sympathetic to the movement.[3] Although Edith Craig's
interest in women's suffrage politics has been associated almost
exclusively with women's suffrage drama in London from 1908 to
1914, it had been kindled in the 1880s. She was involved in a range of
political and cultural activities nationwide. She produced plays in
support of women's suffrage at political events on a freelance basis,
as well as through the Actresses' Franchise League (AFL) and the
Pioneer Players. These cultural organizations were two of many
which supported the movement, operating in a relatively formal,
often pragmatic, way. This chapter will therefore explore what
women's enfranchisement meant to Craig and what contributions
she made to the movement, which had its contradictions, producing
limitation as well as liberation.

Craig's involvement with women's suffrage and her work as producer predated the founding of the AFL in autumn 1908. St John attributed Craig's involvement in the movement to the sight of protesting suffragists at Henry Irving's funeral in 1905. However, Craig revealed in an interview that she had been a suffragist all her life:

> 'When I was at school,' she said, 'I lived in a house of Suffrage workers, and at regular periods the task of organising Suffrage petitions kept everybody busy. Perhaps I didn't think very deeply about it, and my first ideas of Suffrage duties were concerned with the interminable addressing of envelopes; but I certainly grew up quite firmly certain that no self-respecting woman could be other than a Suffragist.'[4]

The failure in 1903 of Ellen Terry's lease of the Imperial Theatre had been blamed by Edward Gordon Craig partly on the disruptive behaviour of a 'suffragette' in the wardrobe department, a shortform for a limited perspective: 'I think she is not to be held entirely responsible for her devilry – for she had become one of the suffragettes – she could not see as the rest of the world saw.'[5] In some ways this was true; the movement produced radically new ways of seeing. Expectations of women's roles were changing. Unconventional approaches to performance and the notion of women writing and directing plays, promoting an independence in decision-making for women, were made available through the organizations which developed from women's suffrage. Some men, such as Gilbert Murray and Laurence Housman, supported the movement. Edith Craig claimed, with a view to increasing their numbers, that the best men in the acting profession were suffragists.[6]

Edith Craig participated in the women's suffrage movement at the level of branch politics, as an ordinary member and informal patron, as well as in the more prestigious roles of director and organizer of fundraising theatrical events. In the event, Rosa Bonheur rather than Rubens became her model. The women's suffrage movement gave Craig a formal meaning to her individually unconventional life and allowed her to attach this to a movement, giving her some creative space and freedom to do what she wanted. In 1905 Christopher St John may have regarded a potential Henry Irving memorial theatre as an opportunity for Edith Craig to develop her career. It was nevertheless the women's suffrage movement which consolidated Craig's opportunities and gave her a means of experimenting and developing her talents. She reached the national and international press. Her most famous nationwide production, *A Pageant of Great Women*, which she devised with Cicely Hamilton, made front-page news in the *Daily Mirror*.

The women's suffrage movement in Britain was a diverse movement campaigning for the enfranchisement of women, which was envisaged as fundamentally transforming the position of women in society. This redefined the 'political', hitherto perceived to be the exclusive domain of men in the so-called public sphere. Women were thought to be incapable of rational thought, appropriately confined to the private sphere of home. The Darwinian argument regarding women's evolutionary inferiority was cited by anti-suffragists to endorse their unenfranchised state. Historians of women's suffrage are currently looking beyond the public/private frame, exploring the role of imperialism in many of the arguments for (white, Western) women's enfranchisement, the sexual politics of enfranchisement, especially entailed in the critique of women's legal position in and out of marriage, a reassessment of the relationship between national and regional suffrage activities, the role of men in the movement for women's suffrage and the reassessment of the cultural politics of the movement.[7] These new perspectives on women's suffrage history in Britain bring Edith Craig into sight.

Craig's support of women's suffrage began at an early age, as one of her teachers played a significant role in the early movement. Elizabeth Malleson had been one of the founder members in 1867 of the Central London Committee for Women's Suffrage of which John Stuart Mill was President. Malleson had made a lasting impression, but Craig differed on some matters of principle. While Malleson was a member of the National Union of Women's Suffrage Societies (NUWSS), Craig was involved with both of the organizations which were to choose more unorthodox strategies: the WSPU and the Women's Freedom League (WFL).[8] The WFL was formed by members of the WSPU in November 1907 in revolt against autocratic methods. Both Edith Craig and Christopher St John worked with the WFL and its President, Charlotte Despard (1844–1939). St John wrote a preface to Despard's influential pamphlet, *Woman in the New Era*. Craig was in correspondence with Despard and party to her negotiations with the Independent Labour Party. Extending the franchise was a concern for socialists who were committed to full adult suffrage, regarding women's suffrage as diversionary and reinforcing class inequalities. Women's suffrage particularly appealed to middle-class women, but arguments about enfranchisement tended to see a conflict between class and gender.

Craig's theatre work in Britain, in the period after Ellen Terry's management of the Imperial Theatre ended and before the establishment of the AFL in autumn 1908, was as diverse as ever. She was taking any and every chance of developing the directorial role. A charity event in July 1908 at the Royal Court Theatre, in aid of the East London Hospital for Children, Shadwell, saw Edith Craig directing Christopher St John's play *On the East Side*.[9] St John was writing as well as translating plays before her commitment to 'suffrage' plays. As early as July 1906 her play, *The Decision: A Dramatic Incident*, was performed at a programme of events at Stafford House.[10] Italia Conti topped the bill at this event, which brought together many of Edith Craig's friends and colleagues. Pamela Colman Smith and Marion Gordon Kerby used the event to advertise their forthcoming 'afternoon of folk lore' at the Aeolian Hall, Bond Street. Edith Craig provided the costumes for Alix Egerton's *The Masque of the Princess*, for which E. Overbeck provided the music. Aimee Lowther's pantomime *Le Madrigal de Pierrot* and Mrs Craigie's *Two in a Tent* accompanied St John's play. Craig is not cited in the programme as producer of St John's play, but the two women were to work together in this way later.

St John's play, *The Wilson Trial*, was directed by Craig at the Royal Court on 14 December 1909. While collaboration was already a reality for St John and Craig, for others it was the women's suffrage movement which introduced them to different ways of working. St John found a co-author in Cicely Hamilton. They wrote plays such as *How the Vote Was Won* and *The Pot and the Kettle*. Craig directed the debut of *How the Vote Was Won* at the Royalty Theatre, London, on 13 April 1909, and subsequently in venues from the modest Corn Exchange, Stratford-upon-Avon (25 October 1909) to the Caxton Hall in London, where the WFL's Green White and Gold Fair was held in April 1909. Craig also acted in both plays: in *How the Vote Was Won*, she played Aunt Lizzie, drawing on the character-acting skills for which she had been commended in Frederick Fenn's *A Married Woman*. In *The Pot and the Kettle*, Craig performed the role of anti-suffragist, Mrs Brewster.

Craig's political position regarding women's suffrage was summarized in retrospect by Cicely Hamilton: 'I do not think that Edy shared these high hopes of a world reformed by the entry of women into politics; she was feminist rather than politician and stood for the franchise chiefly as a measure of justice.'[11] However, Craig's commitment to the justice which women's enfranchisement signified was complete. She was sufficiently motivated to become involved in many suffrage organizations; she did not see this as contradictory. She even claimed that 'one cannot belong to too many'.[12] When interviewed by Margaret Kilroy for *Votes for Women* in April 1910, she was evasive about whether she was 'chief organiser of the Actresses' Franchise League': 'Oh, am I? I organise for every society I belong to, not for any one in particular. That's nearer the truth.'[13] She was one of many women whom Liddington and Norris have described as non-partisan and, contrary to popular opinion, the organizations of the women's suffrage movement were not mobilized into relentlessly antagonistic factions. These organizations rather functioned separately, specializing in different fields and representing diverse groups. Their boundaries were permeable. Craig declared, 'As to joining Suffrage societies – yes, I belong to ten now, but I don't seem to be able to remember more than seven.'[14] The traffic between organizations, developing into informal networks of women, produced a dynamic which, at least for women, was unconventional and productive: 'There was a new Freemasonry amongst women since the movement had begun. For one woman Suffragist to know that another woman held the same views was to trust that other.'[15]

Craig was not bound by party lines. She worked as a freelance director, on many occasions not associated directly with the AFL or any other organization. The AFL was concerned to maintain a neutral stance and organized the performance of plays and entertainments for any of the political organizations, showing no preference for the WSPU or the NUWSS. The ways in which Craig was able to help were diverse and she attracted the image of suffrage shapeshifter:

> The enthusiastic master of our pageants, the kindly daughter of our good friend delightful Ellen Terry, the most genial of workers – and the easiest to work with – the most painstaking of picture-makers, the quickest to grasp a telling incident, and the most understanding of teachers, choose which description you will, and you instantly conjure up the figure of Miss Edith Craig. A very Proteus of Suffragists, she comes continually to our assistance, ... The work which Miss Edith Craig has done for us on various occasions ... has not always received its due notice, owing to her habit of laughing self-effacement.[16]

Identifiable here is Margaret Webster's Promethean image of Edy talking, rather than Marguerite Steen's bossy troublemaker. Craig, like Proteus, possessed the gifts of transformation and prophecy; her enigmatic personality, her ability to transform herself and others through costume and performance were vital contributions to the suffrage movement.

Craig's involvement in the movement extended beyond adapting her professional skills to producing or organizing cultural events for women's suffrage entertainments. She also sold newspapers in the street:

'I love it. But I'm always getting moved on. You see, I generally sell the paper outside the Eustace Miles Restaurant, and I offer it verbally to every soul that passes. If they refuse, I say something to them. Most of them reply, others come up, and we collect a little crowd until I'm told to let the people into the restaurant, and move on. Then I begin all over again.'[17]

Characteristically for Craig, the interview from which this extract comes is not used to seek glory but to provide constructive advice for prospective newspaper vendors:

It was seeing *Votes for Women* sold in the street in an apologetic manner that made me feel that I wanted to do it quite differently, and I began joining societies right away. That was some time ago, you know, and our sellers don't apologise for their existence now.[18]

Craig was often seen in the street. She was involved formally and informally in suffrage street processions. During a working trip when she was organizing entertainments for the WSPU's Glasgow Exhibition, her impromptu appearance in a street procession in Glasgow was caught by a WFL photographer for the *Vote*.[19] More formally, Craig was General Director of the procession in the John Stuart Mill celebrations.[20] She worked with Sime Seruya to develop 'open air work' for the WFL. In this capacity they both attended a meeting of the Willesden and Maida Vale WFL.[21]

Although these plans were realized, and she had worked with Sime Seruya as organizer of outdoor processions in June 1910, it was Seruya who was ultimately named as chief organizer.[22] In the mean time, Craig had collaborated with Laurence Housman, culminating in July 1910 in designing the West procession of the WSPU demonstration.[23] Her expertise in the field of theatre crossed disciplinary boundaries in her work for the Suffrage Atelier. Several of its artists were friends, notably Laurence Housman and Pamela Colman Smith. The Suffrage Atelier, formed in February 1909, produced plays as well as artwork for the movement, and Edith Craig was, as Lisa Tickner suggests, a crucial link between the suffrage art and theatre organizations.[24] The cultural diversity of organizations was widespread. As well as organizing drama, the AFL held debates and meetings, including an At Home meeting led by Lena Ashwell, and discussed the relationship between the 'White Slave Traffic' and enfranchisement of women.[25] The Suffrage Atelier hosted a lecture by Dr Haslam on women in the medical profession.[26]

Sime Seruya, a founder member (with Winifred Mayo) of the AFL, the WSPU and then the WFL, was one of those responsible for developing the cultural infrastructure of the movement, enabling groups to connect and work together. In 1910 she founded the International Suffrage Shop, a feminist publisher and bookseller. In the month of the WFL's census protest, in April 1911, it moved to the basement and ground floor of 15 Adam Street, Strand. It was more a cultural centre than a shop, organizing printing, bookbinding, book searches, lectures and meetings and housing a lending library. The most famous of the meetings it hosted included the debate between Cicely Hamilton and G. K. Chesterton and the W. T. Stead Memorial Meeting.

Edith Craig provided practical help, offering her Bedford Street flat to house the International Suffrage Shop when it was founded. After its move to Adam Street, the International Suffrage Shop had its windows smashed: a sign of its effectiveness not merely as a place to buy radical literature. Seruya had used the shop variously as a venue for the discussion group of *The Freewoman* and as a safe haven for the children of striking transport workers.[27] Ellen Terry and Cicely Hamilton had contributed to the Shop's £900 fund. Hamilton, like many other writers and actors including Craig, was drawn into activities such as public speaking. In July 1910, for instance, Craig spoke at a garden party in Bromley, Kent, organized by Mrs Harvey.[28]

Craig was, like Cicely Hamilton, an active member of the Central London Branch of the WFL, which met at the Bijou Theatre, 3 Bedford Street, just down the road from her flat. Craig was elected Literature Secretary of the Mid-London (renamed Central London) Branch on 14 February 1911. This level of commitment should not be underestimated: attending branch meetings is one of the hidden (and often thankless) but essential parts of democratic political organizations. Craig financially supported women's suffrage by donating money for the WFL's J. S. Mill celebration and to its newspaper, the *Vote*.

Margaret Webster recalled from her childhood, when her parents May Whitty and Ben Webster lived in the top flat at 31 Bedford Street, the activities of the tenants downstairs: 'Some of the most determined of the "militants" would take refuge with them, either before they set out on some mission or after they were released from prison.'[29] No documents survive to support this assertion, except perhaps a couple of letters from Joseph Pennell who lived in the flat above, and who wrote to complain about noises on the roof.[30]

The Bedford Street flat became one of many centres of cultural and political activity. Suffragists opened up their homes for political events. At 1 Pembroke Cottages, Laurence and Clemence Housman played host to a suffrage fair on 21 and 22 October 1910. Craig contributed entertainments with her 'strolling players'.[31] Craig's flat was the venue for the farewell party for Muriel Matters before her trip on a lecturing tour to Australia and New Zealand with her companion (Miss) Violet Tillard. The party, held on 4 April 1910, was reported in the WFL's newspaper.[32] Muriel Matters was an outrageous character; politically courageous and, like Craig, with the broad experience of travel and work. She was born in Adelaide and had worked as an elocutionist and actor before travelling to Britain. Her achievements in the women's suffrage movement were high profile and inventive. She became the first woman to speak in the House of Commons, by chaining herself to the grille in the Strangers' Gallery, and she scattered leaflets from a hot-air balloon over the Houses of Parliament on 17 February 1909.[33] When she arrived in London with an introduction to Prince Kropotkin (1842–1921), she had socialized with, and learned about cultural politics from, anarchists, socialists and Russian refugees. She was one of many women, such as Janette Steer, Stella Campbell and Edith Craig, to be treated to a biographical portrait in the *Vote*. Later Muriel Matters was to study under Maria Montessori (1870–1952) and run a model school for the children at the Mother's Arms, Sylvia Pankhurst's creche in the East End of London.[34] Muriel Matters and Edith Craig had a great deal in common.

Craig was a mover; she made things happen and did not bother much about owning them. She got many authors' plays published, making them available for production. However, she bought the rights to some plays; for two of these she had drafted conditions for performance.[35] Craig's collection of plays included some privately printed by the Utopia Press, which had a reputation for controversial work.[36] One of these, possibly never performed, J. L. Austin's play, *How One Woman Did It*, features a female cross-dressing butler who argues an individualistic solution to women's oppression. Through cross-dressing the woman has access to the otherwise masculine privilege of equal pay for her work and to a social freedom routinely denied to women.[37] Women sent plays to Craig hoping that she would be able to make them known, if not produce them.[38] The manuscript of 'The Masque of Women' by Margaret Nilior Meuron exemplifies the kind of humour widely employed by suffrage artists and writers and the ways in which women were reinterpreting dramatic forms, such as the masque and the pageant.[39]

The women's suffrage movement itself brought about changed relationships even while its campaigns envisaged enfranchisement as the deliverer of new economic and social relationships. The possibility of exploitative relationships, even within a movement explicitly founded to counteract such things, was undeniable. Donation of time and work to the campaigns was regarded as a charitable, even sacrificial, act. As Lisa Tickner noted, Sylvia Pankhurst often felt the conflict between her commitment to the movement and her own needs as a worker.[40] Nevertheless, for women such self-denial, regarded as heroic in male politicos, accrued meanings corresponding to the submissive femininity against which they were arguing. Craig claimed that writing plays about women's suffrage was 'a great work' and urged women to get involved.[41]

A photograph shows Edith Craig, Cicely Hamilton and Christopher St John in a street procession in 1910 carrying the Women Writers' Suffrage League (WWSL) banner.[42] Craig had worked with many of the WWSL's key members since its formation in June 1908 by Cicely Hamilton and Bessie Hatton (Madeleine Lucette Ryley was one of its earliest members). In 1913, its headquarters were located in Henrietta Street, familiar to Craig. Just round the corner from Bedford Street, it was the street where Edith Craig & Co. costumiers was based.[43] Craig owned performance rights to three of the WWSL's published plays: *A Pageant of Great Women*; *How the Vote Was Won*; and *Lady Geraldine's Speech*.

Women's rights were already also women's business for writers, publishers and producers of plays. Craig ensured that her directorial rights over plays which she had brought to the stage for the first time would be safeguarded. The conditions for production of *A Pageant of Great Women*, for instance, detailed the reasonable terms on which Craig was prepared to work; these did not change where friends were concerned. Christopher St John wrote to May Whitty regarding the Theatrical Ladies Guild's attempt to produce *The Pageant of the Stage* for a second time, but without recourse to Craig's directorial role:

> [Craig] gave not only her time and her talents as a present to the charity when the pageant was last done, but a very considerable sum of money. She was much out of pocket by it. She doesnt grudge this at all but she does feel she ought not to let her enthusiasm carry her away a second time.
>
> I am very sorry – but unless this first condition – Edith Craig as producer – is complied with, the pageant must not be performed, I need not go into the others which are all of minor importance.[44]

Craig was, according to St John, 'practically part author, and I cannot hand over her ideas to be dealt with by another'.[45]

Craig's earlier production of *The Pageant of the Stage* had involved Cicely Hamilton as prompter, Regina Laurence as stage-manager, Mrs Haverfield as call-boy, while the wardrobe was in the care of the 'Three Arts Club Girls'.[46] The history of theatre according to St John places Hrotsvit's drama (or Roswitha as St John spelled her) emphatically before the *Quem Quaeritis*, often cited as the 'first' drama. In St John's *The Pageant of the Stage*, Tragedy's statement, following Hrotsvit's lines, emphasizes by juxtaposition the (presumed) male authorship and ownership of the 'first play': 'It was not long 'ere priests began/To make church dogmas sweet to man.'[47] Male dramatists seemed to have had a monopoly on putting words into women's mouths. The historical knowledge of Hrotsvit, a nun who could make drama sweet to women, was used to challenge this.

In typically self-effacing mode, Craig urged women to write plays, emphasizing the role of the writer rather than actor or producer:

> 'I do think plays have done such a lot for the Suffrage. They get hold of naive frivolous people who would die sooner than go in cold blood to meetings. But they see the plays, and get interested, and then we can rope them in for meetings. All Suffrage writers ought to write Suffrage plays as hard as they can. It's a great work.'[48]

Margaret Wynne Nevinson credits Craig with having persuaded her to write a play from her articles in the *Westminster Gazette*.[49] Craig's attempts to encourage men to write were less successful. She could not persuade Ford Madox Hueffer (Ford) to write a play even though his pamphlet, *The Monstrous Regiment of Women*, published by the WFL for 6d, had been so popular.[50] Craig's emphasis on the 'great work' which writing plays constituted places women's suffrage drama in the context of a socially responsible contribution to a socio-political movement for change. If writing plays for the suffrage movement is presented by Craig as almost compulsory, such a view was contested by anti-suffragists and, surprisingly, by some suffragists.

The relationship between politics and cultural form was crucially brought into sharp focus by the highly publicized interventions of suffragists. Lisa Tickner's point that the reception of much women's suffrage cultural production has dwelt upon a perceived opposition between the political and the artistic[51] is relevant to the reviews of women's suffrage drama and to its subsequent historiography by feminist and non-feminist critics alike.

Women's suffrage (or 'suffragette') drama has become associated with a number of plays which have been re-published by feminist critics such as Dale Spender and Carol Hayman (1985) and Viv Gardner (1985). Spender and Hayman's anthology published seven plays, of which *How the Vote Was Won* was directed by Craig. Gardner's anthology contained twelve plays, of which four were amongst those for which Craig owned performance and reading rights. These anthologies have formed a provisional canon, representing some of the most popular plays to be performed at women's suffrage events. In a sense the 'women's suffrage play' or 'suffragette play' did not exist. It was not an autonomous form. As Lisa Tickner has argued, no single image was originated by women's suffrage artists, who appropriated and manipulated existing imagery.[52] In the same way, the drama of the movement drew on existing forms of the monologue, the naturalist play.

Plays performed in support of women's suffrage were reviewed in the mainstream national press as well as the women's suffrage newspapers, in which the critics were often women. It was one of Craig's productions which elicited an energetic critique from Rebecca West in *The Freewoman*.[53] West was twenty years old when she published this review, which vilified a specific play, the Pioneer Players and the AFL in general, and the plays of Cicely Hamilton at a stroke. West had already worked, unsuccessfully, as an actress in Manchester, Eastbourne and Brighton, having performed in Hamilton's play *Phyl*.[54] The hostility centred on the issue of literary merit, which West failed to find in Florence Edgar

Hobson's *A Modern Crusader*. The play, nevertheless, aligns social reforms such as improvements in housing and health care with vegetarianism and egalitarian relationships between women and men. West used her review, as reviewers sometimes do, as a platform for another debate.[55] This incident underlines the fact that women involved in women's suffrage and feminists (sometimes not members of the same group) had opinions regarding the use of drama in the movement and disagreed on the relationships between art and politics.[56] In contrast to Craig, Madeleine Lucette Ryley (a dramatist with whom Craig had worked in 1902) argued that writing plays for the movement could trivialize complex issues and therefore have a detrimental effect. This did not prevent Ryley from acting in *A Pageant of Great Women* and *The Rack* by Mrs Harlow Phibbs.[57] Presumably these plays were, in Ryley's opinion, successful in adequately engaging with complex political issues.

Edith Craig used the term 'propaganda' unapologetically. Her business notepaper was headed 'Propaganda Plays' or 'Suffrage Plays', listing the ones to which she owned performance rights. Strategies for exploiting the press were commonplace and Craig included in her estimate for producing St John's *Pageant of the Stage* the option of advertising. New audiences were being created for women's suffrage culture, including drama. A reassessment of the relationship between gender and value in cultural production was a recurrent feature of the women's suffrage movement and concerned its critics. The AFL was anxious to change the working conditions of women in theatre. The Suffrage Atelier challenged the distinctions between professional and amateur, and, as Lisa Tickner suggests, used its educational role to encourage experiment in the artwork it produced.[58] Many of the women inspired by the movement to write for the first time had not considered themselves as writers and wrote only one or two plays. The WWSL did not make a great attempt to break down the barriers between professional and amateur. To some extent, like the AFL, it was concerned with raising the professional status of women working in a given field. Some of the plays directed by Craig as part of women's suffrage events raised questions about the need for a female tradition or network of support, about the double standard in operation in different fields of work (female performer in theatre, women as writers). The system of values customarily brought to bear on cultural production was rigorously reconsidered. The ideology of the aesthetic was exposed and subjected to a critique taking different, sometimes contradictory, forms.

The claim that women can produce artwork which is of equal value to that of male artists was common, as was a more radical attitude to art or literature. This involved the refusal to distinguish between, for instance, the value of a play and a sketch, a raffle and a recitation, in an all-day women's suffrage entertainment. The use of drama, poetry, recitations and other forms in this context was not merely functional. It actively transformed the cultural forms themselves and impinged on the narrow perspectives of critics who depended on isolating literature and art, just as it threatened male politicians who contended that women did not exist in the public spheres of politics and work. The arguments circulating in women's suffrage cultural organizations reflect on a widely held, contrary attitude amounting in itself to an aesthetic. This was a defiant appropriation of anything useful, a fundamentally experimental mode: try it, if it works, use it. Such a pragmatism was most visible in the suffrage all-day event when the programme shifted from recitations and drama to ju-jitsu displays and raffles. It had its own coherence which, defying the conventions of malestream modernism, has evaded literary critics who have been unable to plot the connections.

Edith Craig directed numerous plays for the AFL. The exact number is unknown. The fact that this went unrecorded indicated the short-term view of the value of the cultural practices of the movement. Cicely Hamilton's anecdote regarding a disagreement between Craig and the AFL executive, in which Hamilton composed letters on behalf of both parties,[59] has unfortunately been taken out of context and used to perpetuate the image of Craig as a troublemaker.[60] There were controversies in the AFL. Eva Moore's performance in a play as a character who appeared to prefer 'kisses to votes' caused a furore.[61] This may form the context for Moore's undated letter to Craig:

> Dear Edie, I have received a letter from Miss Mathers of the Womans Freedom League, saying that you 'suggested that probably I would lend my drawing [sic] for a meeting.' I should have been delighted but I must confess to being humorously annoyed that you who consider me a disloyal member of the A.F.L. should suggest the using of my house. Need I say more. Yours sincerely Eva Moore.[62]

However, the subject of the disagreement to which Hamilton refers is not known, and it did not prevent Craig's continued involvement with the AFL. In October 1910, Decima Moore announced that

Edith Craig was to direct a new department involved with the production of propaganda plays.[63] The dominant narrative of the history of women's suffrage has been of antagonism rather than development, specializing, adapting. Stealthy strategies were needed to negotiate repressive forces. These were manifested a month later, on 18 November 1910, with the brutality of 'Black Friday', when 500 suffragists marched to the House of Commons on hearing that the Conciliation Bill had been shelved. The women struggled with police for six hours, during which time many suffragists were violently and indecently assaulted.

The plays Craig directed for women's suffrage explored a diverse range of representations of women, particularly in relation to work and marriage. The portrayal of women who were questioning marriage occurred in plays such as Jess Dorynne's *The Surprise of His Life*, Margaret Wynne Nevinson's *In the Workhouse*, Cicely Hamilton's, *Jack and Jill and a Friend* and Laurence Housman's *Pains and Penalties*. Characteristic plots involved the confrontation between different generations of women and the condemnation of the Womanly Woman, who is seen to be complicit in the oppression of other women. The representation of the (female and male) anti-suffragist converted to sympathy for women's enfranchisement was common, for example in *How the Vote Was Won* and in Evelyn Glover's *A Chat with Mrs Chicky*. Less common were representations of relationships between women, sometimes posing an alternative to marriage, and an attempt to represent the diversity of women. This was attempted by *A Pageant of Great Women*.

Craig's nationwide productions of *A Pageant of Great Women* were major events in the suffragists' calendar of 1909–11. They were featured in the various women's suffrage newspapers where the play became so well known and popular that it was referred to simply as 'pageant'. The debut at the Scala Theatre, London, on 12 November 1909 made the front page of the *Daily Mirror*. The eight performers photographed included Ellen Terry as Nance Oldfield and Marion Terry as Florence Nightingale. The new photojournalism, its minimal captions and the implication that the-picture-says-it-all depoliticized the play as a gathering of famous and beautiful women in fancy dress. Godfrey Blount in *The Freewoman* referred to the view of a (male) friend who

> attributes the vogue for pageants to that feminine domination which he thinks characteristic of the day. He says it is nothing more than the vanity of the sex, its infatuation for posing and

drapery. I think there is much truth in his suggestion, and that this age will be remembered as a flabby or sentimental period in which women's thoughts directed men's energies, and women's fashions inspired their art.[64]

A few years later the *Daily Mirror* used a similar technique, appropriating and deracinating images of women in its coverage of the Hyde Park meeting. The photographs, as Tickner shows, recorded the natural history of the evolving/degenerating New Women: 'The Suffragette Face: New Type Evolved by Militancy'.[65]

A Pageant of Great Women developed from several tableaux of famous women which Edith Craig had organized and from the imagery in a cartoon of Woman chained at the feet of Justice by the artist W. H. Margetson.[66] Cicely Hamilton wrote the play, as the dedication to the published text states: 'To Edith Craig whose ideas these lines were written to illustrate.' At this time, Cicely Hamilton was co-editor with Marion Holmes of the WFL's Newssheet (begun on 16 September 1909). The need for such a play was urgent and was not simply a response to a cheery array of empowering images of women to motivate suffragists who were becoming physically and mentally destroyed by imprisonment and forcible feeding. It was prompted by a need to alleviate the burden of proof; the anti-suffragists' argument that women were not worthy of the vote was unrelenting. F. E. Smith MP (later Lord Birkenhead) had argued that 'If Sappho had never sung, if Joan of Arc had never fought, if Siddons had never played, if George Eliot had never written, the sum of human happiness to which woman has contributed by her womanly faculties would not have been affected.'[67] Such summary denials of women's place in history and their exclusion from the 'human' category were countered by an alternative, albeit whiggish, history.

The circumstances in which *Pageant* was devised, produced and rewritten provide an insight into some of the more contradictory aspects of the women's suffrage movement. The play was not simply imitating the public ceremonials of power, representing itself to itself. It did not insert women into existing patriarchal history; the great women replace, rather than correspond to, androcentric history. Suffragists became actively involved in producing women's history. Any significant woman of the past could provide a political reference point for contemporary history-making. Margaret Wynne Nevinson followed the example of Amelia B. Edwards in lecturing on Egyptian women as proto-suffragists.[68] The feminist potential of Hatshepsut or Hathor, Egyptian snake goddess (if not Mrs Brown-

Potter's performance as Nicandra), was identified by suffragists as well as anti-suffragists. Bram Stoker's representation of women in Egyptian history in *The Jewel of Seven Stars* is partisan, while *The Lair of the White Worm* associates Lady Arabella, possessed by the serpentine spirit, with 'the want of a principle of a suffragette'.[69] Queen Elizabeth I was added to Stoker's collection of disturbing women in 1910 when he published *Famous Imposters*, which infamously claimed that the woman known as Queen Elizabeth I was in fact a man, the substitution having been made when the real Queen died in childhood.[70]

In *A Pageant of Great Women*, the 'great' women were marshalled into cohorts, responding to each of the most common anti-suffrage arguments. A report of the performance in Beckenham noted, 'It is a splendid thing to bring "Antis" to'.[71] Only one great woman, the eighteenth-century actress, Nance Oldfield, spoke. This part was played by Ellen Terry, in remembrance of the orchestrators of the proposed tableau of silent women for her jubilee. The silence of the other great women is counterpointed by the speech of Woman. Her response to Prejudice's anti-suffrage arguments addressed to Justice constitutes the play. Woman presents the case for woman's right to enfranchisement, arguing against Prejudice, in the court of Justice. The representations of silence and speech, of Woman and women, and the deployment of the only male character in the play as Prejudice and not Man, make the *Pageant* one of the most profound responses to the crisis of gender staged by the women's suffrage movement.

The setting in the court of Justice emphasizes the legal dimension of the arguments, and the need for women to make out their case. Justice, conventionally represented as a blindfolded woman, and therefore impartial, generates further implications in this context. The sex of Justice is conventionally invisible; her blindness allows her to see the truth. The coercive mark of visibility as power, phallogocentrism, is made visible in the *Pageant*. Perhaps crucially for Craig and Hamilton, the representation of women in the play reverses the conventional dynamics of women's history as bringing women from silence to speech.[72] On one occasion Prejudice was even played by a woman,[73] wresting the debates even more clearly from what anti-suffragists liked to regard as a sex war.

The great women were thematically grouped into six categories: the learned women; the artistes [*sic*]; the saintly women; the heroic women; the rulers; and the warriors, the largest of the groups. Some of the representatives in these groups were surprising choices.

Writers were not given a unique group but appeared, like Jane Austen, as one of the learned women or Sappho as one of the 'artistes'. French revolutionary and assassin of Marat, Charlotte Corday, was played at the Albert Hall by Mrs Brown-Potter. She appeared in the heroines' group.

Cicely Hamilton, Edith Craig and the actors playing Woman, Justice and Prejudice travelled to the various venues, where Craig would ensure that the local suffragists comprising the cast of great women were appropriately dressed and trained in their non-speaking roles. Casting amongst local suffragists for the numerous great women negotiated nepotism and vanity. Prospective participants were invited to send their photographs and vital statistics to Miss Tuke,[74] and a 'Measurement Form' was produced to standardize the collection of this information.[75] Craig's 'Descriptive Cast List' provided some guidance for the suffrage societies who were responsible locally for casting appropriate amateurs. The embodiment of the great women was expected to have a literal basis, particularly in terms of age, physique, hair colour and texture. Caroline Herschel and Catherine of Siena 'can be old', whereas Sappho was to be 'tall, young and strong looking, thin, nice hair'.[76] Some characters were more popular than others.

The audiences for the productions of the *Pageant* were actively cultivated. Advertisements were published in the *Vote*, promising that the event would be an enriching and consciousness-raising experience: 'come and realize your beliefs'.[77] Tickets were made available at shops and from private houses (in Sunderland, tickets were sold by Mr Flintoff, Stationers at Borough Road, at 3 Havelock Terrace and at 4 Athol Road). The advertised addresses of ticket-sellers map the pockets of support which women's suffrage found in local small businesses.

The production of plays coincided with political meetings. At Croydon, the WFL members saw Mrs Harvey's play, *Baby*, directed by Craig, and heard Mrs How Martyn give a speech. Muriel Matters's nationwide lecturing visits were used, on at least one occasion, to 'work up an audience' for a forthcoming production of *How the Vote Was Won* in Wales.[78] Such visits incurred some physical danger. Matters reported that the house where she and other suffragists had stayed had been surrounded at midnight by an angry Liberal mob.[79] The massive gatherings which *A Pageant of Great Women* attracted were threatening and provoked much fear.

Although the *Pageant* was a play and not a procession, it had the capacity to generate an event which could – indeed did – fill the

Albert Hall. When it was performed there for the WFL, the play was held not in the theatre where the smaller-scale plays were staged, but in the Great Hall. The Albert Hall production on Saturday 11 December 1909 was part of an all-day event and a star cast was planned. Mrs Langtry was announced as a participant. She wrote to Craig, 'I'll try my best dear. Ask me again a little later – What do you want me to be? One of the witches?'[80] Ultimately, however, she could not appear. The *Pageant*'s large cast of fifty-three to ninety great women demanded a large venue. Craig's conditions of performance warned that the play needed to be performed in 'a large hall (with a large platform) or in a large garden'.[81] Craig could not produce the *Pageant* at the Glasgow Exhibition in April 1910 because 'there was no hall big enough'.[82] In Middlesbrough, the *Pageant* was performed at the Grand Opera House, where it was a 'spectacular treat'.[83] In Sunderland there were over 2,000 in the audience. The advertising, administration, hire of the hall, the orchestra and the casting of the amateurs for the roles of the great women were the responsibility of the local suffrage society or branch. Ticket prices varied across the country. A minimum of 6d was paid, usually 1s, with a maximum of a couple of pounds. There is evidence that children were expected to attend. At the Royal Albert Hall tickets for children were at a reduced rate of 6d, for which they could see the *Pageant* as well as visit the Christmas tree at the WFL's yuletide festival.[84] In Bristol, 'children's revels' and morris dances preceded the *Pageant*. The cast included Edith Craig as (ever) Rosa Bonheur and Lady Constance Lytton as Florence Nightingale. Cicely Hamilton was unavoidably absent, as was Ellen Terry, who was touring in America. In a private box in the Prince's Theatre were Christabel Pankhurst, Mrs Tuke, Annie Kenney, Mary Allen and the Pethick Lawrences.[85] Annie Kenney wrote: 'Congratulations the play went off *splendidly*. You have done as usual wonders in a short time. Oh Edith the life of Pioneers! and yet it is worth it all. It is charming the play and very beautiful in thoughts.'[86]

The play changed as it moved round the country. Famous women of Cambridge were added when it played at the city's Guildhall. Miss Fanny Johnson introduced the play, announcing the 'foundresses' of various Cambridge colleges: Lady Elizabeth de Clare (Clare College); Countess of Pembroke (Pembroke College); Margaret of Anjou and Elizabeth Woodville (Queen's College); Lady Margaret (St John's and Christ's College); Lady Frances Sidney, Countess of Sussex (Sidney Sussex College).[87] The Executive Committee of the Cambridge Association for Women's Suffrage held an extraordinary meeting to abdicate responsibility for the play to Johnson. However, the 16 guineas which the performance made were not refused.[88] An attempt to adapt the play to the various locales emphasized the dialogue between dramatist, producer, actors and audience. The nationwide production of the play was not a message from the metropolis, not merely a provincial tour of a play which had been successful in London.

Craig hired out costumes for the great women (at a cost of 7/6 to 10s each), with reduced rates for repeat performances. Thankfully, her general view that stage costumes should not be cleaned was not strictly followed where these costumes were concerned. They were cleaned and altered for each performance. On many occasions, payment of fees for hire of costumes was devolved to the performers to disperse the costs of the production, yet the responsibility for the collection of fees remained with the suffrage society or branch. Fees were payable within one week of performance. The cost of the production varied according to the number of great women and costumes.[89]

The research required to produce the play was considerable. Lina Rathbone (photographed in costume as Mary Ann Talbot in the 1948 edition) worked in the British Library, reading biographies of Agnes of Dunbar, Christian Davies, Madame Roland, Mary Ann Talbot, Hannah Snell, the Ranee of Jhansi and Vittoria Colonna.[90] The following great women warriors were researched but did not make it into the play. Marie Schelling, a Belgian soldier with the French army at Jemappes, Jena and Austerlitz, was awarded the Legion of Honour in 1806.[91] Maid Lilliard was a soldier at the battle of Ancrum Moor. William Brown, a black woman who fought in Queen Charlotte's navy between 1804 and 1815, was 'conspicuous for agility as captain of main top no less than for her partiality for grog & prize money'.[92] Brief biographical sketches of the great women were listed in the play programme and attributed to Mary Salmon, MA, who played Caroline Herschell in the production for the Swansea WFL.[93]

The play evolved in various ways. The title changed from 'famous' to 'great' women; the suffrage press referred to it as a 'pageant of the world's heroines', sometimes simply 'the pageant' once it had become so famous. In the WFL, the *Pageant* became as quotable as Edward Carpenter's *Toward Democracy*.[94] Characters were added, such as Camargo and the actress Mrs Siddons. It seems, however, that some performances deviated from the published playscript. In Hamilton's manuscript Prejudice's lines, entitled

'Prejudice (Poor Beggar) His Part (Lawd 'elp 'im)', designate a mode of exit inconsistent with the formality of the published text: 'Exit in tears, with a despairing shriek, chased by Miss Chase'.[95] Pauline Chase, famous for her performances as Peter Pan, played Joan of Arc in the original performance at the Scala Theatre.

The ways in which the play changed in performance may have involved more than merely the accretion of other great women. The ridicule of Prejudice by Joan of Arc was consistent with the humour of the music hall. In this respect it was similar in tone to the curtain-raiser which usually preceded the *Pageant*: Cicely Hamilton's 'Anti-suffrage Waxworks'. This piece involved the reproduction on stage of various stereotypes of women from the anti-suffrage perspective. These were self-consciously stage-managed by Hamilton, assuming a Phineas T. Barnum role as the Showman [*sic*], and then routinely deconstructed. At Sutton Coldfield Town Hall, Edith Craig played Elizabeth I, an exceptional woman strangely under-used in women's suffrage iconography.[96] In Sunderland Charlotte Despard praised 'Anti-Suffrage Waxworks' for its complementary function in relation to *A Pageant of Great Women*: 'emphasising the thraldom of the sex in modern times to prejudice and convention, [Waxworks] formed a fitting introduction to the second portion of the programme demonstrating the capacity of women to achieve greatness both in the spheres of mind and action'.[97] The cultural context of 'Waxworks' is to be found in the cartoons caricaturing anti-suffragists in the *Vote*.[98]

Waxworks as a cultural form has its significance in contemporary popular entertainments, in positivist as well as the popular history-making demonstrated by Madame Tussaud, who produced figures of Emmeline and Christabel Pankhurst. Since the eighteenth century the use in scientific education of wax 'anatomical venuses' had been common.[99] As Elaine Showalter has shown, the interest in opening up the female body under the guise of a quest for medical knowledge uneasily sparks off other associations: the objectification, control and possession of women by men; in metaphorical terms, the imperial invasion of countries; and the misogynist fantasies of mutilation which abound in *fin de siècle* culture, exemplified by Arthur Conan Doyle's 'The Case of Lady Sanox' (1894) and, through the Jack the Ripper case, in contemporary crime. Hamilton's dissection is exercised on the stereotypes of women represented by the waxwork-women of anti-suffrage debates. Thus, the conventions of waxworks are superimposed onto the tableau form. As Nina Auerbach has suggested, the *Pageant* was responding to the tableaux at Drury Lane, which involved scantily clad women.[100] Tableaux ordinarily featured women, arranged on stage in some excuse of an artistic pose or re-enactment, essentially for the consumption of a male gaze.[101] The characters in Cicely Hamilton's 'Anti-suffrage Waxworks', with the exception of Queen Elizabeth, are types which powerfully deny as redundant the ideological bases of these images.[102] The force of the parody lies in the re-presentation of images of women which are elsewhere claimed to be 'natural'.

Mimicry could be a politically powerful tool. It was, nevertheless, also used by the anti-suffragists who published a parody of *A Pageant of Great Women* in the *Cambridge Review*. This was incorporated into the review of the Cambridge performance, under the subtitle, 'An Amusing Skit':

> I am the Lady Margaret;
> I am out the vote to get.
> I am the saintly Joan of Arc:
> I head processions in the park.
> I am the pious Countess Clare;
> I riot in Trafalgar Square,
> I am Queen Margaret of Anjou;
> I am a dab at jiu-jit-su.
> I am great Queen Elizabeth;
> Prime Ministers I put to death.
> I am Saint Catherine of Siena;
> Down with George, Winston and McKenna![103]

Craig and Hamilton worked together on *A Pageant of Great Women* collaboratively. Cicely Hamilton dedicated it to Edith Craig but registered copyright in America with the Library of Congress in her name as sole author.[104] Craig published the play, which was one of many for which she owned performance rights.[105] These included sixteen of the most successful and well-known plays, such as *How the Vote Was Won*, *The Pot and the Kettle*, *Press Cuttings*, *A Pageant of Great Women*, *Before Sunrise* and *Lady Geraldine's Speech*. There were concerns amongst authors regarding control over royalties for performances of their plays. Beatrice Harraden wrote to Craig for advice on collecting her royalties due from the AFL for performances of her play, *Lady Geraldine's Speech*. In November 1912, Cicely Hamilton complained to the Society of Authors regarding a performance of *A Pageant of Great Women* in Liverpool which she had not permitted.[106] Craig seems to have been scrupulous about appropriate fees. Her accounts, including those for the WSPU production in Liverpool, charged the standard author's fee of 1 guinea.[107]

A *Pageant of Great Women*, or an imitation of it, was produced in Ireland,[108] whilst the opportunity for the play to be performed in Budapest demonstrated the international reputation which it had acquired. The correspondence between Cicely Hamilton and Countess Iska Teleki, President of the Hungarian section of the International Woman Suffrage Congress, in August 1912, indicates that problematic negotiations were involved. Teleki's letter is direct: 'tell me frankly what is taboo & what we may do'.[109] The specific points of her proposal were clearly presented: to stage the play in Hungarian, roughly translated by herself, preferably at the Royal Opera House where she could rely on the influence of two male patrons, her friends Count Bansby and Count Julius Baskyory. The former 'has great influence in the aristocracy, & can make ladies do many things (that they would not do) if he wants that it should be done. For instance, to take part in a pageant which is propaganda for women's votes!'[110] Three professional actors from the Hungarian National Theatre, Mrs Marie Jasry, Mrs Emilia Markus and Mr Gynels, were envisaged for the main roles. Some of the great women were substituted, replaced by 'Hungarian heroines instead of less known foreign ones'.[111] She welcomed the first condition of performance, that Edith Craig must 'stage manage and produce the performance', but ominously concluded, 'we work & prepare our congress in the teeth of ill will, so we are not rich'.[112]

Hamilton replied on behalf of herself and Craig. The letter reveals their attitude to the play and the spirit in which it was produced. There was no objection to changing the characters, even a suggestion that the substitution proved the international relevance of the play. Thus, the warriors could be replaced by 'three Hungarian women who are known to have done the same thing – they are easily to be found in the history of every country'.[113] The guidelines for selecting the great women was an eye for the dramatic impact, since it was on that basis that the great women had been selected 'with a spectacular effect in mind'.[114] Hamilton explained that Craig's terms were no different from those prevailing in Britain. They involved ten days' to two weeks' work before the performance, travel expenses and accommodation and 1 guinea per day for producing the play. Time was at a premium: 'being a busy professional woman she has only a limited amount of time at her disposal'.[115]

It seems that the *Pageant* may have been considered as a part of the Seventh International Woman Suffrage Congress in Hungary, which Craig was unable to attend. Rosika Schwimmer wrote on 7 March 1913 to say that 'the present political situation keeps us so busy that we cannot afford to occupy ourselves with anything not concerning our political work or preparations for our congress'.[116] Priorities were changing. In June 1913 time ran out for Emily Wilding Davison. A card at her funeral read, 'In her was new England and in her was new woman. She died for women and for men.'[117] Activists were turning to increasingly dangerous and desperate acts, demonstrating perhaps the contemporary provenance of *A Pageant of Great Women* in which Charlotte Corday was a heroine and the women warriors formed the largest group. Representations of the suffrage movement are to be found in the early films of the day. Davison's final act has survived on film. In December 1913, Ellen Terry's third husband, James Carew, acted in a film entitled *The Suffragette*.[118]

The consumption of a play designed to foster a sense of community could ironically give rise to conflicts between women. This nevertheless points to the divisive aspects of capitalism and patriarchy. To what extent was it possible for women to achieve, as Sheila Stowell contends, 'a stage of their own'? Owning property was permissible for women even while they were refused the vote: the Married Women's Property Acts (1870, 1882) preceded women's enfranchisement by some fifty years. Even so, ownership of a theatre, or sufficient funds and the inclination to buy one, was the privilege of very few women. A small number of women were involved in theatre management, and some, like Kate Santley, took risks to present unorthodox drama. Others, like Gertrude Kingston at the Little Theatre, which she had built, and Lena Ashwell at the Kingsway Theatre, attempted to improve the opportunities and conditions for women working as performers and writers in the theatre. The independent theatre societies produced several plays by women. *A Question of Memory* by Michael Field was performed by the Independent Theatre.[119] Suffragists were adept at making the best use of their resources, including people. The involvement of famous names made useful publicity even though organizations such as the AFL decried the star system. Ellen Terry's activities in women's suffrage have been attributed to Edith Craig's suggestion, and Terry's refusal of a prestigious invitation to the Seventh International Woman Suffrage Congress in Budapest (15–20 June 1913) seems to suggest a degree of resistance: 'I can't = for more reasons than that I can't travel nowadays.'[120] In 1911 she remarked in a letter to George Bernard Shaw that Edy had neglected her for all the other women.[121] Nevertheless, Ellen Terry's involvement in *A Pageant of Great Women*, in the only speaking role as Nance (Anne) Oldfield (1683–1730), had numerous meanings. Terry's lines associated her with early actresses such as Nell Gwynn, whom she had played in *Sweet Nell of Old Drury*. Terry was placed unequivocally in women's theatre history:

> By your leave,
> Nance Oldfield does her talking for herself!
> If you, Sir Prejudice, had had your way,
> There would be never an actress on the boards.
> Some lanky, squeaky boy would play my parts:
> And, though I say it, there'd have been a loss!
> The Stage would be as dull as now 'tis merry –
> No Oldfield, Woffington, or – Ellen Terry![122]

The silent women who had been proposed for the tableau commemorating Terry's stage jubilee in 1906 are made to speak through Ellen Terry's self-naming in the role of Nance Oldfield.

It seems, more specifically, that women achieved temporary access to spaces in which to produce plays and entertainments with limited interference; these spaces were often public halls rather than theatres. Access to acting space was therefore a matter of renting or borrowing rather than owning; this has profound implications on the equipment available and on legal responsibilities. Thus Cicely Hamilton's ironic disclaimer regarding the limited extent of the experimental productions available to the AFL's Woman's Theatre suggests that it was not the availability of plays written by men that was the contentious issue for Hamilton,[123] but rather the gendered aspects of theatre institutions and dramatic experiments: this was fundamentally circumscribed by the economics of women's subjection. It did not affect Edith Craig's inventiveness. Her talented use of subtle lighting, coloured cloths and minimal, but judiciously arranged, props was widely praised in the conventional, as well as suffrage, press.

Edith Craig continued to support the AFL, which organized events in the West End of London. At the Theatre Royal, Drury Lane, Edith Craig was given a place on the platform at the AFL's Mass Meeting on Friday 22 May 1913.[124] Craig was at one end of the back row; at the other end was novelist May Sinclair. Ellen Terry and Charlotte Despard sat at the front. On Monday 29 June 1914, the Hotel Cecil in London hosted a sumptuous costume dinner organized jointly by the AFL and the WWSL. Numerous tables each representing a different nation or aesthetic welcomed a distinguished guest list. Edith Craig and Christopher St John dined apart. Craig sat at Cicely Hamilton's 'England' table while St John took her place at Sarah Brooke's 'France' table.[125] The costume dinner represented world history; the evening was rounded off with a pageant, possibly explaining the reference made by May Sinclair when she wrote on 11 July to congratulate Craig.[126]

As Edith Craig's nationwide productions of *A Pageant of Great Women* have demonstrated, the pageant form and the acting out of different roles was wildly attractive for women involved in the suffrage movement. The whiggish aspects of the play's history-making are counterpointed by the destabilizing processes of the play's performances. The fantasy of greatness enacted by women seemed to reinforce individualism, but this was undercut by the circumstances of the play's performances. Greatness became the attribute of more and more women as the play increased its numbers of great women (between 45 and 90) from venue to venue. The diversity of women was emphasized by the collective acting out of greatness by local suffragists. Greatness seemed to be within reach of every woman.

The emphatic choice for Craig, with ninety or so great women at her disposal, was for the artist Rosa Bonheur (1822–99). Craig was prepared to enforce director's prerogative in owning this role at every performance. Bonheur appears on stage in the Artistes' group, after Sappho, Vittoria Colonna, Angelica Kauffmann and Vigée Le Brun. The three lines designated for Bonheur emphasize her masculinity: 'A man? No – Rosa Bonheur!/Back from the horse fair, virile in her garb/ As virile in her work!' [127] While for Cicely Hamilton and Christopher St John, the warriors Christian Davies and Hannah Snell were soul mates, Craig chose an artist not a woman of the theatre. Beatrice Harraden wrote to congratulate Craig for a production of the *Pageant*: 'I meant also to say greetings to Rosa Bonheur. As for your dear mother, well, she was bewitching.'[128] The photograph of Craig in costume by Marie Leon[129] was chosen to decorate the cover of the play programmes for the production in the Albert Hall, Sheffield. Like Rosa Bonheur, Craig is seen wearing a floppy bow tie. Such clothing was emulated by the Suffrage Atelier of which Craig was a prominent member. The uniform was 'bright blue workman-like coat, a black skirt, and a big black bow like that beloved of the artists who dwell near the Luxembourg'.[130] Rosa Bonheur was an artist who demonstrated, as Emmanuel Cooper suggests, 'that women could compete in a male-dominated world'.[131]

Although Bonheur's artwork and her realistic representations of animals appeared to be conventional, in other respects she was true to her Saint-Simonian upbringing, unapologetically unconventional. She referred to her lifelong relationships with artists Nathalie Micas and Anna Klumpke in terms of marriage, with Bonheur as husband, and Micas – and after her death, Klumpke – as wife.[132] Bonheur secured official permission to wear masculine clothes at a time when it was otherwise illegal. She perceived her sexual identity in mystical and androgynous terms as one of 'the third sex', writing about this in an account to the Magnus Hirschfeld Institute of Sexology in Berlin.[133] As a successful and respected artist, Bonheur was internationally famous. It is likely that, at least in some quarters, she signified lesbian in Britain in 1909–10. Her ability to pass as a man was made explicit in *A Pageant of Great Women*, where, unlike the cross-dressing Warriors whose disguise was superficially a prerequisite for battle, this has no other function.

Virginia Woolf famously claimed 1910 as a landmark year.[134] For Christabel Pankhurst it was the 'year of truce'.[135] For Edith Craig it was the year of the *Pageant*, a veritable Who's Who in women's suffrage as well as women's history. It was a hard act to follow. Craig sought out different audiences for her next project in the Pioneer Players, but she was never to find such nationwide success with a single play again.

In retrospect, suffragists were preoccupied with dating, and rating, their commitment to the movement. Some women felt uncomfortable about past acts, perceived as terrorist. In the 1930s politics had come to mean the often dull and uneventful participation in democratic organizations. They needed to remember, meet and re-present their contributions to the movement and to pinpoint the moment when they became involved. On 6 February 1937 at the Glasgow Equal Citizenship Dinner, commemorating the Representation of the People Act 1918, Edith Craig was a keynote speaker. In the chair was Dr Marion Gilchrist, the first woman to graduate in medicine from the University of Glasgow; the Reverend Vera M. M. Kenmure proposed the toast to the pioneers. In her speech, Craig said that the women's suffrage movement was a painful subject to talk about, and expressed regret that she had not been imprisoned.[136] This retrospective devaluing of her contribution to the movement which, in its numerous productions and processions, constituted a major part of her career, is perhaps determined by the definition immediately after enfranchisement of suffrage militancy in terms of law-breaking rather than cultural interventions.[137] Cicely Hamilton recalled Craig's approval of 'militant tactics', but that she had never taken part 'in the active law-breaking that landed so many of her fellow-members in Holloway'.[138] This does not mean that Craig consistently upheld the law. She was involved in the Tax Resistance League which boycotted the 1911 Census. In the 'Pageant of the Leagues', organized by Mr Tripp Edgar, Edith Craig represented the Tax Resistance League.[139] Laurence Housman published advice on strategies for resistance to the Census and details of the relevant legislation which applied only to occupiers of houses, not inmates and travellers. A refusal to answer the Census, or a false answer, was liable to a £5 penalty.[140] Thus women refused to appear in national statistics, defiantly imitating their obliteration from history and democracy. Margaret Wynne Nevinson described this as 'passive resistance' in response to a government which failed to represent women.[141] Although many interpretations of militancy obtained, only a small number of the most sensational have persisted in public memory.

Although Craig avoided imprisonment, she did appear in court, not as a defendant but as a witness, when Sime Seruya was charged with obstruction outside the Lyceum Theatre on 27 October 1911.[142] In a sense Craig's regret characteristically undervalues her achievements; it also represents a wider, internalized devaluing of women's cultural production, which was perceived to be ephemeral. The nationwide recognition of her productions of plays like *A Pageant of Great Women*, her performances as Rosa Bonheur or Lizzie in *How the Vote Was Won* had faded in the memory. They had served their purpose well. The categorization of these plays as political rather than artistic by pro- and anti-suffragists backfired. It condemned them to obscurity and prevented any of the many women writers of the women's suffrage movement from replacing the utopian figure of Judith Shakespeare in Virginia Woolf's selective female tradition in *A Room of One's Own* (1929).

Chapter 5

THE PIONEER YEARS
1911–20

Before Edith Craig launched the Pioneer Players in London in May 1911 her greatest achievement to date had been *A Pageant of Great Women* seen by thousands of people in public halls, rather than theatres, in major cities nationwide. As a freelance director and organizer, Craig had been in great demand. In producing plays with whatever came to hand, whether it was personnel or acting spaces, she was faced with an unrelenting pressure on her imaginative powers. Working for women's suffrage had been an exhilarating and exhausting experience. The AFL had benefited from the *Pageant* sufficiently to 'launch into offices'.[1] The changes in the AFL and the WFL, however, did not satisfy her. As Margaret Webster noted, the Pioneer Players developed from Craig's work for women's suffrage and for the AFL,[2] and was to take up much of her time for the next decade, forming a significant stage in her career. It was one of only two London-based theatre societies to survive the First World War.

The Pioneer Players developed from Craig's work with the *Pageant* and represented a broadening of the base of her work. Just as the *Pageant* performances and the At Homes were aimed at drawing in the reluctant or undecided, the Pioneer Players was formed 'to produce plays dealing with all kinds of movements of interest at the moment' and 'to assist social, political, and other Societies by providing them with plays as a means of raising funds'.[3] If the Pioneer Players seemed to represent Craig's desire to settle and consolidate her work in one organization, it was not intended to end her travelling. The society's fundraising function was put into action. A few productions were given outside the metropolis. *A Pageant of Great Women* was produced in Liverpool and in Nottingham, and *How the Vote Was Won* was staged at the Royal

Albert Institute for the Windsor and Eton Branch of the London Society for Women's Suffrage. The Pioneer Players had many political and dramatic lives. It has appeared as a footnote in theatre histories, more recently regarded as a women's theatre, a theatre company associated solely with women's suffrage or political drama, or in many ways as owned by Edith Craig. None of these designations adequately represents its work.

The form of organization adopted by the Pioneer Players has a history in European avant-garde theatre as much as the amateur theatricals of the English middle classes. Its models in Paris were Marya Chéliga's Théâtre Féministe[4] and Antoine's Théâtre Libre; in London the Mummers and the Stage Society. The Pioneer Players was dependent for its income on members' subscriptions. In one sense 'free' from the burden of commercial success, in many others it was burdened by the lack of a permanent venue, reliant on borrowing or renting theatres for its (usually) one-off performances. A significant motivation for women to develop informal, experimental theatre spaces was to be liberated from the sexual harrassment prevalent in the commercial theatres. The Pioneer Players was not a replica Lyceum Theatre, although Edith Craig pulled off a production of George Bernard Shaw's *A Man of Destiny* with the society, something which Henry Irving had not been able to manage at the Lyceum.

The Pioneer Players had a formal structure, holding annual general meetings, operating through an executive committee or council of management, publishing annual reports and lists of members. Its offices were run from Craig's Bedford Street flat. Membership was available at different rates for acting and ordinary members, acknowledging the low pay of many actors, which was in itself an issue debated in women's suffrage newspapers.[5] In this respect it differed from its major competitor, the Stage Society, which had a flat-rate subscription, but a consistently larger membership. Since actors and audience were drawn from the Pioneer Players' membership, a fundamentally different relationship was established compared with the anonymous audience in a commercial theatre, which hires and fires actors for a specific run of a play. The Pioneer Players' actors included amateurs as well as professionals. As funds increased, the society was able to pay rehearsal fees, but until then it relied on actors donating their time and work. They did this in the hope that the play would be successful and be taken up by a commercial theatre for a long run, or that their performance would be noticed by prospective employers. For just such a reason a later theatre society was named the Shop Window Players. The Pioneer Players' membership fluctuated as its agenda changed. The rising cost of living and economic crises of the First World War impinged on the private budgets of individuals as well as on the commercial domain of the Entertainments Tax.

Edith Craig founded the Pioneer Players, acting as Director, with Ellen Terry as President. The core of its Executive Committee comprised Craig's friends and family: Christopher St John, Gabrielle Enthoven,[6] and Olive Terry.[7] Ellen Terry's lecture on 'Shakespeare's Triumphant Women' was well publicized when she performed it for the Pioneer Players. She remained more than a figurehead as President, performing in several of the society's plays.[8]

Although the Pioneer Players has been considered to belong to Edith Craig, Christopher St John pointedly remarked that in the society Craig had lacked 'complete control'.[9] The choice of plays and cast was not determined unilaterally by Craig but by casting committees, whose work was minuted from 1913 to 1920. A play by Edith Ellis, *The Pixey*, was considered, but ultimately not chosen for production.[10] Claude Rains was discussed for the role of Bortsov in Chekhov's *On the High Road*, but the part was ultimately performed by William Armstrong. Ethel Smyth was unsuccessful in persuading Edith Craig to produce Vernon Lee's play *Ariadne* with the Pioneer Players in 1911, before the Casting Committee was set up.[11] Sometimes controversial decisions were taken by this committee. *The Swan Song* was rejected in favour of Chekhov's *The Bear*. The Pioneer Players produced guidelines, 'Notes to Authors', stating the terms on which the society accepted plays and intended to work with authors and translators.[12] No more than two performances of a play would be produced. No fees were paid to authors but, in the event that the play was subsequently taken up by a commercial theatre, the society claimed rights to 25 per cent royalties up to (and in order to redeem) the cost of the society's production. These rules protected the interests of authors and the financial liability of the society. It devolved responsibility for securing the author's permission for translation to the translator. The Casting Committee invited the author's suggestions for casting, and the producer of the play was required to carry out the author's wishes in the production.

The number of plays which Craig co-produced with the dramatist was formally endorsed as a criterion in the society's guidelines. It also testifies to her ability to collaborate with others. She had worked relatively autonomously in the women's suffrage movement, and had operated as patron to many writers and activists. In the Pioneer Players, Craig spread financial liability thinly across the membership, incurring a loss of personal power and a greater requirement for her to work with and for others. While the society had its internal disagreements and controversies, these were greatly outnumbered by its successes.

The assumption that the Pioneer Players was a women's theatre or one which was solely concerned with the women's suffrage movement is inaccurate. The sex ratio of the society's membership showed a consistent majority of women at all levels, but men were present as members at all levels.[13] The sex ratio of dramatists whose work the society produced favoured women in the first three years of its existence, coinciding with the high points of the women's suffrage movement and before the First World War. Nevertheless, even though such a form of organization was possible and celebrated in the women's suffrage press,[14] the Pioneer Players was not a women-only organization. While it was advertised in the women's suffrage press as founded to produce 'propaganda', its membership was not exclusively pro-suffrage. Indeed some of its members were opposed to women's suffrage.[15] In many ways its attitude to women's suffrage as an inevitable part of contemporary life was reflected in its membership: a coalition which was open to all manner of plays and ideas. This fundamentally experimental attitude was equally at home in women's suffrage cultural practices as it was in the theatre societies.

Edith Craig was outspoken on the issue of stage censorship. Since 1737 plays intended for public performance needed to secure a licence from the Lord Chamberlain. Playscripts were submitted to the Lord Chamberlain's office and were passed, refused or granted a licence subject to alterations. The criteria for licensing were obscure, arbitrary and subservient to the presumed sensibilities of the dominant groups of monarchy and government.[16] Some criteria were explicit: for instance, swear words were taboo, as was the representation on stage of monarchy or God. The founding of the Pioneer Players coincided with a growing campaign against the powers of the Lord Chamberlain, and several of its productions were explicitly given in defiance of the law which affected plays publicly performed in theatres. Thus, Edith Craig stated that the forthcoming triple bill of plays would be performed in the King's Hall, a venue in the National Sporting Club, 'that there may be no fuss about any possible censoring'.[17] This interview, conducted by

'MOK',[18] took up an entire column on the 'Every Woman' page of the *Pall Mall Gazette*. Other articles on the same page covered Lady Domville's travelling gown after her marriage to Sir James Domville, nursery nursing for hospital nurses and the current craze for buttons. The incongruity of these juxtapositions which modern readers might register reveals that campaigning, whether on the issue of censorship or women's rights, was commonplace for middle-class women.

Unorthodox representations of monarchy featured in two of the Pioneer Players' most controversial productions. Christopher St John and Charles Thursby[19] co-wrote a play called *The Coronation*. This showed the monarch in an imaginary kingdom on the way to his coronation being converted to socialism by the testimony of a destitute woman whose poverty had led to the death of her child. The play lent itself to the possibility of change being brought about by the actions of a single person, specifically a woman; and it showed the instability of ancient institutions in the face of a widespread desire for change. At the end of this production the audience was called upon to form The Coronation Society to campaign against censorship of the stage. An imaginary monarch was perhaps less persuasive than a real historical example. Queen Caroline provided just such an opportunity.

It was the Pioneer Players which produced Laurence Housman's play, *Pains and Penalties*, appropriating Queen Caroline for the women's suffrage cause and comparing George IV's exclusion of Caroline from the coronation on 19 July 1821 with the exclusion of women from parliamentary democracy. Interest in Caroline's life had led to the reprinting in 1908 by John Lane of the diaries of Charlotte Bury, lady-in-waiting to Queen Caroline. Virginia Woolf had reviewed Bury's diaries in the *Times Literary Supplement*.[20] Laurence Housman reinterpreted Caroline as representative of disadvantaged woman knocking on the door at Westminster. Caroline was found guilty of adultery but that of George IV was ignored. Housman emphasized the role of scheming politicians and injustice at the hands of an abusive husband determined to dispense with an unwanted wife. Historians Leonora Davidoff and Catherine Hall have shown how the alternate sympathies for, and condemnation of, Caroline marked a founding moment of the middle-class family, subsequently represented by the monarchy.[21] Interest in Caroline's predicament has been revived recently in the wake of debates about morality and the royal family.[22] In spite of the injustice of the double standard by which she was judged, Queen

Caroline was more offensive to an English middle-class sensibility for her vulgarity. This aspect of her character was played down by Housman. Immediately after the Pioneer Players' production of the play at the Savoy Theatre, Harley Granville Barker and Elizabeth Robins, neither of whom were ever members of the society, took to the stage to rouse the audience to campaign against stage censorship and, to that end, to join the Caroline Society.[23] George Bernard Shaw had claimed that, for the English middle classes, the theatre had taken the cultural space and status of the church. They were now prepared to stand on the pews and shout at the vicar. When interviewed about the play, Craig was characteristically enthusiastic and preoccupied with the challenge of re-creating on stage the interior of Westminster with a minimum of resources.[24]

It is in the context of this involvement in the campaign against the Theatre Licensing Act that the Pioneer Players and Edith Craig have entered theatre history. Consistent with its aims and objectives, the society became involved in other topical campaigns, and many of their plays made connections between various social reforms. The performance of an adaptation of Reginald Wright Kaufmann's novel, *The Daughters of Ishmael*,[25] about enforced prostitution, known in racist terms as the 'white slave' trade, was even more controversial because Boots' lending libraries had recently banned the novel. Some reviewers were equally shocked by the enactment on stage of violence against women and remarked on its allusion to the Queenie Gerald case, a recent scandal in which Gerald was charged with living off immoral earnings from her brothel in Piccadilly, an address that was frequented by influential figures whose names were protected.[26] A couple of plays responded specifically to the implications of the Insurance Act in 1912. Jess Dorynne's *The Surprise of His Life* designated the Act 'Lloyd George's little bill of all right' for its welfare provision for mothers, which could provide an excuse for the father to renounce his responsibilities.[27] Women's financial independence is unexpectedly interpreted as disempowering for women in relationships with men. Cecil Fisher's *The Great Day* explored the psychological impact of overwork on men in the insurance industry. Florence Edgar Hobson's *A Modern Crusader*, a play which presented a holistic vision of social reforms in housing, food production, vegetarianism and women's rights, argued that 'all reforms meet underground'.[28] This liberal view, placing women's suffrage in the context of social reforms, was attractive to the Pioneer Players, which refused to identify with women's suffrage in isolation. Such a strategy may have made arguments for women's enfranchisement more widely available, like the Drawing Room meetings, aimed at the unsuspecting and the apolitical. The reviewer for *The Times* who sat through the society's inaugural subscription performance in May 1911 felt that s/he had been deceived: 'We had walked in so innocently, imagining that the pioneering of the Pioneer Players was to be dramatic, not (if we may be pardoned the ugly word) feministic.' [29] Similarly, Lady Cynthia Asquith, herself never a member of the society, claimed in 1918 that the Pioneer Players made tickets available to non-members and thus the 'private' production of the play was a bit of 'chicanery'.[30]

The Pioneer Players produced plays which represented women in an unorthodox manner. Women were seen to be, variously, workers, claiming rights within marriage, female prostitutes arguing that their predicament was caused by ineffective education and feckless parenting. The womanizing of the prostitute, rather than the usual patronizing depiction of her as victim, either to be saved or scapegoated for social evils, was extremely controversial. *Honour Thy Father*, written by H. M. (Tottie) Harwood,[31] gave voice to the prostitute, even implying that her economic power and good sense made her a valuable mentor for, rather than a threat to, her sister. The play ends with the two going off to the Café Royal for tea. The socialist newspaper, the *Daily Herald*, praised the play's rare, unsentimenal treatment of such a complex issue.[32] The Pioneer Players' response to women's suffrage did not therefore emerge crudely through the ubiquitous suffragist character, or a plot which involved the suffrage campaign. The question of women's rights was given a more detailed treatment, illustrating the implications of a society which oppresses and exploits. The Pioneer Players' production of Herman Heijermans's *The Good Hope*, the play which Christopher St John had translated and Ellen Terry had successfully performed in Britain and America, was reviewed by *Vote* as 'a suffragist play by accident'.[33] Like *Honour Thy Father*, *The Good Hope* examined the causes as well as the effects of oppression.

The endorsement of women's history made by Craig and Hamilton in *A Pageant of Great Women* was sustained in the Pioneer Players' productions of Laurence Housman's *Pains and Penalties* and Christopher St John's two plays, *The First Actress* and *Macrena*. Margaret Hughes is claimed by St John, with no mention of the other contenders, as the first actress on a London stage in 1661.[34] Hughes's debut is not glamorized, but is revealed, rather, as the product of male machinations, setting Hughes up as a stooge, her performance subjected to ridicule and criticism. It is only in

Hughes's despondent dream that a number of great actresses of the future appear to persuade her to continue. The actress is attributed a representative role in the battle for women's rights. Margaret Hughes was played by Nancy Price and Nell Gwynn was played by Ellen Terry.

In *Macrena*, the Polish nun, Irena Macrena (fl. 1840) is claimed as a revolutionary role model in her battle against apostasy in the face of the imposition of the Russian Orthodox religion in Poland in 1840.[35] Macrena matched Joan of Arc as a heroic figure. The Catholic Women's Suffrage Society, whose patron saint was Joan of Arc, approached Christopher St John to organize a performance of the play for them. Macrena excelled in her leadership of a group of nuns dissenting only in their refusal to abandon their faith. In this respect, Macrena is revolutionary in a different way from Joan of Arc. While Joan dies alone for her beliefs, Macrena and the other nuns survive. Macrena's values are endorsed by a community of women, views that are held tenaciously even under threat of rape and death.

The Pioneer Players was actively involved in making history. Its legal challenges on the issue of stage censorship made a footnote in theatre history. The society's production, and Christopher St John's translation, of Hrotsvit's *Paphnutius* was historic in an international context. It was published in *The Plays of Roswitha* (1923), but by 1951 it was already becoming lost to theatre history.[36] Her plays manipulated the conventions and dramatic form of Terence.[37] The significance of Hrotsvit as the first female dramatist attracted many reviewers. *Paphnutius* was one of several plays produced by the Pioneer Players about prostitution, but the character of Thais appears to be the most orthodox representation of the prostitute as disruptive of society and the object of widespread activity to transform her. Thais's redemption is brought about by privation, her imprisonment resulting in death. The dramatization of the dancing women accompanying Thais called for a sumptuous decor. Craig excelled again, and her stage design received comparisons with Leon Bakst.[38]

In many ways, this production exemplifies the complex readings available from the Pioneer Players' productions. It could be read as an endorsement of the restriction of women's sexuality. In the context of the imprisoned suffragists, it could be interpreted as granting their suffering a sacrificial status. Irrespective of its content, as a play written by Hrotsvit, it symbolized the existence of women as writers, specifically for the stage, since the tenth century. The translation of the play and its performance constituted an under-standing of the political aspects of getting involved in women's history, which had given rise to *A Pageant of Great Women* and *The First Actress*.

The Pioneer Players made the social columns of newspapers too. The society's costume balls were advertised. Participants were photographed in the *Tatler* in outrageous, possibly Futurist, costume and in self-dramatizing poses.[39] Suzanne Sheldon, in a costume attributed to the contemporary play *Kismet*, stares defiantly down the camera. Olive Terry and Hilda Moore are shown facing each other, practically nose to nose. Cicely Hamilton in trousers and 'Futurist' wig stands next to 'an "Arab" friend', who looks more like Hamilton than the betrousered woman. A miserable looking Elsie Craig, dressed as Columbine, is the only subject who appears not to have taken charge of her representation. The Pioneer Players held two 'mi-careme' balls,[40] at which prizes were awarded for tango dancing and dances invented for the Mazurka. The costume ball was a typical Edwardian upper-class pastime and, through the class constituency of activists, it featured as a fundraising focus in the women's suffrage movement. The class background of suffragists had been exposed by the awarding of a fancy-dress prize at a 'hard-up social' to the participant who had interpreted the theme by going as 'a lady in a sack'.[41] Fancy dress provides the opportunity of temporarily playing a different role, acting out a fantasy. A photograph records the fancy-dress choice of Cicely Hamilton as George Eliot and Christopher St John as George Sand.[42] Some of the Pioneer Players' dramatists and performers appeared in the social pages of the press. George Plank's costume designed for Cicely Debenham in *A Merry Death* at the Savoy Theatre on 2 April 1916 was photographed by E. O. Hoppé in the *Daily Mirror*. Gwen John, the dramatist, wrapped in coat and turban, was photographed in the *Bookman*.[43]

In the first three years of its existence, the Pioneer Players favoured women writers, but it was always an actors' society, providing special low subscription rates. It was a society for theatrefolk and politicos rather than writers with nice literary pretensions. Actors, such as a young Basil Rathbone, applied on the off-chance of being considered for any role in forthcoming productions.[44] In a sense, the society's accommodation of actors allowed Craig to develop her skills in teaching. As a perennial theatregoer she was always on the lookout for new talent. Many of her theatre programmes were often annotated with a code of crosses and dashes next to the members of the cast, sometimes explicitly marked with 'good' or 'very good'. When she attended the Academy of Dramatic Art performance on 3 April 1914 Colette O'Niel, J. Leslie Frith, Miles Malleson and Fabia Drake caught her attention.[45] All of these were to become prominent performers for the Pioneer Players.

The Players had just enjoyed acclaim for its performance of *Paphnutius* when the First World War began on 4 August 1914. The society's initial response to war was to distance itself in an attempt to continue with business as usual. In September 1914 Cicely Hamilton went hop-picking in Kent with Edith Craig and Christopher St John, a last fling before her departure to the abbey at Creil where she worked as a clerk for the Scottish Women's Hospitals.[46] The difficulty of securing theatres increased, as did the cost of living, especially after the introduction of an Entertainments Tax. The 'khaki-clad and khaki-minded world' was one which the society did not at first wish to join.[47] Some Pioneer Players' members were well-known pacifists, such as Irene Cooper Willis, Florence Edgar Hobson, Laurence Housman and Mary Sheepshanks.[48] The society produced several plays to raise funds for charities to alleviate the suffering of casualties and non-combatants, which could perhaps be divorced from war work. Later, female ushers at a Pioneer Players' production were reported to be appropriately dressed in khaki. Independently of the Pioneer Players, Edith Craig was involved in entertaining troops home on leave at the Shakespeare Hut in London. This temporary venue was set up in 1916 by the YMCA on the site intended for the prospective National Theatre.[49] The site, an acre of land just behind the British Museum at the corner of Gower Street and Keppel Street, had been bought in 1914 for £50,000.[50] On 21 April 1916, possibly when the Shakespeare Hut opened, Craig directed a selection of scenes from Shakespeare.[51] The Hut was the training ground of actors Fabia Drake and Angela and Hermione Baddeley.[52] In 1918 the Shakespeare Memorial National Theatre Committee decided to form a 'special company of players' to perform Shakespeare's drama in particular. The New Shakespeare Company was formed to produce the Stratford-upon-Avon summer festival. After the retirement of Sir Frank Benson, Mr W. Bridges-Adams was appointed director.[53] Such a post may not have appealed to Craig, but it received a sizeable guarantee of £3,000, a level of financial security which her projects were rarely to enjoy. Craig's involvement in the Shakespeare Hut was not recorded in Geoffrey Whitworth's narrative of these events.

In 1917 Edith Craig participated in Madame Clara Butt's matinee at the Chiswick Empire.[54] This was given in aid of the War Seal Foundation, raising money to build accommodation for disabled servicemen in Fulham Road. Craig appeared as Nerissa in the trial scene of *The Merchant of Venice*, Ellen Terry resumed her role as Portia, while Matheson Lang was Shylock. Other features included an excerpt from Louis N. Parker's *The Pageant of Fair Women*. 'The Women's Tribute' represented women's war work through abstract types such as Faith, Hope, Love and Courage, and figures such as Britannia, played by Lady Tree. It was as if Cicely Hamilton's 'Anti-Suffrage Waxworks' and *A Pageant of Great Women* had never been. Ten years before, Edith Craig and Cicely Hamilton had appropriated great and famous women for the women's suffrage movement. Parker showed just how readily the great and the good who happened to be women could be reduced to the 'fair', how easily such images could be used to fix femininity to an imperial vision.

Responses to the First World War by women were, of course, varied. Some of those who, only a short time before, had been extremely fastidious about their political principles became involved in 'war work', including aid for injured non-combatants and refugees, for a variety of different reasons. Some women regarded the war as an opportunity to prove their capabilities which, although the battlefield was denied them, could be achieved through working for the numerous charities. This line was taken by Christopher St John.[55] Women worked as an ancillary police force and as ambulance drivers (the latter famously represented in Radclyffe Hall's novel, *The Well of Loneliness*). Pamela Colman Smith illustrated the tensions of these roles for women in her design for a play programme cover, using a visual metaphor of women carrying unfeasibly high piles of plates.[56] A steadfast resolution to continue life as usual and to respond to the difficulties the war posed was the route chosen by the Pioneer Players and by Edith Craig.

The Pioneer Players, unlike its competitor, the Stage Society, attempted to sustain its profile rather than to adapt to circumstances during the First World War. While the Stage Society deliberately suspended its production of new and controversial plays in favour of inoffensive comedies and revivals, the Pioneer Players seemed intent on tackling as many extremely sensitive topical issues as it could.[57] On 13 May 1917 two plays were performed which explored two deeply disturbing wartime issues concerning gender as well as national disobedience: soldiers deserting their duty; and the infidelity of soldiers' wives at home. *Luck of War* by Gwen John dealt with the potential for bigamy created by the uncertainty of verification of death of soldiers in action. *The Quitter* (directed by its author, Sewell Collins) explored the temptation to desert and the involvement of Americans and non-combatant services in the war. The representation of female desire through the figure of the dancer, in Gabrielle Enthoven's *Ellen Young* and Nikolai Evreinov's *The Theatre of the Soul*, risked the condemnation of the critics. Performed in April 1916 at the Savoy Theatre, *Ellen Young* dramatized the dilemma of a working-class dancer who shot to fame in the music hall as The Don't Care Girl. Her talent seems to depend on her consumptive illness and her drug taking, since her holiday from the stage leaves her uninspiring and the play ends with an expedient, if implausible, marriage. The use of drugs and their prevalence amongst dancers and performers had preoccupied the newspapers for a year, to erupt finally with the trial of Willy Johnson.[58]

The Pioneer Players was unconcerned by criticism. At a time when Edward Knoblauch,[59] like many others, changed the spelling of his second name to disguise his German heritage, the Pioneer Players produced numerous plays in translation representing the cultures of France, Belgium, Russia and Spain. Christopher St John's linguistic skills were used in the translation of Herman Heijermans's *The Rising Sun*. Unusually she collaborated on translation on one occasion. Marie Potapenko[60] is cited as co-translator from the Russian of Evreinov's *The Theatre of the Soul*, published by Henderson's, the bookseller and publisher, which identified its publications with missiles, advertising itself as 'the bomb shop'. The bill in which this play was produced was advertised as a tribute to the Allies. Many of these plays met with a degree of suspicion, not least *The Theatre of the Soul*. Perhaps this was to be expected from the dramatic representation of a man in the process of psychological disintegration during wartime. Craig's production of this formally innovative play brought expressionism to a London stage in 1915.

Although selected for inclusion in a charity matinee organized by Lady Minnie Paget at the Alhambra Theatre, *The Theatre of the Soul* was pulled at the last moment by the manager of the Alhambra, André Charlot. Lady Paget was mortified. Charlot was not explicit about the precise offence caused by Evreinov's play. The irony of Charlot adopting the role of censor was not lost on Christopher St John. The Lord Chamberlain had passed the play for public performance subject to a couple of alterations.

The play was weird in every respect. As an expressionist play it was enough to shock an audience used to naturalism. The action takes place over eighteen seconds. The scene is set inside the protagonist's body where his thoughts are embodied by actors. A pulsating heart was represented by a pulsing red light, nerves signified by jangling noises. The play explored the inner conflict of a man in the process of deciding whether to leave his wife or his mistress. Ultimately, the decision is overpowering and he commits suicide. The man's vacillating perspectives on the two women in his life are embodied by female actors. His view of his mistress's beauty as false is symbolized by the actor removing a wig to reveal a bald head and false teeth. Such misogynist imagery was exposed by the absence of concomitant humour and when the objectified women were played by well-known, independent and forthright women, such as Ethel Levey (1881–1955) and Margaret Morris.[61] The casting of actual dancers to perform the role of the dancer was more than a gesture towards realism. In A Pageant of Great Women, the role of Marie Camargo (1710–70), the famous eighteenth-century dancer, had been performed by a number of dancers, such as Miss Locke, Miss Badshah and Mademoiselle Dolli.[62] It provided a metatheatrical dimension to the play, staging women's professional competence. An added dimension to Morris's performance was her relationship with (married) John Galsworthy.[63] To Morris at least, an ironic reading of Evreinov's play was therefore possible. Some of the Pioneer Players' productions, like those of other theatre societies, exploited the intimacy and shared knowledge of a knowable audience.

Whatever the reasons André Charlot had for pulling the play, they were not made known. Strong letters were exchanged in complaint about the damage to Edith Craig's reputation, about bad faith, spoiling for a breach of contract case. The incident was headline news and later became part of the society's history. The carefully preserved newspaper hoardings screamed 'BANNED PLAY'.

Sometimes it seemed that the Pioneer Players could not win. The society was accused of being partisan one moment, impartial at the next. In response to the Easter Rising in Dublin, W. F. Casey's play Insurrection was produced to reviews which charged it with fence-sitting, for refusing to condemn the revolution. The play did not survive. Casey wrote to Craig of his intention to 'bury' rather than publish it, concluding with the miserable plea, 'I wish I didn't go on hearing those sturdy gentlemen who hissed! And those kindly fellows the critics!'[64] Christopher St John's translation of Hrotsvit's plays also fell victim to the political turmoil in Ireland when her manuscript was destroyed by fire at her Dublin publishers.[65]

Some of the plays produced by Craig with the Pioneer Players displayed a peculiar, often self-referential, sense of humour. Two plays, *The Conference* and *Pan in Ambush*, produced on 6 February 1916, exemplify this. Lady Margaret Sackville (1881–1963), under the pseudonym Delphine Gray, wrote *The Conference*, which satirized the New Woman as well as the aristocracy. A cheap running gag about congenital deafness signified the ignorance of the aristocratic older generation, who failed to notice that the New Woman was out of date. That kind of woman had already been a suffragette and was about to become a flapper. As a threat to the status quo, rejection of marriage is replaced in *The Conference* by inter-class marriage. Poetic drama had been employed subversively in *A Pageant of Great Women*. In Marjorie Patterson's *Pan in Ambush* it was used satirically, in a rewriting of *L'après midi d'un faune*.[66] An extremely articulate, argumentative Faun (performed by the author) represents the values of classical mythology, where marriage is a curse, in contrast with those of early Victorian England.

The production of Evreinov's *The Theatre of the Soul* in 1915 had marked a shift in the Pioneer Players' agenda.[67] The formal and technical experiments in art theatre by male theatre practitioners at this time have been well documented. Edward Gordon Craig's ideas had been tried out with *Hamlet* at the Moscow Art Theatre in 1912. In France the Théâtre de l'Oeuvre of Lugné-Poe and Jacques Copeau's Théâtre du Vieux-Colombier were both working towards an anti-realist drama, while in Germany Max Reinhardt became associated with the effective management of huge crowd scenes. Gordon Craig acknowledged the influence of Adolphe Appia, who argued that stage lighting should take into account shade as well as light. Gordon Craig's vast screens were used to absorb light, and cast great swathes of shade. Considerable technical difficulties arose in fitting such structures into the inflexible spaces of available theatre buildings. The screens also met with resistance and suspicion because they dominated the stage, reducing the significance of the actor. Edith Craig shared her brother's interests and those of Lugné-Poe, Reinhardt and Copeau. However, although subject to similar influences, she deployed the principles in a different manner from that of her brother. Her use of light and shade always ensured that the actors, the script and every other element were balanced. In 1907 she had publicly rejected the common practice of garish lighting as if the stage were a saloon. Since then, she had put these ideas into effect in numerous productions. Perhaps the most innovative of these had been *The Theatre of the Soul*. While Lugné-Poe was responsible for bringing Paul Claudel's play to a Parisian stage, it was Edith Craig who brought *The Tidings Brought to Mary* to London in 1917. Her production was highly praised, but in some quarters it was assumed that the success of its scenic artistry was due to Edward Gordon Craig's influence.[68]

Edith Craig wanted the Pioneer Players, a society without a permanent theatre and comprising a couple of hundred (transient) members, to be England's principal art theatre. Her route to such an achievement was very different from that taken by her male contemporaries in Europe, America and Russia. In spite of this Saint-Georges de Bouhélier retrospectively rated Craig as a better director than Antoine, Lugné-Poe and Gemier.[69] When the Pioneer Players produced Christopher St John's translation of de Bouhélier's play, *The Children's Carnival*, in June 1920, he had already heard of the Pioneer Players and Edith Craig, although he was not an English speaker.[70] He viewed the Pioneer Players in the context of a European battle against naturalism, a struggle against convention. In his view, Edith Craig formed the Pioneer Players, 'pour lutter contre les routines dont souffrait notre art' ('to struggle against the conventions from which our art was suffering').[71] He failed, however, to acknowledge the society's other struggle against convention, through the production of plays which explored the issues surrounding women's suffrage. Even those who had been involved in the early suffragist days of the Pioneer Players were unlikely to mention it in their memoirs. They tended instead to focus on its later work, more comfortable with remembering the Players as an art theatre.

The society's choice of plays by Spanish dramatist, José Echegaray, Paul Claudel and Anton Chekhov linked it with Lugné-Poe's work at the Théâtre de L'Oeuvre. Unfortunately the ambitions of the Pioneer Players had been identified at perhaps the worst moment in theatre history. The time was not propitious. Wartime Britain saw rising costs and the introduction of an Entertainments Tax. The borrowing of theatres had been something on which the society had depended. Venues were hard to find and the Pioneer Players was a theatre society without a theatre. Members thought twice about paying subscriptions at a time when personal budgets were scrutinized and frivolous spending was associated with treason. Patrons were sought, but in spite of the increased number of

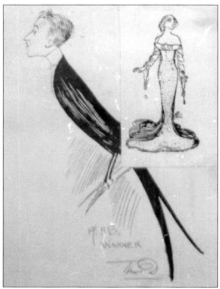

Caricature by
Pamela Colman Smith
depicting herself
and Edith Craig.

Sketch by
Pamela Colman Smith
of Nicandra costume
designed by Edith Craig.

Caricature by Pamela Colman Smith depicting Edith Craig as 'The Puck'.

Sketches of scene designs by Pamela Colman Smith and Edith Craig for W. B. Yeats's play *Where There Is Nothing*.

Caricature by Pamela
Colman Smith depicting
herself and Edith Craig.

Christopher St John
(sitting, centre) in costume
as Herod in the
Early English Nativity Play,
Rye Monastery, 1919.

Left: Edith Craig on a camel near the Sphinx, Egypt, 1923. *Right:* Press coverage of Edith Craig's camel rides during a film shoot in Egypt, 1923.

Left: 'Our First Border' in the garden at Priest's House in Tenterden, Kent. *Right:* Edith Craig in monk's costume while directing the Mount Grace Pageant, 1927.

Left: Christopher St John at the summer house in the garden at Priest's House in Tenterden, Kent in 1910. *Right:* Edith Craig and Christopher St John at the well in the garden at Priest's House.

Left: Christopher St John and Edith Craig in the garden at Priest's House.
Right: Christopher St John and Tony Atwood on the beach (location unknown).

Christopher St John, Edith Craig and Gabrielle Enthoven.

back row, standing:
Christopher St John, unidentified;
middle row, sitting:
Edith Craig, Pamela Colman Smith,
unidentified; *foreground, sitting:*
Reggie (Regina Laurence),
unidentified, Tassle.

Edith Craig, Christopher St John and Tony Atwood at Sissinghurst, Kent.

Edith Craig, Tony Atwood and Christopher St John in the garden at Priest's House.

aristocrats in the membership, the society's future was not secure. Lady Randolph Churchill had fixed the performance of *The Theatre of the Soul*, seen later at the Shaftesbury Theatre and repeated at the Savoy for Lady Paget's matinee for the soldiers' and sailors' buffet. Craig was forced to work within extreme conditions. Venues were changed at the last minute, and any attempt to develop the manner of staging the plays could not rely on the availability of equipment or even a particular shape or size of stage. Funds for costumes, props and sets were minimal. Nevertheless, Craig's productions were repeatedly praised for their clever use of draped, colourful cloths and subtle lighting effects. Her resources were always limited but she used them to advantage. Like William Poel she favoured minimal scenery for her anti-naturalist drama. This was fortunate. Minimal scenery was the most she was ever likely to get.

1916 was the most successful year for the Pioneer Players. It was also the year of conscription. The Pioneer Players' work, if not membership, flourished during the war. Perversely, it was the society's productions of plays by Paul Claudel which met with the greatest success. Claudel described his work as 'musical drama'.[72] Claudel's use of a musical structural analogy for building up characters and plot was to appeal to Jean-Louis Barrault in his concept of 'total theatre'.[73] The musical basis of Claudel's poetic drama attracted the musician in Craig. Like Tairov at the Kamerny Theatre, she was often at work on musical accompaniment to her productions. On some occasions she was assisted by Lady Maud Warrender, who sang unaccompanied plainchant in *The Tidings Brought to Mary*. On others she worked with Christopher Wilson, and later Ethel Smyth. In *Paphnutius* Craig experimented with antiphons, and in the mime production of the ballad, 'Death and the Lady',[74] with cantillation, a kind of musical chanting of verse. Early music and musical instruments had been promoted by Arnold Dolmetsch, attracting such as George Bernard Shaw, Violet Gordon Woodhouse and W. B. Yeats at the time of The Masquers.[75] Other traces of The Masquers' influence may be detected in the Pioneer Players' intention to produce Yeats's *The King's Threshold*. It seems that this was never realized.

The drama of Paul Claudel presents several difficulties. As poetic drama and drama in translation it is demanding on performers and audience alike. The subject matter and ideological base of Claudel's drama was Roman Catholicism. Sybil Thorndike's performance as Synge in *The Hostage* on 23 March 1919 at the Scala Theatre was, in her opinion, her best work.[76] The part has some parallels with

Thorndike's later role as Joan of Arc. For Edith Craig, Claudel's drama was compatible with her lifelong interest in pageants and her increasing interest in the relationship between drama and the church, the effect of making theatre in a spiritual context. Christopher St John may have influenced Craig in this to some extent, but the productions of Claudel's plays did not represent a crude promotion of Roman Catholicism.[77] They also make some sense in view of the wartime need for cultural and spiritual support. Just as poetry became a focus for the psychologically war-damaged and desperate, drama was identified for its potential as a means of building communities, of propagating ideologies.

In 1916 Atwood joined the Bedford Street flat, which was to be described in Futurist terms as a factory for (cultural) missiles.[78] She does not seem to have been involved in Edith Craig's women's suffrage theatre productions although Craig and St John may have met her at the Stage Society.[79] Atwood remembers Craig visiting her studio. It is an image of peaceful time spent together, sharing the view of the Thames:

> It was a great day when Edy would come to spend it, complete with bags and baskets, knitting and books, in a certain studio, now no more, on Bankside looking over the river towards St Paul's. How quickly those hours flew! A run through of canvases, finished or begun, drawings and designs for future work; then, when she was tired, she would sit in a big chair, mounted on a platform before the open window, and watch the river traffic.[80]

The Bedford Street flat became a more intense cultural centre as well as a *ménage à trois*: a hive of activity, where art, writing and theatre flourished. Atwood's skills were exploited by the Pioneer Players. She had trained as an artist at Westminster and the Slade School, where her teachers had been L. C. Nightingale and Professor Frederick Brown. In 1912 she had become a member of the New English Art Club where she had been exhibiting work since 1893. Atwood became known for her portraits and interiors, and her work was widely exhibited in London, Liverpool and Scotland. She was distinguished as one of the few women to receive an official commission during the First World War. In 1919 the Canadian government commissioned her to paint one of the large decorations for the Canadian War Memorial Exhibition at Burlington House. And in 1920 she was commissioned by the Imperial War Museum. With the Pioneer Players, Atwood designed props for Claudel's *The Hostage* and held the post of Play Secretary from 1917 to 1918, responsible for reading numerous plays.[81] The Edith Craig Archive is almost silent about Tony Atwood, with the exception of some letters Atwood drafted on Craig's behalf.

Wartime arguments about the ownership of Shakespeare and the introduction of concert parties to entertain troops, led by women such as Lena Ashwell, Gertrude Jennings and Cicely Hamilton, demonstrate that the ideological power of drama was becoming widely recognized. This power had largely been proven by the women who had organized drama for the women's suffrage movement, some of whom were now lending their services to a government with which they had hitherto been at war. Lena Ashwell initiated a meeting with the Ministry of Propaganda to suggest the use of drama as propaganda.[82] Edith Craig was involved in the making of a propaganda film, *Victory and Peace*, also known as *The Invasion of Britain*, or *The National Film*, directed by Herbert Brenon for the National War Aims Committee in 1918. She is credited for her performance as Mary Rowntree. She later claimed to have been floor manager and to possess a 200-foot section of the film.[83]

Edith Craig and Frederick Whelen had been signed up by J. T. Grein, founder of the Independent Theatre and sponsor of the new drama in Britain, to work for his War Players. Grein wrote to Edith Craig, addressed as usual to 'my dear friend' ... 'delighted that you will accept the post of Manageress of the Southern Company. I have immediately handed in your name to the Ministry.'[84] A couple of weeks later he offered her the post of Assistant Director at a salary of £6, involving her travelling to Holland.[85] Grein planned to send a company of actors to Holland to entertain interned prisoners of war.

The Pioneer Players' performance of Torahiko Kori's play *Kanawa* on 16 December 1917 attracted xenophobic (and misogynistic) responses from critics even though it was written in English. Kori felt that it was 'a sincere effort at the unaffected interpretation of Japanese rhythm (as [Mrs Christopher Lowther's] personification struck both me and my compatriots among the audience though it may not have appealed to dilettante orientmongers)'.[86] Craig had evidently changed her stance on cultural imperialism. A few years earlier, she had declared that translations should make the characters 'talk like English people'.[87] Grein had been the target of racism on two counts: for his involvement as a Dutch man in developing British theatre; and for encouraging the production of plays in French or Italian, rather than in English translation.[88] The Pioneer Players not only performed plays in translation but on one unusual occasion also translated a play written in English (by Christopher St John) into Italian.[89] The French Players, of which Grein was President and Jules Delacre was Artistic Director, produced plays by Molière, Sacha Guitry and Alfred de Musset.[90] Such cosmopolitan sponsorship appeared threatening to those attempting to forge an English national identity in the metropolis, represented by an English national theatre.[91]

In the context of this cultural controversy, Grein became embroiled in defending one of his performers in court. In April 1918 Grein produced Oscar Wilde's *Salome* with Maud Allan in the title role.[92] The story of Salome had particular significance for Craig, as John the Baptist was the source of Christopher's self-naming. The head of John the Baptist was Salome's price for her much-demanded dance in front of King Herod. Elaine Showalter suggests a relationship between the claim to power of Salome in determining her own erotic dance and the symbolic castration of John the Baptist.[93] In some cases *Salome*'s author, Oscar Wilde, had only to be mentioned to provoke anxiety attacks. Maud Allan claimed that she had been libelled by Noel Pemberton Billing, MP for Hertfordshire East. The court case, financially backed by Grein, brought lesbianism into public debate. Presumably, the failure of the case and Grein's departure for Europe,[94] meant that Craig's new job with Grein's War Players fell through. It had come too late. The possibility of Craig working in Europe faded just as Cicely Hamilton returned from France.

The image of the female dancer symbolized the unleashing of desires which threatened the social order. As Marek Kohn has demonstrated, women and 'foreigners' were targets of cultural panic during wartime.[95] Myth and reality coalesced in Mata Hari (Margaretha Zelle MacLeod), who had been executed in 1917 as a spy. She had worked as an 'oriental' dancer accompanied until 1914 by musician, Inayat Khan. Khan then moved to London where he founded a Sufi order.[96] Khan's Eastern musical event and lectures on mysticism at 86 Ladbroke Grove was advertised by the Pioneer Players in December 1915. In June 1918 Edith Craig was invited to hear Khan and his musicians at a private event at Grein's London home.

In February 1918, just over a week after some women were enfranchised, the Pioneer Players sunk most of its available funds in a remarkable production. This was a dramatization in English of Pierre Louÿs's short story, *The Girl and the Puppet*. The story seems unpromising and unlikely to interest a Pioneer Players' audience committed to women's empowerment. The male protagonist is obsessed with a girl who is persuaded to dance naked for him in a bar. As in Evreinov's *The Theatre of the Soul*, the representation of women seems to be irredeemably misogynistic. However, the title provides a clue to the society's choice of such a play. The 'puppet' in the play is the male character who, while he believes that he is in control of the girl, is ultimately subject to her dance. In terms of Craig's developing experiments in subtle lighting, the play was praised by one member of the audience. Lady Cynthia Asquith recorded in her diary that she was impressed by the use of gauzes and lights which simulated the nudity of the dancing girl.[97] Asquith also noted that Louys was the author of an 'unspeakably improper' novel, presumably *Aphrodite* (1896).[98] The Pioneer Players did not trouble to apply for a licence for this production.

The productions of *Ellen Young* and *The Girl and the Puppet* in 1916 and 1918 were audacious. They attracted Radclyffe Hall and Una Troubridge, and possibly brought them into the social life of Craig, Atwood and St John before Hall and Troubridge moved to Rye in 1930. In February 1919 the Pioneer Players produced *Trifles* by Susan Glaspell at the King's Hall, Covent Garden, one of the few plays by women in the society's later years. It was one of two plays by Glaspell to be directed by Edith Craig. The second was *The Verge*, the society's final production, staged after Sybil Thorndike had put pressure on Craig to resurrect the society in 1925. Many reviews of plays were anonymous, but the Pioneer Players' mid-life success was praised by critics such as Desmond McCarthy and Virginia Woolf in the *New Statesman*, Cicely Hamilton in *Time & Tide* and by *G. K.'s Weekly*, owned by Hamilton's old adversary, G. K. Chesterton.

Edith Craig achieved a nationwide reputation for producing nativity plays. Her interest in the genre, like the pageant, developed from the use of theatre by the church. As early as 1902 Craig had been involved in her brother's production of Housman's play *Bethlehem*. Nativity plays were becoming increasingly popular. Cicely Hamilton's *A Child in Flanders* showed that such plays could become a communal focus, reinforcing the ideology of heroism through Christianity, mapping the nativity story onto the European battlefield.

As early as January 1915 at Westminster Cathedral Hall Edith Craig staged *The Shepherds* by Father Cuthbert in aid of the Franciscan Hop Fields Mission. The play was described in unconventional terms, 'written in a racy, colloquial style, precisely that style which the secular dramatist who associates religion only with church on Sundays seldom succeeds in achieving'.[99] The author, Father Cuthbert, was a Capuchin friar and Warden of the hostel for Franciscan students at Oxford University. He had published a biography of St Francis. The funds raised by the play would be used to support the 10,000 Catholics employed in Kent during the hop-picking season. A number of stalwarts took part in the event. Rosabel Watson – otherwise conductor of the Aeolian Ladies Orchestra seen at many a suffrage event – directed the music, and the irrepressible Gwen Lally played First Roysterer.[100] In December 1915, Rutland Boughton's play, also called *Bethlehem*, was produced at the Glastonbury Festival, where it was to be repeated in later years. Christina Walshe designed the scenery of the play, which was publicized as emphatically 'not a modern "stunt"'.[101]

Craig's most frequently produced nativity play was written by the scholar E. K. Chambers.[102] Chambers's explanatory note in the play programme states that *An Early English Nativity Play* was adapted from the extant texts of the miracle plays performed by the trade guilds at Coventry and York. The principle of the adaptation was to 'preserve the mediaeval simplicity of speech and motive'.[103] The production at Rye Monastery, on 13 and 14 January 1919, was organized by Lady Maud Warrender. In the Procession of Saints and Martyrs, Warrender appeared as St Cecilia, George Plank as St Crispan and Gabrielle Enthoven as St Damien. Ellen Terry read the Prologue. Enthoven also appeared as Calchas. This fundraising event in aid of the Borough Nursing Fund excited the locals. The Mayor thanked all concerned especially Ellen Terry as the 'Queen of the theatrical world'.[104] For the participants, the play clearly appealed for a number of different reasons. Local police sergeant, Arthur Lefevre, must have enjoyed promotion in his role as St George of England. A number of the characters were cross-dressed in performance: the Angel Gabriel, Herod's soldiers, the Third King and of course Herod. Christopher St John is convincing as Herod, seen centre stage, flanked by attendants.[105] She was praised as a 'grand elocutionist', clearly showing no sign of the lisp which Marguerite Steen attributed to her.[106]

At the Wigmore Hall, probably in the previous year, the same play had been given to raise funds for women war workers. Edith Craig had directed Mrs Geoffrey Bowes Lyon as St George, but the costumes were different. Designed by Pamela Colman Smith, the simple lines and spare use of surface design, possibly screen printed, were lavishly photographed by E. O. Hoppé with whom the Pioneer Players were already familiar.[107]

The Pioneer Players kept up to date with contemporary work in the theatre, in particular that of their members. It took out a subscription to a theatre society called The Plough.[108] Active members included Hoppé and artists such as Margaret Mackintosh, Charles Rennie Mackintosh, George Sheringham and Stella Bowen. In June 1918 at the Royal Court, The Plough produced Clifford Bax's play, *The Sneezing Charm,* in which several members of the Pioneer Players took part.[109] Clifford Bax and Rosabel Watson (who conducted the music which had been written especially by Gustav Holst) were ordinary members of the Pioneer Players. The play capitalized on the imperial fascination with the East, just predating E. M. Dell's novel *The Sheik* (1919). The eleven 'Ladies of the Harim' [sic] came from the Margaret Morris School. The second production by The Plough was to be hosted in June by wealthy patron of the arts, Baroness D'Erlanger, at her home, 139 Piccadilly.[110]

The peak of the Pioneer Players' work was marked by Paul Claudel's religious drama rather than plays associated with women's suffrage. A very different impression is provided by the society's later work. The Pioneer Players effectively had two lives: one as a theatre society committed to a range of political campaigns; the other as an art theatre. The two lives of the society have been seen as distinct. Although Edith Craig's success was rooted in women's suffrage drama, she was consistently committed to theatre work. As Cicely Hamilton said, she was not chiefly a politician. The theatre was her chosen field of work. A lot has been invested in associating her exclusively with either women's suffrage drama or art theatre. Celebrated by some, dismissed by others, as political, as feminist, she wanted financial backing to make the Pioneer Players a permanent feature; she needed a theatre building in which to develop her experiments. Although the society increasingly attracted aristocrats, significant patronage was not forthcoming. At the same time Ellen Terry's financial situation collapsed and her increasing frailty meant that Edith Craig had to take care of her mother. Craig was forced to reassess her own career. There was no time to waste.

In 1918 an article surveyed the Pioneer Players' work as producing the best of every kind of play in 'kaleidoscopic fashion'. It was therefore a crucial testing ground for plays, but this made its work hard to define.[111] The future of the Pioneer Players was dependent on its audience, possibly following a repertory season such as that launched by Sir Thomas Beecham.

In August 1919, the British Drama League (BDL) was founded 'to encourage the Art of the theatre both for its own sake and as a means of intelligent recreation among all classes of the community'.[112] Edith Craig was one of the twenty-three members of the BDL Council. At Stratford-upon-Avon where the BDL was launched, an exhibition of scenic models and designs was organized by Craig, Norman Wilkinson, Randolph Schwabe and Norman MacDermott. The Pioneer Players lent several items: four designs by George Plank of *A Merry Death*; one design of *Death and the Lady*; and one model by Teoo Imakaroa for *Kanawa*.[113] It was proposed that the Pioneer Players might benefit from sharing administrative costs with other play-producing subscription societies. A number of ideas were mooted about organizing the production of drama by providing technical advice and support, costumes and scenery. With this aim, Edith Craig and Tony Atwood became members of the Workshops' Committee. Later in the year, on 30 November, the BDL held a dinner at the Florence Restaurant. Its motto was Matthew Arnold's influential injunction, 'organize the theatre'. Among the numerous speakers was Christopher St John representing the Foreign Drama Committee.[114]

Some members of the Pioneer Players felt that the BDL's involvement threatened the society's autonomy, but Edith Craig appears not to have taken this view, and appeared as a keynote speaker at the BDL's inaugural summer conference at Stratford-upon-Avon. Here she spoke on 'Reform in Production', sharing the panel with Norman MacDermott and Norman Wilkinson. Possibly referring to the furore over Grein's production of *Salome* the previous year, she quoted Oscar Wilde, to the effect that 'reforms in art were as tiresome and unprofitable as reforms in theology'.[115] She cited numerous reformers, including Henry Irving and Charles Kean. Kean's historical knowledge had liberated stage costume from the limited choice between a shirt and a shape, distinguishing between pre- or post-Elizabethan age. She argued for progress, for transformation rather than reform, and openly disagreed with her brother. While he believed that 'the whole thing should be the creation of one mind ... she believed the theatre should be run entirely by the men and women of the theatre'.[116] In the open discussion which followed, Christopher St John was outspoken: 'there had been too much of the introduction of the studio on the stage. Chelsea artists had invaded the theatre, and thought production was quite an easy job. They did not bring about the reform that was needed.'[117] It is not clear whether this was directed at Norman Wilkinson or The Plough, which had benefited from Baroness D'Erlanger's patronage.

Ellen Terry was unable to attend the BDL conference. Instead she sent a letter on the subject of 'Dramatic Art in National Life and the Case for a British Drama League'. The letter was read by Edith Craig. It was published in full in *The Stage*, but elsewhere was reduced to the inflammatory claim that audiences were in need of improvement. Other speakers included Elsie Fogerty on the need for a dramatic university, and Lewis Casson on the repertory movement.

Edith Craig's role was increasingly turning towards education. Although the opportunity to teach at Rosina Filippi's school in 1917 did not materialize,[118] Craig taught at the Florence Etlinger School in 1924 where her friend Rosabel Watson was in charge of the orchestra. Etlinger's operatic and dramatic school at 60 Paddington Street had a comprehensive curriculum: modern comedy, Shakespeare, elocution, grand opera, light opera and musical comedy in 1916–17. The Physical Culture department taught dancing, fencing, gesture, deportment and Dalcroze eurhythmics. A few years later, Craig was a member of the Committee of Theatre Practitioners formed to discuss the founding of a university course in drama. The diploma in Dramatic Art was to be sanctioned by London University and hold its first examinations in July 1925.[119] Other members of the committee included Sir Johnston Forbes-Robertson, Kenneth Barnes, Sir Israel Gollancz, Sir Frederick Mott, Norman McKinnel, Athole Stewart, Alfred Lugg, Dr Aiken, Lena Ashwell and Elsie Fogerty. It took longer than many expected to establish drama as a university discipline.[120]

By the time Edith Craig directed Susan Glaspell's weird play, *The Verge*, for the Pioneer Players in 1925, the society had suspended its activities for several years. The last official subscription production had been Saint-Georges de Bouhélier's *The Children's Carnival* in 1920. This performance met with a hostile reception. In the event, the BDL effectively took over the administration of the Pioneer Players, which was put on hold. The bank account was put in order and Geoffrey Whitworth, at the BDL, dealt with correspondence. However, as will be seen in the following chapter, Edith Craig was far from idle in the 1920s. The Pioneer Players had been responsible for testing numerous plays. It was pioneering work, doing whatever it took to launch new plays and plays new to a London stage. Playscripts were translated and commissioned as well as the necessary designing of scenery and costumes and the difficulties of finding an appropriate cast and venue. Edith Craig was let down on several occasions when the venue in which she had rehearsed and set the stage was withdrawn at the last moment. In 1934 Charles F. Smith recalled the story of Craig's last-minute haul of props and scenery across Covent Garden to transfer her play to the Savoy. She had dressed as a monk to enable her to be on stage to prompt and direct unobtrusively.[121] This production was the historic performance of *Paphnutius* by Hrotsvit. The Pioneer Players had been subject to internal disagreements, some of which were not officially recorded. H. F. Rubinstein wrote cryptically about 'unpleasantnesses' surrounding the production of his play.[122] Obstacles may have been considerable, but Craig overcame them. Her career was characterized by a contrast between the critical acclaim she received for a production and the lack of material assistance which she found in the theatre. In the end, Edith Craig wanted to dispense with the role of the pioneer. It was a freedom in the theatre which cost too much. She wanted to know what it felt like eventually to have arrived.

Chapter 6

THE CALL OF THE SUBURBS:
The Little Theatre Movement
1920–28

Just as the Pioneer Players was suspended, other theatre societies were springing up like 'pilchards at St Ives'.[1] Although the Pioneer Players was a significant predecessor of the Arts Theatre in London and provided a training ground for many actors, stage-managers and directors, its work has received little critical attention. The reasons for this state of affairs are diverse. The unevenness of historical constructions demonstrates that histories are always made in the present, shaped by current concerns and perspectives. There is consistent evidence in contemporary newspapers of the high value of the Pioneer Players' work. Craig's outspoken views were also occasionally reported. She had accused the repertory theatres of intellectual snobbishness,[2] and although she condemned the nepotism of amateur dramatics, claimed that 'English theatre was firmly rooted in an amateur tradition.'[3]

Edith Craig was a national figure in the movement to encourage the founding of 'little' theatres all over the country. The demise of the Pioneer Players was gradual. It put an end to Craig's ambition to establish an art theatre in London. For Craig, the call of the suburbs was hard to resist. It was far enough away from London that she could work with greater autonomy and to consistently high acclaim.

The countryside had a particular significance in Craig's life. It had provided many of her mother's bolt-holes from London and, for Craig, St John and Atwood, was where they spent their time when not in Bedford Street. The perception of the country by cityfolk as an escape, a retreat promising safety, innocence and rest has a long history, throughout eighteenth-century British literature back to the writings of Horace and Juvenal. Such values were embodied in the plays which Craig produced by exponents of the 'regional novel', Sheila Kaye-Smith and Constance Holme.[4] Although Craig was a member of the English Folk Song Society (with its rather narrow view of 'folk song' which excluded workers' songs of the urban industrialized world), her interests were broader. Her collection of published music and song included her favourite Hebridean music as well as Hungarian dances, Russian folk songs and the *Labour Song Book* published by the Independent Labour Party (ILP). Life in rural Kent was, for Craig, not a holiday. She was a regular during the hop-picking season and raised funds for rural workers, with whom she seemed to identify. Friends could spot her at a distance by her distinctive hand-loomed blue or red smocks.[5]

Towards the end of the nineteenth century, middle-class cityfolk were reassessing the countryside as an appropriate environment in which to live out some radical ideas. While the country was used as a playground to act out fantasies of feudalism, it signified for others a place in which to establish new ways of living, a new organization of space and building, to experiment with new relationships. After the First World War this was consistent with rebuilding and the regeneration of communities. The development of the garden cities had been an attempt to plan not only new housing but also communities following a new way of life in the suburbs. In Letchworth, the first garden city, the local theatre was a valued part of garden-city living. Craig was involved in the early stages of the development of the theatre in Letchworth and she worked for the Everyman Theatre in the suburb of Hampstead.

Norman MacDermott (1890–1977) founded the Everyman Theatre in Hampstead between 1920 and 1926 and wrote its history, *Everymania* (1975), guaranteeing it a place, however small, in theatre history. The Everyman Theatre has been acknowledged for its productions of plays by dramatists Eugene O'Neill, Noël Coward and Luigi Pirandello. The prospectus for the Everyman Theatre sets out MacDermott's manifesto, citing Jacques Copeau of Le Théâtre du Vieux-Colombier in the need for the new movement in the theatre to 'begin at the beginning' and to develop theatre through practice rather than theory: 'practice, continued effort, self-sacrifice, to work obscurely, to construct slowly. And this alone bears fruit'.[6] No short cuts would produce a new art theatre. It needed to start afresh, finding new acting spaces and performing all types of plays in order to relearn the Greek meaning of theatre as 'a place of seeing'. The architecture of the stage was crucial in American theatre where they 'built [their] own theatre (or perhaps remodelled a barn), so that the building might have some suitability to the work to be done'.[7] The Everyman Theatre was run in the drill hall, formerly used by Martin Shaw and Edward Gordon Craig for rehearsals of their Purcell productions. MacDermott criticized the West End productions for their 'spurious gaiety, bright colour ignorantly used, movement absurdly misapplied'. Lighting was innovative at the Everyman and drew critical attention. MacDermott agreed with Edward Gordon Craig in the need for a ' "new man of the theatre", his Artistic Director, who brings unifying vision to the whole work', but emphasized the role of the audience. MacDermott's disagreement with Gordon Craig was unpopular. However, while it lost MacDermott the support of Rutherston, Wilkinson and Lovat-Fraser,[8] it did not trouble Edith Craig. The missing link for MacDermott (and Edith Craig) in conceptualizations of an art theatre hitherto was the support and enthusiasm of the audience. He concluded his manifesto thus: 'It remains for the public to do its part.'

MacDermott's founding of the Everyman Theatre followed a brief career designing theatre models, lecturing on scenic history and teaching and he remembers meeting Edith Craig at the BDL's Stratford Exhibition. He was on the same panel of speakers at the BDL conference in 1919 when Edith Craig had given a keynote speech on reform. Immediately after the suspension of the Pioneer Players' activities at its AGM in October 1920, Edith Craig turned her energies towards Hampstead where she worked as a producer independently and with Norman MacDermott. In November and December 1920 she arranged crowd scenes, fights and dances for *Romeo and Juliet*, which was produced by MacDermott. In December of the same year she produced Israel Zangwill's *The Melting Pot*, E. K. Chambers's *An Old English Nativity Play* (a revival from Craig's 1918–19 productions at the Wigmore Hall and Rye Monastery) and *Through the Crack* by Violet Pearn and Algernon Blackwood. The latter was a mawkish play about a bereaved family on the death of the child Misty Love. At night the children find that they are able to visit the spirit world through the crack between night and day. In 1920 Craig was working on a production for at least eight months of the year. In November she took part in the Sydney Valentine Memorial matinee at the Alhambra Theatre, an event to raise funds for the Valentine Memorial Pension Fund. Its first beneficiary was to be Valentine's widow.[9]

Craig's role in the Everyman Theatre seems unclear from MacDermott's history, in spite of his careful acknowledgement of her work and the support of Christopher St John and Tony Atwood. They were remembered as three musketeers wearing the black *capa* of the Italian cavalry. He states clearly the 'unusual arrangement' of

Craig's employment whereby she was cited as producer 'under the general direction of Norman MacDermott'.[10] The emphasis on her geniality reads suspiciously like an unsolicited testimonial: 'I found her delightful to work with, easy, good-humoured and loyal.' [11]

At the Everyman Theatre between January and August 1921, Craig produced eight plays by George Bernard Shaw, including *You Never Can Tell*, with which she had been so unimpressed in her youth. MacDermott recalls that the unpopularity of Shaw's stance on war meant that producing her work was a financial risk. One of the Shaw plays produced at Hampstead, *The Showing Up of Blanco Posnet*, took Craig to the Albert Hall, Leeds. This was to lead to further work and a new departure for her.

Edith Craig shared MacDermott's views, and later spoke on the important functions of architecture and audiences, the need for an eclecticism where dramatic form was concerned. The relationship between director and audience was paradoxical. In identifying that the audience had a role to play in the success of a production, practitioners such as MacDermott were challenging many assumptions. Power had been shifting from the managers of theatres to the dramatists and gradually to the actors. The audience now was assigned a role in the performance, in the form of a duty to appreciate, that is understand, dramatic form and convention and, of course, to support it financially by attending and paying for tickets. The introduction of the audience into the equation seems to challenge the prevailing Modernist view that the work of art is autonomous. It is distinctly different from the contempt in which Futurist theatre held its audience. Such theatrical ventures may exemplify the 'conservative modernity' which Alison Light has suggested evade the Modernist-preoccupied literary histories of the twentieth century.[12] Ultimately the role of the audience was fixed by MacDermott and others whose views on the 'new theatre' were prescriptive and hierarchical, the artist-director leading the revolution and imparting his [sic] knowledge to an unenlightened audience. Perhaps what distinguished 'artists' of the stage such as Isadora Duncan and Edward Gordon Craig from Norman MacDermott and Edith Craig was the constituency of their audience. Duncan's art had always been designed for an elite. Edith Craig and others were committed to the virtues and values of dramatic art. Their determination was conceived in terms of inspiring, educating and elevating a mass audience to the (perceived) higher culture, more commonly associated with the genre of poetry and the sentiments of the Newbolt Report 1921.[13]

The participation of women in the theatre in the context of this gendered construction of the 'new theatre' appears to have been overlooked. The suburbs had become associated with the feminine.[14] The year 1920 saw the launch of *Time & Tide*, for which Christopher St John was a regular music critic.[15] Following the partial enfranchisement of women in 1918, there was a premature sense of arrival. Since so much had been invested in legislative change, it was expected that the inclusion of women in institutions amounted to an equal society. As time went on, however, many women became disillusioned; others shrewdly continued to campaign for equality in all aspects of life. The WFL, for instance, continued to exist as a campaigning body, its last bulletin dated 1961. Other bodies such as the Six Point Group and the Women's Institutes provided women with political and cultural space. Elsewhere women were taking part in politics at a national and local level.

The year 1922 was special for Craig as a year of children's theatre and some single, very remarkable productions. For Ellen Terry it was the year of academic honours, as the University of St Andrews awarded her an honorary doctorate. J. M. Barrie was installed as its Rector. In January Ellen Terry and her daughter saw Laurence Olivier perform in *The Taming of the Shrew*. In March Edith Craig produced John Dryden's *All for Love or the World Well Lost* at the Shaftesbury Theatre for the Phoenix Society. Her old friend Tom Heslewood designed the costumes. Later the same month she produced *Pride and Prejudice*, by Eileen H. A. Squire and J. C. Squire at the Palace Theatre. The design of the costumes was attributed to Lovat-Fraser (1890–1921), a colleague from the BDL Workshop Committee, who had died the year before. This was one of several dramatizations of novels which Craig produced (the others being *Wuthering Heights* and *The Secret Agent*). In April she produced *Shakespeare* by Clifford Bax and H. F. Rubinstein for the Fortune Players at the Royal Court. In April and June she produced Beatrice Mayor's *Thirty Minutes in a Street* and *The Girl in the City* at the Kingsway Theatre for the Playwright's Theatre. Rehearsals were under way in March and Virginia Woolf attended to provide moral support to one of the performers, Betty Potter, sister of Beatrice Mayor.

Woolf recorded her experiences of the rehearsal in her diary, including a portrait of Edith Craig. She had attended a production of the Pioneer Players in 1920 and reviewed *The Higher Court* for the *New Statesman* in 1920, but she did not mention Craig. Her portrait dramatically scripts her memories of 1922:

Miss Craig is a rosy, ruddy 'personage' in white waistcoat, with black bow tie & gold chain loosely knotted.

Stop those monkey tricks, do Saunders – & let us have some light.

Miss Craig (Saunders stands right up to the footlights & shouts through her hollowed hands:) 'There's a short on the batterns, Miss Craig.'

Let's have the floats then . . .

Now, all of you. I want you to listen carefully to the music. Make the movements that suggest themselves to you.

Beautiful lady, you go up to the balcony. Can you step to the left? No: I won't take risks. Young man, Dunlop, you walk straight – straight I say – straight – Can't you move that table? No? Well then to the right. Miss Potter (this with some acerbity) you needn't dance.

Poor Betty looked like the skeleton of a sheep. She is at one of her crises, & may be dismissed the stage over this affair.

But it is, as usual, the atmosphere I want to get. The supple, candid, free & easy good sense of theatrical manners, as I noted them at tea. 'My dear boy', drinking out of the same cup. Little Lanchester said, when I asked if she walked in her pyjamas, 'Oh do stop being funny' – I don't think one could use one's brain without being warned off. Still, it don't much matter. I walked with Miss Litvinne, mother of an illegitimate child, down Longacre, & found her like an articulate terrier – eyes wide apart; greased to life; nimble; sure footed, without a depth anywhere in her brain. They go to the Cabaret; all night dances; John Goss sings. She was communicative, even admiring I think. Anyhow, I like Bohemians. Then we went into the theatre, & there was the light on, the group significant, (Bobo's children) gold tissue; something stimulating & unreal.[16]

In spite of the unintellectual character of proceedings, or perhaps even because of this, the resulting scene was 'something stimulating & unreal'. The distance in Woolf's narrative, elsewhere formally impressive, is here somewhat melancholy. She is an onlooker, an outsider who does not quite fit in. Theatrefolk were always to be a fascination to her, a mystery beyond her ken.

Edith Craig devised her own play for children, *The Shoe*. A narrative woven from nursery rhymes and set to music by Max Pirani, this was performed on 27 June as part of a fundraising event at the Palace Theatre in aid of the Women's League of Service for Motherhood's infant welfare centres.[17] Dame Clara Butt announced the proceeds. Ellen Terry played the Old Woman, and May Whitty's daughter, Peggy Webster, also took part. Monica Disney played Buy-a-broom by kind permission of Italia Conti.[18] Lady Diana Cooper made an early theatre appearance at this event which predated her worldwide tour as the Nun in Max Reinhardt's *The Miracle*.

Edith Craig's interest in children's theatre and nativity plays was shared with many others. Mabel Dearmer's children's theatre tea party at the Royal Court was opened by Ellen Terry, where Noël Coward sang 'Fairy Shoes', and there were performances by Margaret Morris's dancing children and the Aeolian Quartet. Iris Rowe was subjected to Edith Craig's talent-spotting gaze. Her name was underlined several times in Craig's programme.[19] Jean Sterling Mackinlay ran a children's theatre with her husband Harcourt Williams. Pamela Colman Smith designed the programme covers and Martin Shaw arranged music. The sets were credited to 'Messrs Let's Pretend'. The development of children's theatres evolved from the annual Christmas pantomime tradition and the Little Theatre movement. The interest in simple drama and the assumed importance of involving children in theatre coincided with a belief in the humanizing effects for adults of performance and play-making which could elevate individual souls and consolidate entire communities. Theatre-making or theatre-going had been twinned with citizenship. National identities were associated with large, visible national institutions, of which the proposed National Theatre had long been a linchpin. The notion that a national culture needed to be organized was essentially a metropolitan directive motivated by middle-class anxiety.

The promotion of amateur theatre activities coincided, and sometimes conflicted with the professionalization of acting. The notion that everyone has a bit of acting in her feeds a democratic impulse which has its place in labour history. E. K. Chambers's note to *The Early English Nativity Play* had explained the function of the trade guilds in producing such drama, performed to an indeterminate public audience from pageants or mobile stages. The role of craftsmanship in the training provided by the medieval guilds was rediscovered by Arthur Penty. Penty's *The Restoration of the Gild System* (1906) was to be influential on the socialist movement in Britain. The combination of beauty and work as an essential antidote to postindustrial alienation had been identified by William Morris and the exponents of the Arts and Crafts Movement. Such Romantic beliefs persisted, transmuted by Modernism, even captured in the wartime paintings of Paul Nash, the strangeness of aircraft, the unnatural beastliness of their mechanical flight. Paul

Nash and Martin Shaw joined Edith Craig in the League of Arts' Dramatic Circle in October 1922. The League of Arts itself had been founded by Martin Shaw and his brother Geoffrey and Charles Kennedy Scott a few days after the armistice. It was based at the Guildhouse, Eccleston Square, in London. In the Dramatic Circle, Edith Craig was in charge of drama, Martin Shaw of music and Paul Nash was scenic artist.[20] In January 1923, the League of Arts produced *The York Nativity Play*.[21] Just before this, Craig had directed *The Shoe* and *A Real Old Fashioned Harlequinade* at the Albert Hall, Leeds, as a Christmas show for the Leeds Art Theatre.

The year 1923 saw the publication of Christopher St John's translation of Hrotsvit's plays. An extant diary of Edith Craig's productions running from 1923–9, possibly notes for her memoirs, provides an insight into her activities and how much she was paid for some productions.[22] Craig's directorial talents were applied to both ancient and modern this year. On 24 June 1923 she directed *The Faithfull Shepherdess* by John Fletcher at the Shaftesbury Theatre for the Phoenix Society and under the auspices of the Incorporated Stage Society.[23] She had already directed for the Phoenix Society at the Shaftesbury: the production in 1922 of John Dryden's *All for Love*. Montague Summers wrote an explanatory note on *The Faithfull Shepherdess* in the play programme, sketching the history of the play and its productions. The play had intimate associations with Craig. The dramatist was, for Craig, a local and his play had been produced by Edward Godwin, Craig's father. Fletcher was born in Rye, only eight miles from her home in Smallhythe Place. In 1885 Godwin had produced the play in the grounds of Coombe Place, Wimbledon, with a distinguished cast, including the Lord and Lady Spencer Churchill. The play had been revived in 1903 by Philip Carr at the Botanical Gardens when several familiar names featured in the cast, including Leonard Craske, later Prejudice in *A Pageant of Great Women*, who played the Old Shepherd. In 1923 Craig seemed to be treading in her father's footsteps. However, Montague Summers remarked that Godwin's production had been conventional. Presumably Craig's was not. Perigot and Amoret were played by Harcourt Williams and Cathleen Nesbitt respectively, while Harold Scott took the part of a Satyr and Audrey Cameron was one of the ubiquitous Shepherdesses.

The productions in January of the nativity play for the League of Arts and in June the seventeenth-century play by Fletcher were followed by a staging of modern drama which presented its own difficulties. Authors were still alive to provide opinions.

C. B. Cochran had suggested to Harold Hobday that Craig produce Arthur Richman's *Ambush* for the London Theatre Guild.[24] The co-operative principle of the medieval guilds seemed elusive. Relationships were strained all round, between actors and management, between director and author. The leading performers made the papers when Madeleine Marshall slapped George Elton. Both Craig and the actors (including her mother's estranged husband, James Carew) had already been engaged when Harold Hobday temporarily suspended rehearsals pending negotiations with Cochran for securing the theatre.[25] The co-operative spirit was revived when a letter of complaint was sent to Hobday on behalf of the entire cast.[26] Richman wrote to Craig making firm suggestions about lighting certain scenes and informed her that Chance Newton, critic of the *Referee*, wanted to see the dress rehearsals.[27] Hobday insisted that more work needed to be done to speed up George Elton's speeches and was critical of the plain walls of the set.[28] The performance on 1 September 1923 at the Garrick Theatre must have come as a relief to all concerned. Craig earned £70 for her troubles.

More work followed. Craig coached Miss Hawkins, daughter of Sir Anthony Hope, for her part in Sutton Vane's *Outward Bound*,[29] and read plays for the Theatre Guild. The procedure was to anonymize the scripts to ensure that the selection process was not biased. Other readers included Robert Minster, Fisher White and Clifford Heatherley.[30]

A few months before her production of *Ambush*, Craig travelled to Egypt to take part in Tom Terriss's Gaumont film, *Fires of Fate*, based on Arthur Conan Doyle's novel, *The Tragedy of the Korosko*. This was not her first venture into film. She had appeared with Ellen Terry in *Her Greatest Performance* (1916), in *Victory and Peace* (aka *The Invasion of Britain* or *The National Film*) (1918) and *God in the Garden* (1921). She was a keen filmgoer and a member of the Film Society. As a theatre practitioner, Craig had a progressive view of film, yet she felt that it would never replace the theatre. On 8 February 1923 she travelled to Egypt with the crew from Victoria Station, London. She was away seven weeks, returning on 11 April.

The filming in Egypt in 1923 followed a significant year. Egypt had gained independence from the British and Howard Carter and Lord Caernarvon had discovered Tutankhamun's tomb. The plot of *Fires of Fate*, concerning the kidnapping of an English woman by Prince Ibrahim, fed imperial anxieties about Eastern sexual incontinence and its threat to English womanhood. The girl is saved by Colonel Egerton, played by Nigel Barrie. The film was remade at another pertinent moment in international political tensions. In 1932 Ibn Abd al-Rahman al-Saud became first King of Saudi Arabia. In the same year, the son of American aviator, Charles Lindbergh, was kidnapped and murdered, an incident which influenced Agatha Christie's novel, *Murder on the Orient Express* (1934).

In 1923 journalists were interested in the American film star, Wanda Hawley, who had travelled 6,000 miles to take part in *Fires*. Shortly before she joined the crew she was in the news, having filed for divorce from her husband Allan B. Hawley on grounds of cruelty and desertion. Craig's role was a 'character' part, Miss Adams, Wanda Hawley's aunt. Before her departure, Craig was forthright in her expectations of the film: 'This film will be something utterly unlike the Los Angeles things.'[31]

Scenes were filmed in a mosque and 'an entertainment at an Arab banquet in the desert by the Sheik of Mena'. The filming at Marg in the Nubian desert was witnessed by British army officers, as one newspaper recorded: 'British Generals See Film Dervish Charge'.[32] The said officers were Generals Herbert and Hunter. Brigadier General Herbert (1866–1936) had retired in 1920, but by March 1923 he was Commandant of the Military School in Cairo, although newspaper reports cited him as Resident Commissioner. The *Sunday Express* remarked, 'everybody dead or alive seems to be mixed up with Egypt just now'.[33] Several photographs appeared in the British press showing Craig riding a camel.[34] It was reported that she got up at 6 a.m. every morning to ride her favourite camel called Princess, a champion at the races.

On her departure for Egypt, Craig was given rosemary by Ellen Terry. Several newspapers printed photographs of the parting at Victoria Station and recorded the fact that, on her return, Craig was given a welcome-home supper by her mother. Extraordinarily, one gossip column reported that Craig's cat was missing her.[35] No reference was made in any of the reports to Christopher St John or Tony Atwood. Speculation about the effect on Craig of her travels and her reception by theatre managers was the opportunity for a wry joke in the *Era* newspaper. The entire report ran: 'Edith Craig who has been filming in the East, has come home crazy about camel riding. Quite a number of London managers have got the hump.'[36]

On her return to England, Craig worked on her London productions, *The Faithfull Shepherdess* and Arthur Richman's *Ambush* at the Garrick Theatre. However, it was Leeds rather than London where Edith Craig's work was to develop in the 1920s. Since bluntness has been regarded more a virtue than a vice in Yorkshire, she was more likely to be accepted.

As the Art Director at the Leeds Art Theatre (LAT), Craig worked closely with Charles F. Smith who subsidized the theatre.[37] He was a supportive friend to Craig with perceptive advice to offer. When they were planning a production of the sixteenth-century morality play adapted by Hugo von Hofmannsthal, *The Great World Theatre*, Smith was on the lookout for a suitable local church as venue. St John's, Holland Park, was rejected,[38] in favour, eventually, of St Edward's Church, Holbeck. Smith's advice was to involve Railton, church warden and amateur actor, since he 'would be very useful' and 'has some good ideas & a lot of influence'.[39] *The Great World Theatre* was highly acclaimed but exposed some problematic working relationships. L. B. (Laurie) Ramsden, business manager of LAT, and C. F. Smith did not get on. Something of Ramsden's attitude can be discerned from his letter to Craig about casting for the play: 'It is rather unfortunate, however, that you mentioned the matter of the Morality Play to Mrs Wigoder as one of the conditions is that all of the people performing in it are good Church people.'[40] Ruby (Mrs) Wigoder had played Winnie Verloc in *The Secret Agent* with Reginald Tate at Skipton and at the Albert Hall, Leeds.[41] Wigoder's performance in particular had been praised by critics. Advice was also forthcoming, probably from Ramsden, on the George Bernard Shaw plays and royalties.[42]

Smith's differences with Ramsden finally came to a head. He sent Craig copies of his resignation letter addressed to Ramsden. Ramsden had claimed that Smith's personal unpopularity would prevent him from raising money for the LAT. Money was the issue: Ramsden wanted a guaranteed salary and more power. Smith's stinging response was privately shared with Craig: 'I don't see how he can expect the security of a paid servant and the prestige of a theatrical pioneer.'[43] The question of money was considered to be beyond the expectations of pioneers.

Craig also seems to have fallen out with Ramsden. He had written to her demanding the prompt copy of Arthur Richman's *Ambush*. Tony Atwood drafted Craig's response.[44] She questioned whether he had permission to perform the play, pointing out that she was not supervising the production and, in any event, did not possess the prompt copy. Craig produced a burlesque of *Ambush* and a 'sensational melodrama in two acts discovered by Edith Craig', possibly *Marion's Crime* for the LAT At Home in the ballroom of the Scala Picture House on 29 April 1924.[45] *Ambush* was seen by the anonymous letter-writer from Harehills Avenue, 'a sincere admirer of your genius from Leeds'.[46] Anonymous statements provide a measure of the intensity of any controversy.[47]

Before the final conflict between Smith and Ramsden, Edith Craig directed some acclaimed productions for the LAT. In 1922 Ethel Smyth directed her opera, *The Boatswain's Mate*, for the LAT. The performance was notable for the unexpected absence of a cello. Smyth saved the day by singing the part. Smyth's article on the event was published in the *Yorkshire Post*, praising the quality of the performers and of Edith Craig as producer. She was particularly impressed by the abilities of the performers to learn new and difficult material. The contrast between the margin for error in musical comedy and that in more complex musical pieces is expressed in terms of a spatial, suburban metaphor. The musical comedy 'is like stepping off the asphalt path across a municipal common – no fear of losing your way!' The article provides helpful advice for amateurs, including the often overlooked matter of anticipated expenses of £28 at union rates for three rehearsals of three hours.[48]

Joseph Conrad wrote his own dramatization of *The Secret Agent* which had been produced in London in 1922. Craig's production for the LAT in November 1923 met with Conrad's approval. His telegram 'thanked the players for their production of his play and wished them success in their project'.[49] In the LAT prospectus for 1923–4, C. F. Smith announced that realism had become a prisonhouse. It was time to break out.[50] The LAT hoped to produce ballets, mimes and operas, not restricting itself to producing plays but 'theatrical productions'. During this second year, Craig directed Hugo von Hofmannsthal's *The Great World Theatre*, Joseph Conrad's *The Secret Agent*, Oscar Wilde's *Lady Windermere's Fan*, John Galsworthy's *Punch and Go*, Eugene O'Neill's *In the Zone* and Lord Dunsany's *A Night at an Inn*.

The production in Holbeck Church of *The Great World Theatre* took up much of her time in January 1924, but in February she was free to do some adjudications of amateur dramatics in Huddersfield, followed by a show at Chilham in June. In November 1924, Craig produced John Masefield's *Philip the King* and Lascelles Abercrombie's *The Deserter* for the LAT at the newly built venue. The LAT had moved from the large Albert Hall venue in the Mechanics' Institute to the Blue Triangle Hall of the YWCA in Cookridge Street. Craig had advised on the adaptations of the new venue.[51] Princess Mary and Viscountess Lascelles were present. The compliments of Princess Mary were sent via Walter Boyle, the Lord Mayor's secretary.[52]

Ramsden recorded Edith Craig's departure from the Leeds Art Theatre in the programme for the 1925–6 season of plays. Craig had effectively been replaced by Mr F. Owen Chambers. Chambers was credited with producing the Winchester pageant of 1908 and working with Mr Bridges-Adams at the annual Shakespeare festivals at Stratford. Plays were to be performed in a new theatre, in the Alexandra Hall.[53] Ramsden graciously acknowledged Craig's 'genius and devotion to the Leeds Art Theatre' and reported that 'She feels, as a pioneer, that now the Theatre is firmly established, her work may be said to be complete.'[54] Edith Craig's talent was to set up new projects, but she rarely saw them mature. She delegated this to others, who ultimately took the credit.

Both Edith Craig and C. F. Smith had more work to do in Yorkshire. Craig was, according to Smith, responsible for 'building up' the York Everyman Theatre. An *ad hoc*, provisional company of players drawn from the LAT, appropriately named The Between-Time Players, was set up to produce plays for the York Everyman Theatre. Craig may have drawn on the experience of forming the Pioneer Players from the actors who performed in *A Pageant of Great Women* and *How the Vote Was Won*. Out of the ashes of one theatre another would rise.

Smith provided some advance publicity for Craig in the *Yorkshire Post*, where his biographical sketch declared her to be the inspiration behind the forthcoming York Everyman Theatre.[55] An unorthodox article, it remarked on her 'stimulating personality', her 'merry eyes and a rich laugh' and the fact that she could be 'a little unreasonable'. Smith took the opportunity to mark out an aesthetic difference between Edith Craig and her brother: 'One couldn't imagine Edith Craig attracted by puppets; her interest in humanity is too keen.'

In November 1924, the York Everyman Theatre revived *The Mollusc* by H. H. Davies at the Art Gallery, York, originally performed at the Criterion Theatre in London in October 1907. The Between-Time players performed the play. Although Edith Craig is not cited in the play programme as producer, an acknowledgement runs thus: 'It will be easy to detect the masterly influence of Miss Craig in this production.' Edith Craig was one of the four directors of the York Everyman Theatre, the others being Charles F. Smith, Margery W. Patterson and Herbert M. Duke. The play programme explained that Elmer Rice's *The Adding Machine*, intended as the third production, had been postponed 'owing to censorship difficulties'. Rehearsals of the substitute production of *She Stoops to Conquer* had been interrupted when Craig was taken ill.[56]

The next production of the York Everyman Theatre was the *Nativity Play* by E. K. Chambers (often incorrectly cited in programmes as 'G. K.'). The aims of the York Everyman Theatre were announced as supporting the 'Theatre as a Repository of artistic tradition' and as an 'arbiter of a correct pronunciation of our glorious language'.[57] Margery W. Patterson's note in the play programme claimed that modern drama was born with the church. The play was to be given one week's run in January 1925 at the Guildhall, York, with musical arrangements under the direction of Dr Bairstow and Mr J. L. Slater. Music was considered an integral part of a play rather than a frivolous accompaniment according to the York Everyman Theatre's principles:

> While disowning any doctrinaire spirit, the York Everyman Theatre will avoid elaborate staging and extravagant decor.
>
> Apart from financial considerations it is felt that scenic accessories should be sufficiently adequate to illustrate the intentions of the author, while allowing perfect freedom to the imaginations of the beholders.
>
> For the same reason there will be no music, unless it is an integral part of the play. Good music would be unworthily employed as an accompaniment to the animated discussions that it is hoped will be indulged in during our entr'actes, while indifferent music would be an impertinence.[58]

In 1920 Jacob Kramer had given a lecture, at the Leeds Art Club illustrated with examples of Kandinsky's paintings, on music as a non-representational art form.[59] The Leeds Art Club crowd had long been interested in a broad range of symbolism and mysticism, a pursuit of the spiritual, an organicist, Romantic modernism and socialism. In placing the author, actor, words, music, the verbal and visual in harmony, the York Everyman was reminiscent of one of Edith Craig's earlier ventures, the short-lived Masquers.

The York Everyman Theatre's 1925–6 season prospectus emphasized its aim to reach 'all classes of the community'. Although the subscribers' fee of £1 precluded this broadly targeted audience, provision was made for a number of free seats to non-subscribers at every performance. An extension of the facilities at the York Everyman Theatre fostered a social and cultural milieu in the library at Mr Watts Dyson's Bookshop, 1 Bridge Street, and the founding of the Hot Pot Club, where inexpensive refreshments and invited speakers were provided. These facilities were presented as 'privileges' to develop the York Everyman 'along club lines' and in the context of 'a club movement'. It was affiliated to the BDL.

In autumn 1924 Edith Craig became involved with theatre work in Letchworth. Beatrice Ensor of the Theosophical Educational Trust was the principal correspondent with Craig about her work for the St Christopher's Theatre, which was to open on 19 December. When the St Christopher's School needed a new hall it was decided to make it available to the local community as a theatre and public meeting hall:

> Just as the ideal of the School, as is now well known, is to train the young citizens in the rendering of service, so the ideal of the Theatre is also that of giving service to the whole community, and of helping its members to understand and appreciate more fully the beautiful things of life.[60]

Craig was invited to speak at the opening night on 'the value of the Drama and the Little Theatre Movement'.[61] Unlike the LAT, stage direction at the St Christopher's Theatre was not to be Craig's alone. In the opening prospectus, three producers were announced. Edith Craig's credits were associated with the Pioneer Players. The other two producers, Beatrice Wilson and Norman V. Norman, came with credentials from the Lena Ashwell Players and the Old Vic Theatre respectively. Norman had been a member of the Pioneer Players and had acted in the society's performance of *Romanticismo*.

The St Christopher's Theatre's first production, a play entitled *Through the Crack* by Algernon Blackwood and Violet Pearn, was not a new experience for Craig, as she had directed it at the Everyman Theatre. The play had just caught the attention of the New York Theatre Guild.[62] Pearn was enthusiastic about the Letchworth production, but the authors had been asked to waive, or reduce, their fees. Algernon Blackwood wrote: 'It is rather difficult to waive a fee altogether, because of other requests and as a matter of principle.'[63] He agreed to reduce the fee from £5 to 1 guinea on condition that his co-author consented. Such requests were common in the lean beginnings of theatre societies. On this occasion, Craig earned £30 4s for her work. On other occasions she seems to have waived her fees as producer, expecting the same from others when limited funds dictated. This was a dangerous precedent to set and Craig did not heed the warnings. The issue was to arise again when

Nigel Playfair wrote a brief note refusing to act, even for charity, without a fee.[64]

Craig's standards were not always shared by others. Her commitment involved self-sacrifice which others would regard as exploitation. She set high standards for herself but sometimes did not consider that others were unable to meet them. Some of the parents whose children were expected to appear in *Through the Crack* for nine nights in a row had complained, and it was suggested that the main role be shared between three children to 'satisfy the parents' and reduce the number of shows for each child.[65] Craig's exacting schedule, working between York and Letchworth, had its price. She was ill in November, but in spite of this managed to fulfil her commitments. Beatrice Ensor was disappointed by the attendance figures in the 600-seater theatre, but the production had been a success and arrangements were in hand for the next. Although Craig had suggested *A Doll's House*, Ensor found little interest in it. Instead, the plays for the new year were Gertrude Jennings's *The Young Person in Pink*, Lady Gregory's version of Goldoni's *Mirandolina* and Lady Florence Bell's *The Fog on the Moor*. Jennings wrote to Craig, 'I'm so relieved you don't ask me to do without the fee which is the request of most people.'[66] Lady Gregory accepted a reduced fee but pointed out that this would not be repeated.[67] The actors were each paid £6 with one exception. Craig was doubling up her productions, and some misunderstandings regarding bookings ensued. Herbert Duke, Manager of the York Everyman Theatre was blamed. Florence Bell wrote to Edith Craig in his defence.[68] *Mirandolina* and *The Fog on the Moor* were produced at York and then Letchworth. Perhaps unusually, Craig paid two organizations, the Red Knight and the Florence Etlinger School, to conduct rehearsals for her.[69]

Rose Quong's appearance in *The Fog on the Moor* had Florence Bell's patronage. Mirandolina was played by Ruth Bower. Craig lent Yew Tree Cottage, opposite Priest's House, to Bower where photographs show Bower comfortable in knee-breeches and sitting in a tree. Craig may have emphasized the subversive aspect of the production. The performance of Mirandolina by a boy in the 1787 production of Carlo Goldoni's play *La Locandiera* had seemed to defuse the threat posed by Mirandolina's final words about the 'infinite tricks of women'.[70]

The Pioneer Players' last subscription performance was given in March 1925. The final Annual General Meeting of the society had been held on 25 October 1920 when activities were suspended. The last subscription performance was *The Children's Carnival*, staged in June 1920 at the Kingsway Theatre. Since that time, Craig's credits were numerous and distinguished. At the Everyman Theatre she produced a season of eight plays by George Bernard Shaw. She had devised and produced her own play, *The Shoe*, several times. Her commitment to the Little Theatre Movement had taken her to Yorkshire where she had worked as Art Director at the LAT and at the York Everyman Theatre. Community theatre in Letchworth had benefited from her talents at the St Christopher's Theatre. Some plays were revived several times. *Through the Crack* was directed by Craig at the Everyman Theatre in 1920, at the Apollo Theatre in December 1922 for the Actor's Commonwealth, as well as at the St Christopher's Theatre. The nativity play was revived numerous times. The staging of the *York Nativity Play* at the Florence Etlinger Theatre School, in which Margaret Webster appeared, was described as in 'the Reinhardt or the Elizabethan Stage Society manner'.[71] After this success, Edith Craig was to start classes at the school.[72] The range of her productions was broad. Ellen Terry remembered her daughter's direction of *The Toils of Yoshitomo* by Torahiko Kori at the Little Theatre in October 1922. As in several of Craig's ventures, she was not responsible for scenic design, or in this case costume design. Kori's partner, Hesther Sainsbury, designed the costumes after careful research in the Victoria and Albert Museum.[73] In December 1925 and January 1926 Craig's work as director of *The Beggar Prince* by Cicely Hamilton at the Q Theatre brought her 5 per cent of the profits.[74] Each production was well received, attracting interest and praise and raising questions about what Craig might do next. In 1924 she acted as the Policeman in *Pan in Pimlico*, part of the dramatic entertainments at Castle Hall, Chilham.[75] In 1924–5 she seems to have been a member of the Casting Committee for the Maddermarket Theatre, Norwich, run by Walter Nugent Monck.[76] She also performed in two films, one of which involved travelling to Egypt.

Craig's thoughts were evidently not dwelling on the Pioneer Players. Since its suspension she had not been idle, although she tended to work on one-off productions. Her work in Leeds seemed to be the most likely to develop into a permanent role. A description of Craig's role in the Pioneer Players was endorsed, if not drafted, by Craig in 1924: 'She has shown her devotion to the art of producing by the way in which she, regardless of every kind of difficulty, ran the Pioneer Players from 1911 to 1919 [*sic*], a company in which Meggie Albanesi and Sybil Thorndike rose to fame, and which offers opportunities for original parts not found elsewhere.'[77] The emphasis on the heroic sacrifices which Craig's work with the Pioneer Players entailed suggests that she was unlikely to be interested in resuming her role in the society. Her directing days for the Pioneer Players were assumed to be in the past. She was no longer offering her services, even though the society's continued vitality is suggested by the present tense.

Times had changed. The Pioneer Players had developed from Craig's women's suffrage activism, from the early productions of *A Pageant of Great Women* and *How the Vote Was Won*. In May 1923 Cicely Hamilton received an enquiry regarding a revival of *How the Vote Was Won*. Maude Scott, Director of the Dramatic Art Section of the Mary Ward Settlement, Tavistock Place, London, wanted to perform the play for the Settlement Club. Ironically Mary (Mrs Humphrey) Ward was a famous anti-suffrage campaigner. Hamilton sent the letter to Craig with the following postscript: 'These people must have passed the last ten years in a cataleptic slumber – you might explain, if you ring them up, that there has been an extension of the franchise & likewise a war.'[78] Craig had certainly not been dreaming or even resting. The Pioneer Players had not turned into the art theatre which Craig had so much hoped for and she had moved on. She never expected that in March 1925 she would be producing another play for the society.

It was Sybil Thorndike, rather than Edith Craig, who was responsible for the Pioneer Players' production of Susan Glaspell's *The Verge*. Craig took some persuading but Thorndike wanted desperately to act in Glaspell's disturbing expressionist play. Its exploration of femininity and creativity dispenses with the ubiquitous creative metaphor of motherhood, turning instead to scientific experiment. Perhaps the most disturbing aspect of the play for many reviewers was the tremendous energy of Claire Archer, obsessed with creating a new species of plant, Breath of Life, which transforms her relationships. The three men in love with her, Tom, Dick and Harry, and her daughter, Elizabeth, are cursorily treated by the preoccupied Archer. As Elaine Aston notes, American productions of *The Verge* received hostile reviews, representative of male reviewers' 'engendered approach' to women's writing and productions for the stage, which are consequently marginalized.[79]

Many of the reviews of Craig's production of *The Verge* in London were no different from those of Glaspell's production for the Provincetown Players in 1921, in their preoccupation with the difference represented by Claire Archer, who, in some cases, is conflated with Glaspell herself. In these gendered readings the questionable sanity of Archer/Glaspell displaces the play's most challenging ideas. These are left unexplored, unseen. A review of the play by 'G. J.', possibly Gwen John, interprets it as 'a modern and feminist American version of the problem of Marlowe's Dr Faustus' and employs psychoanalytic terms to describe Archer's character, an 'over-developed ego'.[80] Although the review does not pursue the Faustus analogy, the point resurfaces in the concluding paragraph: 'It is the eternal battle in the dual nature of man no less strikingly conveyed because the prototype is the most modern of intellectual women.' Such a comparison entailed the possibility of a female tragic hero. This was unthinkable for most reviewers. Nevertheless, a subject position for women in drama was feasible in this period, largely as a result of women's suffrage drama. Sybil Thorndike was attracted to the role of Claire Archer. *The Verge* is a difficult play to perform, to sustain the extreme pitch of Archer's character, even to maintain the dialogue, which is disrupted, unconventional.

Craig's production gave reviewers the opportunity for a retro-spective on the Pioneer Players. Many regretted the demise of the society and anticipated the revival of the organization. This was not to be realized. Craig resumed her usual busy schedule of the customary innovative productions. In October 1925 at the Scala Theatre, London, she directed Webster's *The White Devil* for J. T. Grein's Renaissance Theatre, a play that had not been performed since the seventeenth century. Critics did not appreciate Webster's predeliction for dead bodies. Craig's production cut four murders, but it still met with distaste from many of the reviewers, one of whom endorsed Samuel Pepys's low opinion of the play.[81] Nevertheless, Craig's simple and effective staging was widely praised, as were the performances of Laura Cowie as Vittoria Corombona, Viola Tree as Isabella and those of actors Cedric Hardwicke and Esme Percy. Wilfrid Hyde White, later to appear in many films, played an ambassador. Florence Bell's protégée, Rose Quong, played Zanche.

By December the gruesome murders of *The White Devil* were forgotten. Craig returned to the tranquillity of *An Old English Nativity Play*, which she revived once again. The worthy charity on this occasion was the Children's Country Holidays' Fund. The willing volunteers at Daly's Theatre were drawn from the acting world (John Gielgud, Gladys Cooper, Zena Dare), and included a number of children, the most notable being Christopher Robin Milne.[82] At the piano was the gloriously named Daisy Bucktrout, accompanist to the singer Marcia Van Dresser, who sang carols in the concert which preceded the play. Fay Compton played Mary, George Skillan was Joseph, while the minor roles revealed John Gielgud as Second Shepherd, Peggy Webster as Page and Raymond Massey as Third Soldier. Edith Craig appeared as First Monk, a disguise that would prove useful in future productions. Tony Atwood was responsible for props, and Doreen Erroll acted as wardrobe mistress. In the concluding tableau, *Visions of Saints*, St Francis was played by Prince Nicholas Galitzina, St Joan by Sybil Thorndike. The local paper in Bath noted that Craig's production benefited from the assistance of the Bath Citizen House Players. Helen Hope designed the angel dresses. Miss C. M. de Reyes was a performer and general assistant and costumes and props were on loan from the wardens of Citizen House where Craig had been staying in November.[83] The play programme shows that de Reyes played the Second Monk, but cites neither Helen Hope nor Bath Citizen House. In November 1925 Craig had seen two nativity plays staged by members of Boston University in the crypt at St Paul's Church, Covent Garden.[84] Craig revived her own *Nativity Play* at St Paul's in January 1927, giving newcomer Catherina Ferraz an opportunity.[85]

The influence of the Pioneer Players can be detected in many of the little theatres and civic theatres. Croydon Repertory Theatre produced Christopher St John's translation of Herman Heijermans's *The Rising Sun* in 1932 by Henry Cass, with scene design by Ruth Keating and performances by Robert Eddison and Clifford Evans.[86] The Arts Theatre Club produced Claudel's *The Tidings Brought to Mary*, which had been directed by Craig for the Pioneer Players in 1917. Many of the Arts Theatre Club actors, directors and some of its dramatists were ex-Pioneer Players. The Gate Theatre Studio, directed by Peter Godfrey and Velona Pilcher (at 16a Villiers Street, Strand), performed a new play once a month on a Sunday evening to an audience of no more than 200. In the years 1925–7, the production of fourteen one-act plays was recorded. Two of these had previously been performed by the Pioneer Players: Susan Glaspell's *Trifles*; and Nikolai Evreinov's *The Theatre of the Soul*, the latter to be repeated in 1927–8. Even André Charlot, who had objected so strongly to Edith Craig's production of *The Theatre of the Soul* in 1915, was President of a theatre society, the Sunday Play Society in 1928. Charlot's new society explicitly claimed the middle ground: 'To further the Sunday Theatre movement, we propose to form a society for the production of Sunday shows. Its object will be to produce plays that are neither highbrow nor lowbrow, and its aim will be to give shows that will interest and entertain.'[87]

Craig's work for the British Empire Shakespeare Society led her to direct two dramatic readings at the Lyric Hammersmith in June and the Haymarket in December 1926, a year of ill-health.[88] She had already taken part as an adjudicator in the extremely popular British Empire Shakespeare Society (BESS) elocution competitions. These competitions, and the amateur theatre field which gave rise to them, promoted a particular accent and mode of speech propagated in the same period by the BBC, consolidating notions of Englishness between the wars.[89]

Lady Florence Bell had supported Craig's production of de Bouhélier's *The Children's Carnival* in 1920 and of her own play, *The Fog on the Moor*, at the St Christopher's Theatre, Letchworth, in 1925. In September 1927 she enlisted Craig's skills in directing her pageant of the history of the Carthusian monks at the Mount Grace Priory, Northallerton (Elizabeth Robins had apparently been first choice).[90] The production was ambitious, with a cast of 1,500. Craig took up residence in some disused railway carriages, which formed her centre of operations.[91] She was assisted by Jacko (Vera Holme). Jacko had been a fearless activist in the women's suffrage movement, working as chauffeur to the WSPU. Sylvia Pankhurst recalled her as 'a noisy, explosive young person, frequently rebuked by her elders for lack of dignity'.[92]

The press photographers had a field day capturing ironic juxtapositions. When it rained, Henry VIII's court put up their umbrellas, to take cover, and two chain-mail clad men riding a motorbike were concisely designated 'Anachronism'.[93] The apparent conflict of interest for C. P. Trevelyan, Lady Bell's son-in-law and Labour MP for Central Newcastle, in playing Richard II attracted several captions: 'Labour on the throne' and 'A Labour MP as an autocrat monarch'. More appropriate casting was employed where the monks were concerned, the roles being taken by Church of England clergy from the North Riding.[94] Two of the pageant players had not met for thirty-two years: Major E. A. Pollard (Thomas Cromwell, Earl of Sussex) and Mr C. L. Hudson (St Bruno) had been to the same school. The Queen also made a surprise visit. After the event, Lady Florence Bell wrote: 'My dear Edy, Thank you again. It's no good repeating it. But it was worth all the ups & downs, wasnt it?'[95]

In January 1928 Craig had produced *Marion's Crime* at the Cave of Harmony. This melodrama, which had been produced for the LAT in 1924,[96] was revived at Harold Scott's request. The Cave of Harmony was a nightclub which Harold Scott and Elsa Lanchester ran from 1920 to 1927. Scott's book, *The Genesis of the Music Hall*, referred to the club's 'special feature ... the performance of nineteenth-century popular songs'.[97] The image of the club given by theatre historians, Wendy and J. C. Trewin, is of antiquarian interest, a 'Victorian cabaret in Seven Dials'.[98] The same club is hardly recognizable in Vera Brittain's account. Brittain cites the club in her book about the trial for obscenity of Radclyffe Hall's novel, *The Well of Loneliness*, in homophobic terms, as one of many clubs and societies which welcomed gays and lesbians:

> In spite of the still dominant Victorianism and pseudo-respectability of the period, clubs and societies existed where those believed to be specialists in the practices vaguely known as 'vice' were welcome. The greater their interest in sodomy, lesbianism, pederasty and kindred topics was thought to be, the more welcome they were as associates. Radclyffe Hall frequented one club known as 'The Cave of Harmony', where Katherine Mansfield gave amateur stage performances. Frank Harris was also a member.
>
> The locked-cupboard atmosphere of these places gave them their attraction, and still does, in so far as they exist today.[99]

It is likely that theatre societies such as the Pioneer Players and the LAT, which functioned along comparable lines, may have attracted a similar public image. The 'club' was a site of popular anxiety, with its alternative culture, unregulated practices and the connotations of recruitment, membership as well as informal associations. In the theatre, such organizations had directly challenged in only a few years many aspects of the law: theatre licensing, as well as the franchise, the law of coverture, the National Insurance Act and the divorce laws. In 1933 Radclyffe Hall and Una Troubridge often went to the Arts Club and the Ivy Restaurant when they were dividing their time between London and Kent.[100] Brittain's inclusion of 'societies' as well as clubs picks up on the oppositional spaces provided by these numerous organizations. Edith Craig, Christopher St John and Tony Atwood are cited early on in Brittain's book in an inventory of Radclyffe Hall's friends:

> Other friends included such well-known personalities as Edith Craig, Christopher St John, Tony Atwood, Francis Yeats-Brown, and Naomi Jacob at Sirmione on Lake Garda. It is justifiable to assume that some of these men and women had homosexual interests or tendencies. There is no doubt that one was Naomi Jacob, who made no secret of the fact. Her style of dressing was

far more aggressively masculine than that of Radclyffe Hall. She wore dress suits in the evening and few men had a greater addiction to the whisky bottle.[101]

Unusually this omits the tag which dogged Edith Craig: 'daughter of Ellen Terry, sister of Gordon Craig'.

Ellen Terry died on 21 July 1928. Craig's grief was compounded by the implications of the public onslaught against lesbians which the court case against Radclyffe Hall's novel was to become. On 16 November 1928 *The Well of Loneliness* was found to be an obscene libel and its destruction was ordered by the courts. An unsigned article (one of many published by the press) in *Time & Tide* referred to it as dealing with 'a distasteful form of excess',[102] but emphasized the issue of censorship, specifically the impact of the trial on a free press in Britain. At appeal on 14 December 1928, the court deemed the novel to be 'dangerous and corrupting'.[103]

The trial effectively put Hall personally, and lesbianism generally, in the dock. The case legislated against the representation of lesbianism in the novel but was widely interpreted in terms of legislation against lesbianism itself. The effects were devastating. Michael Baker claims that by 1933 Hall and Troubridge felt that Gabrielle Enthoven had betrayed them. She had been involved in their production with the Stage Society of *Cheri* by Colette in 1931. But 'they now felt she had "ratted" on her breed by deliberately distancing herself from her homosexual friends'.[104] Craig would not have been tempted to such a betrayal. After her involvement with Grein and his support of Maud Allan in the libel case, Craig had quoted Oscar Wilde in 1919 at the beginning of her BDL speech. In the late 1920s Craig demonstrated similarly steadfast principles, and she was not alone. She proved that it was possible to live and work while openly living with other women.

Edith Craig set about guaranteeing her mother's place in history with a memorial. The Shakespeare memorial had set a precedent. A living, acting memorial, in the form of a theatre, would provide the best means of remembering Ellen Terry. Norman MacDermott had reported that in America the conversion of barns into theatres had enabled exponents of the new theatre to build their own space, rather than work within the constraints of existing theatre architecture. Edith Craig was to make the Barn Theatre a memorial to her mother, a place of experiment as tradition.

Chapter 7

THE ART OF AMATEUR THEATRE 1928–47

When Ellen Terry died on 21 July 1928 a book was found at her bedside, *The Imitation of Christ* by Thomas à Kempis, in which she had inscribed a poem by William Allingham. Next to the lines, 'No funeral gloom, my dears, when I am gone', she had noted her wish that on her death her relatives should follow these sentiments. Consequently, her funeral, held at the sixteenth-century Dutch church of St John's, a few hundred yards from her house at Smallhythe Place, was a simple affair.[1] Edith Craig ensured that arrangements were simple and effective. She directed the funeral with care. It was her most significant production. Women wore white. A number of labourers formed a guard of honour with scythes, hoes and hay forks. Herbs – hyssop, rosemary, lavender and rue – were strewn on the floor of the church. Lady Maud Warrender sang a hymn solo. Martin Shaw played 'The Londonderry Air' on the organ. The white ash coffin in the shape of a cradle was designed by Edward Gordon Craig and draped with a cloth of gold and pale blue, made from a dress worn by Ellen Terry. The Reverend J. Watson of Wittersham read the lesson. The four pall bearers were Major Robson, the Mayor of Tenterden, Major H. Neve, the Squire of Smallhythe, the actor Norman Forbes-Robertson and the Reverend A. R. Rylett, the Unitarian Minister of Tenterden.

The multi-faith spirit of the funeral was sustained at the memorial service at the actors' church, St Paul's, Covent Garden, in the shadow of beloved Bedford Street. The Reverend H. Kingsfort, director of the Catholic Faith Society, conducted a requiem celebration of the Holy Eucharist. Rosemary had been picked from Ellen Terry's garden and was distributed amongst the congregation. The cremation at Golders Green attracted massive crowds. Her ashes were then taken to St Paul's where, in August 1929, Edith Craig unveiled the silver casket designed by Edward Gordon Craig and Paul Cooper, in which Ellen Terry's ashes were enshrined in a niche in the church.[2]

Ellen Terry's executors were her daughter and her solicitors. She left an unexpectedly small estate, and on 12 December 1928, some of her effects were sold at auction. Almost immediately the press, relatives and friends began to organize a means of preserving her house at Smallhythe Place. A fund-raising committee was formed and a campaign was launched. The fund had four objectives: to acquire Ellen Terry's house and to pay the salary of a custodian; to keep two rooms in the house as they had been during Terry's lifetime; to devote another room to a library; and to adapt the barn in the grounds of the house to become a theatre in which an annual dramatic festival in July would remember Ellen Terry. The sum of £15,000 was needed to achieve these objectives. The Honorary Organizer was Miss J. M. Harvey, a ubiquitous name where organization and management in the theatre were concerned.[3] The chairperson of the Executive Committee was Gertrude Kingston. The Honorary Legal Adviser was Irene Cooper-Willis and the Honorary Treasurer Lady Maud Warrender.

A fundraising matinee at the Palace Theatre, London, on 23 April 1929 was organized by Edith Craig and James Carew, Ellen Terry's third husband. Tony Atwood had a minor acting part. Three months later, on 21 July 1929, the Barn Theatre at Smallhythe Place gave its first memorial performance, albeit of a simple kind. Car headlights, detached and placed inside biscuit tins, were used for stage lighting.[4] It was the start of an annual event which became a tradition. Craig did not wait for funding before launching the Barn Theatre. By August 1929 a disappointing £2,000 had been raised, although this represented a very large number of small donations.

The Barn Theatre anniversary performances are held every year in July, as near as possible to 21 July. The format of the performance began and, in later years, ended with a speech. A welcome speech was followed by a tribute to Ellen Terry, and, after her death, to Edith Craig also. Scenes from Shakespeare's plays were regularly performed by actors such as John Gielgud, Sybil Thorndike, Lewis Casson, Edith Evans, Gwen Ffrangcon Davies, Margaretta Scott and, on occasions, by Donald Wolfit and Robert Donat. Songs were often performed by Jean Sterling Mackinlay. The Barn Theatre floor was strewn with herbs and posies of sweet peas were hung from the central lighting rig.[5] Before the performance, a memorial service was held at St John's Church nearby and afterwards Craig served supper to the guests in the grounds around the barn.[6] The tribute speech was given by a number of distinguished speakers. From 1930–8 the speakers were Dame May Whitty, Clemence Dane, Lawrence Alma-Tadema, Margaret Webster, Sir William Rothenstein, Lady Maud Warrender, Lena Ashwell, Violet Vanbrugh and Harcourt Williams. In 1943 Edward Percy Smith gave the lecture, while in 1945 Vi Pym did the honours. Some of the speeches have survived.[7]

Margaret Webster's speech in 1933 referred to her appearance in the nativity play at the Florence Etlinger School when Edith Craig had brought her mother to watch a rehearsal. Ellen Terry's praise, 'Very good, Peggy, very good!', prompted Peggy to trip over her draperies and tumble downstairs. Webster claims that Terry's approach to Shakespearian acting eschewed 'academic rules' and 'preconceived theories', instead leaving 'something far deeper and more imponderable'. In 1931 Clemence Dane reflected on the ephemeral nature of acting, compared with the more tangible artworks of the painter and the architect.

The tone of the speeches was part testimonial, part sermon. Lawrence Alma-Tadema's speech was mystical and moving, claiming that Smallhythe Place would be 'a living shrine' to Ellen Terry long after the death of those gathered to remember her and when Ellen Terry would seem but a 'perfumed name upon a printed page'. Vi Pym recalled her childhood memories of Ellen Terry and her own performance as the Angel Gabriel in the nativity play at Rye Monastery. She said that Edy *would* keep coming into her story about Ellen Terry: 'so many of my early memories of Ellen Terry are really Edy, & when I think of Edy in those long ago days I seem to see her beloved Mother. Are they so very different after all?' From the beginnings of the Ellen Terry Memorial and the founding of the Barn Theatre, Edith Craig's identity became ever more closely attached to that of her mother. If the Barn Theatre seemed to provide the 'complete control' which Christopher St John assumed Edith Craig had desired, it was always already Ellen Terry's theatre.

Although the anniversary performances at the Barn Theatre brought Edith Craig home to Smallhythe Place in July, she continued to work as a freelance director, adjudicator at drama festivals, a lecturer and teacher. She was committed to keeping her mother's memory alive and to passing on her own knowledge and skills to anyone with a sincere interest in theatre. The commercial theatre did not recognize the value of her contribution and increasingly she worked with amateurs, and on occasions without pay. This seems to have been the case for her involvement in an anti-capitalist play for the new socialist theatre in London in 1930.

Harold Scott asked Edith Craig to direct the first play to be given at the Apollo Theatre, London, on 9 February 1930 by the Masses' Stage and Film Guild. This venture was associated with the ILP and endorsed by members of the cabinet, George Lansbury, J. R. Clynes, C. P. Trevelyan and F. O. Roberts. The chairperson was Fenner Brockway MP. The play was Upton Sinclair's *Singing Jailbirds* about the 1923 dock strikes in America organized by the International Workers of the World, known as 'The Wobblies'. Striker, Red Adams, is imprisoned and dies in his prison cell. As the note to the play programme suggests, the representation of police brutality and appalling prison conditions accurately reflected conditions in America and Poland and had some parallels in Britain during the General Strike.[8] Eugene Leahy rejected the offer of a role. He felt that it was too gloomy and would be bad for his health.[9]

Harold Scott's choice of director was, of course, a professionally judicious one. It was also, coincidentally, a kind thought. For Craig, 1929 was a sad and dramatically barren year; a year of adjustment, of acceptance. Much of her energy was devoted to launching the Barn Theatre and the Ellen Terry Memorial. Immediately after her mother's death, in the summer of 1928, Craig had been involved as adjudicator for the Women's Institute and was working at various summer schools at Battle, Shrewsbury and Newcastle, probably for the BDL. The *Singing Jailbirds* project was just what she needed to reaffirm her identity.

Preparations began in November 1929. In December, Tony Atwood wrote on behalf of Edith Craig to ask Mary Eversley to be assistant stage-manager, a post she shared with Edward Carrick (Craig). Craig relied on Mary Eversley for the preliminary arrangements because she spent the New Year in Swanage recuperating until 6 January. Tony Atwood was relieved that the rest was doing her good.[10] The details of the stage set were precise. Letters were sent to Heinz & Co., Del Monte Foods and the British American Tobacco Company Ltd. Authentic American posters were promised. May Whitty was scouting, on Craig's behalf, for someone to play One Lung, the Chinese cook. Bryan Tuke wrote to offer his services, confident that Craig had appreciated his performance in *The Amorists*.[11]

Singing Jailbirds is a play which makes considerable demands on the director. An aptitude for music was essential as the imprisoned wobblies' singing plays a significant part in the plot. The favourite song was Joe Hill's anti-capitalist song, which included the memorable line, 'You will get pie in the sky when you die.' Many of the scenes consist of the dreams of Red Adams as he lies in his cell. He dreams of a restaurant for working men, and that his dead wife Nell is still alive. The most striking dream scene is that of the 'hall of hate', a surreal court in which the officers are seen wearing animal-head masks. The judge is a senile old man in a tiger suit, the clerk is a rat and the policemen are bulls. Tony Atwood made the masks and Edith Craig ensured that the shifts from present-time reality to the projected dreams of Red Adams were staged convincingly. One reviewer disliked the play but praised Craig's work, claiming that she 'could produce a dramatic version of the multiplication tables without boring me'.[12]

Christopher St John reviewed the event. She was critical of the play and the organization, asserting that it 'does not seem to have any genuine representatives of the masses among its members'.[13] She was, however, 'enraptured by scene after scene of beauty, contrived out of those odds and ends of material with which the producer of a Sunday show...has to make shift'.[14] As with her review of Craig's production of *The Great World Theatre* in 1924, St John made a public pronouncement on Craig's lack of opportunities in the commercial theatre: 'It is strange indeed that we see so little of Edith Craig's work in the "commercial" theatre. Is this explanation to be found in what Ethel Smyth calls "this obscurely-working, self-unconfessed anti-woman spirit"?'[15] Sexism could be identified but it was difficult to speak about other prejudices which were having a significant effect on women who were feminist, unmarried, lesbian. Craig's work had been seen at its best in numerous plays which were undeniably uncommercial, plays which would attract a minority audience. Nevertheless, her ability to work in any theatre on any kind of play had been proven.

Christopher St John's defence of Edith Craig implies that Craig had wanted a job in a commercial theatre. It also raises the question about the marginalization of Craig in her field of work and the extent to which this was Craig's self-representation. One article stated: 'It is a tragedy to her friends – she herself cares little about it – that her worth has never been fully recognized or her genius properly exploited.'[16] Many of Craig's colleagues followed Ellen Terry's example in that they knew about, and seemed to have accepted, her relationships with Atwood and St John. It may be that the doors of commercial theatres would be closed to Craig by the new owners, the entrepreneurs, who regarded theatre as big business and knew more about box-office receipts than what happened on stage. However, heterosexuals' tolerance of lesbianism has its own coercive powers, tending to dictate its own terms. Edith Craig, like many of her friends, would have regarded such tolerance as an impertinence, as insufferably patronizing. Nevertheless, a plea for tolerance of lesbianism appeared to be the subject of *The Well of Loneliness*, causing a furore in 1928. It bears very little resemblance to the sociable community which Edy and the Boys enjoyed.

In 1930 Radclyffe Hall and Una Troubridge had moved to Kent, living in rented houses while their house, the Black Boy in the High Street, Rye, was being restored. For the next three years they were to spend much of their time with Craig, St John and Atwood.[17] They attended productions in the Barn Theatre and spent Christmas together two years running. Una Troubridge recorded one of the reasons for their liking for the women: 'There is great consolation and gratification to me in the company of these friends who like us & want to be with us because they know us for what we are and respect what John has done for her kind.'[18]

If the commercial theatre appeared to be closed to Craig, opportunities for work were still vital in Yorkshire where she had no shortage of admirers. The Leeds Civic Playhouse had been going for five years in 1930. By this time it had the support of 5,000 subscribers, with a further 2,000 in Bradford. Some of its most remarkable productions were Craig's responsibility. In May 1930, as the Leeds Civic Playhouse's fifth anniversary celebrations, she produced George Bernard Shaw's *Back to Methuselah*. It was, C. F. Smith recalled wryly, the only production of the play to make a profit. It had toured the region, showing at the Theatre Royal, Huddersfield (5 May), the Albert Hall, Leeds (12 May) and the Jowett Hall Little Theatre, Bradford (26 May). As usual, Craig was imaginative in her use of resources. In her production of Ansky's *The Dybbuk*, she had achieved 'a Rembrandt effect with old velvet curtains which had been in stock for years'.[19] By January 1933, the Leeds Civic Playhouse, like the LAT, was looking for sound financial backing. Recalling the Playhouse in 1934, C. F. Smith included Craig in his list of distinguished producers who had worked there, alongside Nugent Monck, Norman Marshall and A. E. Filmer. The Leeds Civic Playhouse, as Tom Steele states, was remarkable 'in that entrance was entirely free, the only free theatre in existence, it claimed', and it was intended by C. F. Smith to be 'a radical/popular theatre'.[20] Its success was confirmed by its survival until 1945 when it was formally patronized by the local authorities and became the Leeds Civic Theatre.[21]

Amateur dramatics was becoming Craig's speciality. In March 1931, the *New Era* published an interview with Craig on the subject. Many of her suggestions are now widely accepted practice in schools and theatres. In a sense they appear so commonplace to be imperceptible as aesthetic strategies or theatrical conventions. In this respect, the ordinariness of amateur dramatics reveals its place in conservatism between the wars in Britain, which, as Alison Light's study has suggested, was self-effacing and inward-looking. Edith Craig argued for drama to become an ordinary part of the school curriculum and to be taught alongside dancing or elocution rather than limited to English literature. School dramatics required little equipment: a magic lantern or cinema light would suffice for diffuse lighting with a few plain curtains as backdrop. Such minimal equipment was expedient, but it also served a useful purpose in making demands on imagination which could enhance the performance. In this respect she cited Chinese and Japanese theatrical traditions. The interview concluded with an advertisement for the BDL, for which Craig was working nationwide. She had plans for Smallhythe Place too, expressing her wish that the Ellen Terry Memorial become a place where people could 'study drama and the history of the drama'.[22] Craig was becoming nationally known outside the acting profession for her work as a teacher and lecturer.

The first four months of 1932 saw Craig travelling to Edinburgh, Nottingham, Louth in Lincolnshire, Kent and Sheffield, variously adjudicating at an elocution festival for BESS and drama competitions for the BDL and Women's Institute. In April she lectured on 'The Drama in Relation to Villages' for the Milsted and Kingsdown WI in Kent. Her novel advice included the use of a lorry as a stage and motor lamps for lighting, which could be used at some distance from the stage and therefore achieve a subtle, diffuse effect. This strategy had already proved effective for her in the first anniversary performance at the Barn Theatre. She also suggested that the quality of the play was worth considering: bad acting was more noticeable in a bad play, whereas 'a good play acts itself'.[23] The Dickensian Tabard Players took her advice. The press coverage of their performance of *The Old Curiosity Shop* on the back of a lorry in a courtyard at the George Inn, Borough, caught her attention and found itself in her ever-increasing scrapbook collection. In a sense Craig's suggestion about the use of a lorry was updating the medieval pageant tradition, and the carts which provided the mobile stage for civic performances. Another allusion is possible. In Soviet Russia, trains were used as makeshift mobile cinemas to take film to remote areas. In any event, the use of lorries is commonplace in late twentieth-century city carnivals, such as Leicester's Caribbean Carnival, but the idea was novel in the 1930s. Craig monitored developments in Russian theatre. The programmes for the Moscow Theatre Festivals for 1933 and 1936 suggest that she may have considered attending. Post-revolutionary theatre was attractive. As the programme for 1933 stated, the audience for pre-revolutionary theatre was 'narrowly esthetic [sic] and apart from life. New forms were evolved, new technique'.[24]

The British Empire Shakespeare Society, founded in 1901 by Miss Morritt, was proud of its motto: 'to spread the knowledge of Shakespeare, by means of study readings (both private and public), production of plays etc.'. The BESS held annual competitions for drama and elocution. On 19 February 1932 Craig adjudicated at the St Andrew's Church Hall, Edinburgh, where fifty competitors took part. The sex ratio of competitors astounded newspaper reporters, who indignantly recorded how 'Girl Elocutionists Outnumber Boys in Edinburgh Shakespeare Festival'.[25] Craig was frequently enlisted to give out the prizes at the BESS award ceremonies. In November 1929 she had presented the Ellen Terry Cup to Eileen Hann in the 'Macbeth' class.[26] She shared the stage on many occasions with Princess Marie Louise, President of the society, and with Lilian Baylis. Baylis and Craig presented BESS prizes at the Ambassador's Theatre in 1933 and, in 1934, at the Haymarket Theatre.

As might be expected, the determination and lack of self-awareness of amateur actors sometimes collided with Craig's direct professional appraisals and her refusal to appease. The Eastern Area Drama Festivals at Leicester and Nottingham elicited the judgement from Craig that one particular play, *The Lovely Miracle* by Philip Johnson, 'needed a woman producer'. Objections must have been intense, since they were recorded in the press. Mrs Atkey thought Craig's comments were 'unnecessarily severe'.[27] Competitors in the Lindsey County Drama Festival, Louth, and the festival organized by the Rural Community Council at the Festival Theatre, Cambridge, were to meet Craig in the role of adjudicator in the next couple of months. Shortly before she was taken ill after this period of intense, and stressful, activity, she opened a short course in drama at the YMCA Hall, Sheffield. This was arranged by the BDL under the auspices of the Sheffield Playgoers' Society.[28]

The constituency of amateur dramatics in this period was diverse. The parochial scene-stealers felt compelled to categorize people in terms of relative acceptability as either 'village' or 'not village', 'county' or 'not county'. Boundaries were drawn ruthlessly in many a village hall. Casting for a play could be a means of re-creating the medieval beating of the bounds, deciding who belonged and who was to be excluded. For others, amateur dramatics was an empowering, even politicizing, experience, particularly for those who were used to working in groups in trade unions or political organizations. Craig's role as the BDL's troubleshooter was in some cases unenviable. She was, however, used to dealing with the pompous, the talentless and the shy. She seemed to be able to identify quickly which group was producing the difficulty. C. F. Smith remarked on Craig's 'hatred of shams' and that she 'loathes pretence'.[29] For those who became involved in amateur dramatics in order to acquire status and power, she had little time. The only difference for Craig between amateur and professional theatre was income, not quality of performance. In many ways she did not adapt her expectations when she was working with amateurs. Her primary concern was the production; personalities were not allowed to interfere with the proper functioning of the performance. She was never dazzled by stars. On one occasion she astonished a journalist by referring to Robert Donat as the man who occasionally helps out in the Barn Theatre.[30]

The audience was also expected to meet high standards in its awareness of dramatic form and conventions. Craig believed that 'misreadings' were possible and would not have welcomed the critical free-for-all which is regarded as liberating the reader or audience. She often referred to the need to educate the audience to respond to innovative performances rather than to misread the play by referring to irrelevant dramatic conventions. In 1934 at the annual BDL conference in Halifax she was reported as asserting that audiences did not know what they wanted.[31] She had made a similar point in an earlier interview, emphasizing the audience's consumption of dramatic performance with a memorable culinary metaphor: 'who wants an earnest omelette or a serious souffle?'[32] While the notion of educating audiences seems coercive and elitist, it nevertheless addresses, in characteristically blunt fashion, what other critics had chosen to ignore. The concept of an audience (as if a cohesive body) approaching a play with an open mind, responding freely and organically to whatever is presented, mystifies the specialized knowledge of dramatic conventions. At a time when literary critics were emphasizing the inherent literary value of the text and the exceptional qualities of the author, and emphatically ignoring the diversity of readers (and consequently readings), Craig's outspoken views opened up some difficult and untheorized issues.

After her badly timed illness in April 1932 and subsequent rest, she enjoyed the retreat to Smallhythe Place. As ever, Craig's rest periods were equal to other people's work. In July she produced her children's play, *The Shoe*, at the local fete and flower show opened by Lady Geddes. Clare Atwood was enlisted to paint the Shoe and Jean Sterling Mackinlay played the Old Woman. One of many children's plays with which Craig was involved, *The Shoe*, was to be one of her last productions.[33]

Although Craig's work was not fostered in the commercial theatre she held high status amongst theatre practitioners. Two events in the actors' calendar called on Craig to represent the profession in honouring their dead. On 8 June 1931 it was the centenary ceremony for Mrs Siddons. Edith Craig was the representative for the BDL, placing a wreath at the base of the statue to Mrs Siddons's memory, a statue which had been unveiled by Henry Irving in 1897.[34] Four months later she placed rosemary on Irving's grave on the anniversary of his death.[35] Increasingly, she was involved in honouring her contemporaries, as well as her illustrious elders, in theatre. A sense of being left behind was beginning to impinge on Craig.

On 20 January 1932, Craig attended a reception at the American Woman's Club, London, in honour of Susan Glaspell who had been awarded the Pulitzer Prize the previous year. A newspaper reported that Glaspell's play *Trifles* was shortly to be staged by Nancy Price at her People's National Theatre.[36] The same article briefly noted that Craig had directed Glaspell's plays and would like to do so again. It mentioned neither the Pioneer Players nor the two productions of plays by Glaspell. Craig created her own opportunities. In September 1934 she produced *Trifles* at the Barn Theatre for members of the Barn Theatre Society, formed in 1932 along familiar subscription lines.

Even Craig's protégés seemed to be winning glittering prizes. In September 1931, Gilbert McConnell-Wood, who had worked with Craig as a scene designer for the Windsor Repertory Company, was appointed as film set designer for Paramount in London.[37] In Leeds, Ronald Giffen had been an assistant producer, working with Craig in 1930 for her production of *St Paul* at St Aidan's Church, and was a producer at the Eyebrow Club. In 1934 he had been appointed stage-manager of the Grand Theatre, Southampton.[38] Audrey Cameron, former member of the Pioneer Players and on several occasions stage-manager for Craig, worked with BBC Radio, standing in for Aunty Muriel on *Children's Hour*.[39] Craig felt dismayed that a long apprenticeship was no longer valued. She remarked, without naming names, that even 'call boys were becoming producers'.[40]

The year 1932 proved to be a troubling one for Edith Craig in many aspects of her life. Disturbing changes in both of her families – biological and chosen – tested her resolve. Her inner strength was seldom defeated but physically she was frequently in pain, sometimes incapacitated. If the Leeds Civic Playhouse was running out of steam, it had taken its toll on Craig. In a lecture to the Hastings Branch of the WFL, Craig warned prospective actresses that a reputation for ill-health could affect the opportunities of work.[41] This may have been a painful acknowledgement of her own position. Ill-health had beset Craig towards the end of her time with the Leeds Civic Playhouse in 1932, as it had in 1924 at the end of her work for the LAT and York Everyman Theatre. In April 1932 illness prevented her from attending a religious play, *The Prodigal Son*, produced by the Reverend Seaward Beddow at the Wycliffe Congregational Church in Leicester.[42] It was unfortunate timing: Craig's illness coincided with attempts to raise money for the Leeds Civic Playhouse. In October 1932 she was to attend the opening of the Eyebrow Club, 'the only Private Play Producing Club outside London' and to 'read extracts from the Shaw–Terry love letters, with a running commentary'.[43] Christopher St John had edited the Shaw–Terry correspondence. St John was to revive her skills as a correspondent.

In 1932, according to Radclyffe Hall's biographer, Vita Sackville-West's fleeting relationship with Christopher St John disturbed the Smallhythe Place household to such an extent that the plans for Hall and Troubridge to build a house next to Priest's House were abandoned.[44] Even though the affair was short-lived the equilibrium had been shattered by St John's adoration of Sackville-West. On Vita's part it was casual, for Christopher it was intoxicating passion. She wrote letters and a love journal to Vita, referring to 'the complete human being who transcends both [sexes]'.[45] What did Edy and Tony think of this? In September 1932 Vita Sackville-West had read her poem, 'The Land', at the Barn Theatre. In November she visited the Bedford Street flat and on 20 December she slept with Christopher St John. Extraordinarily it is possible to put a date to this because it was quite self-consciously recorded. Much to St John's regret this was not to be repeated.

As regards the family battle over ownership of Ellen Terry's story, 1932 was for Edith Craig the year of speaking out. Craig and St John collaborated on a revised edition of *The Story of My Life*, renamed *Ellen Terry's Memoirs*, with extra chapters and explanatory notes. This was published explicitly in response to Edward Gordon Craig's *Ellen Terry and Her Secret Self*. In 1932 Craig had other responsibilities. She became a (surrogate) mother. Robinetta (Ruby Chelta) Craig, the daughter of Edward Gordon Craig's eldest son, Robin, had become her adopted daughter.[46] Craig had, in a sense, like her own mother, taken on the responsibility of caring for the extended family. Nina Auerbach has identified the allusiveness of casting Ellen Terry as the Old Woman in Edith Craig's play *The Shoe*. Ellen Terry had generously supported Edward Gordon Craig's children and ex-wives or partners financially or through donating her precious time. Robinetta attended Priory House School and Kindergarten, Alexandra Road, Forrester's Hall, Kilburn. She was becoming involved in school drama. Inevitably, this attracted the attention of the press in view of her theatrical relatives. Robinetta was a senior prizewinner for her performance in April 1932 as the Prince Shee Ma Guin in Clementina Ward's operetta, *Princess JuJu*. Her thank-you letter to Craig for lending costumes was signed 'Your Robin'.[47] Robinetta also appeared in *Little Snow White* and *Beauty and the Beast*. Her school reports were despatched for Craig's opinion.[48]

Craig's extended family had flexible borders. Jacko (Vera Holme) was a frequent visitor to Smallhythe Place and particularly to the Barn Theatre. In 1932 during the first season of the Barn Theatre Society, Jacko gave a lantern-slide lecture, 'Serbia in Wartime'. An explanatory note to the programme ran: 'Miss Holme was attached to the Women's Scottish Hospital Unit as a motor driver during the war.' In spite of her Perthshire home, she attended the Ellen Terry anniversary performance every year. In 1935 and 1936 the Barn Theatre hosted another anniversary: a tribute to Jacko. On 29 August 1935, the 'Grand performance in honour of Jacko's Birthday' involved Edy, Chris and Tony in comical sketches. St John played Captain Corker, the Mayor, announcing Vera Holme as the new Carnival Queen for the ensuing year, replacing Edith Craig. Part two contained 'A Pageant of Smallhythe Life'. The atmosphere of the Cave of Harmony seems to attach itself to the self-referential humour. The following year, on 30 August 1936, an even grander skit was staged: the 'Annual Celebration of the Illustrious Chevalier Jacko'. It had become a tradition in itself and was feted by actors such as Sir Seymour Hicks, Owen Nares, Sybil Thorndike and Yvonne Arnaud. Jacko was treated to a tribute which referred to her combat in two wars: the 'war to end women' and 'the war to end war'. The combatants in the 'war to end women' continued to fight.

When the *Vote* devoted its front page to an interview with Edith Craig on 31 March 1933, it opened with an optimistic perspective on the prospects for theatre during the depression.[49] Craig argued that good plays were succeeding and endorsed the strategy of lowering West End ticket prices to bring plays to a wider audience. Her responses were snippets of advice, emphasizing the practical. She aimed her comments, as ever, towards the amateur rather than the professional. Radio plays should make a demand on the imagination of the listeners. While the cinema's popularity appeared to threaten the theatre, the career for an actor in film was much shorter. The Little Theatre Movement was described as a training ground, since opportunities in commercial theatres had diminished. Doubtless a great number of actors in the 1930s gained valuable training in amateur dramatics as well as at the numerous acting schools and with freelance tutors.[50] One of the few articles Craig was to write was entitled 'Make-Up Secrets for Amateurs'.[51] The economic climate was not propitious for fields of employment which provided such little security. Nevertheless, the theatre seemed to have no shortage of resourceful actors and producers.

Edith Craig was always willing to produce plays to raise funds for charities and worked in several different ways to fight poverty. She had directed three of Laurence Housman's plays for the People's Concert Society, which appears to have provided entertainments, albeit rather sombre ones, to a particular class: 'It carries concerts to the dwellers in mean streets to men and women whose lives are on a dead level of monotony and dullness.'[52] In March 1933 she directed *The Liars* by H. A. Jones at the Garrick Theatre in aid of a charity based in East London. Edith Craig was a member of the Committee of The Fellowship of St Christopher for Unemployed and Homeless Boys. Once again Princess Marie Louise lent her support as patron. Small hostels were run with the principle, 'Any boy under 18 taken in regardless of race or religion'.[53] The hostels were emphatically not for 'temporary relief but stabilization'. In the couple of years of the Fellowship's existence it had helped 1,000 boys. The majority had been found work, a small proportion had been returned to their homes, while a minority were regrettably deemed 'unhelpable'.

Theatrical benefits are events which, however financially successful, tend to have their ironic moments. The *Birmingham Mail* featured the occasion, but the use of twenty debutantes of the year as programme sellers made the byline rather than the charity or its beneficiaries.[54] The choice of play may have been suggested by committee member Irene Vanbrugh who had appeared in the original production of *The Liars* at the Criterion in 1897. Nigel Playfair's appearance may have provided the context for his letter to Craig refusing to act without a fee even for a charity matinee.[55] Craig was able to exercise her skills in period costumery.

The devastating effects of the depression in the 1930s gave rise to numerous political and economic responses. In retrospect, the sinister associations of eugenics prompt a sense of incredulity that such ideas were widespread. Edith Craig, Sir Dan Godfrey, Val Gielgud and Hazel Terry were featured in a film made jointly by the Eugenics Society and Gaumont-British Instructional Films. The *Gloucester Citizen* reported: 'Film of effects of heredity: how children take talents from parent'.[56] Biologist Julian Huxley provided the introduction and commentary to the film, which explained 'by means of diagrams the behaviour of the mysterious chromosomes which, according to modern theory, determine heredity'. Craig's sense of being exceptional was compounded by the attribution of inherited genius. If Craig shared Radclyffe Hall's views on lesbianism as inversion, a pathological variation, the sentiments of the Eugenics Society would have been an attractive endorsement of her identity, accommodating her sense of her difference and her genius. Compared with that of Craig's other contemporaries Cathleen Nesbitt's autobiography is unusual in that it mentions lesbianism explicitly and without condemnation. However, Nesbitt recalls numerous acting colleagues, but not Craig. While her approach is emphatically tolerant, she also claims for lesbians and gays a 'natural' inclination towards genius. This is predicated on the perceived 'abnormality' of same-sex desire. By contrast, but ultimately not much more disempowering, is Violet Vanbrugh's cursory reference to sexual perversion.

An opportunity arose for Edith Craig to act as patron when the Commonwealth Theatre produced a play which was of special significance to Craig: John Fletcher's *The Faithfull Shepherdess*.[57] The play was directed by Ida Teather in the summer of 1933 at the Playhouse, Oxford. Two special matinees were given in New College Gardens, with the permission of the warden, H. A. L. Fisher. The twelve patrons included Fisher, Edith Craig and Virginia

Woolf.[58] Wilfrid Rooke Ley, who wrote the explanatory note in the play programme, seems to perceive Modernist features in the sixteenth-century play from which, he states, 'you are to expect no element of "plot" in the modern sense, that is to say, no ingenious "situations", no surprises'. A surprising emphasis is placed on the play's representation of desire: 'You shall find that chastity is the pattern of this Pastoral, but no negative or frustrating chastity; romantic rather, flashing bright like a sword blade, or like a flame white-burning in a windless air.' Edith Craig appears to have attended the performance on 1 August, possibly attracted as much by the play as the production by a woman.

On a couple of occasions Craig lectured on the topic of women in theatre. The fairly detailed newspaper reports of her lectures suggest that she tended to speak informally, often humorously, choosing an episodic form with an emphasis on practical advice deliberately aimed at amateurs and novices rather than experts. In May 1933 she spoke to the Hastings Branch of the WFL. She condemned the age restrictions in the theatre, criticized the tendency towards sloppy curtsying and warned against being ill: 'They will be sorry for you the first time, but the next time it is stamped upon your forehead for ever, and every manager knows it, and then you do not get jobs easily.'[59] She encouraged women to consider the role of producer rather than actor. In response to a question from the audience about female producers being resented by actors, she remarked that women who knew their jobs were not resented. However, 'there are a lot of men who do not know their jobs and get away with it, but I do not think an actor would let a woman get away with it'.[60]

Records of a number of social events in June and July 1934 unusually escaped the selective destruction of Edith Craig's papers. The Kent branch of the English Folk Dance and Song Society invited her to a Rose Festival and Fair on Saturday 2 June in the grounds of the Friars, Aylesford.[61] Over the next two weeks invitation cards were sent to two London exhibitions: Frederico Beltran Masses' oil paintings at R. W. S Galleries,[62] and the photographs of John Flower and Anthony.[63] Women's suffrage comrades kept in touch. On Sunday 17 June a syllabub party at Backsettown, Elizabeth Robins's house in Sussex, run as a rest home for women, promised the company of Elizabeth Robins and Octavia Wilberforce.[64] On 6 July Charlotte Despard's ninetieth birthday party was held at Caxton Hall. Then it was back to Smallhythe Place for the Barn Theatre memorial performance.

Summer 1934 saw Craig giving a class for amateur producers at the Cambridge summer meeting. She illustrated her class with scenes enacted by members of the University's dramatic society in the garden of King's College.[65] Another university also recognized her work that year. Liverpool University for the first time appointed four individuals to the Shute Lectureship on the art of the theatre in 1934–5. The other lecturers were J. W. Van Druten, Sydney W. Carroll and Paul Rotha. Craig was the only woman to be appointed that year and it was to be the most prestigious public lecture she would give. When, in February 1935, she spoke on the performance of plays, it was reported nationally. Her lecture was evidently humorous. During the course of her historical sketch on the introduction of the proscenium arch, her reference to the exclusion of women from the stage elicited some laughter from the audience: 'Boys were also replaced by temperamental and untrained women (laughter).' [66] She argued that the 'fourth wall' of the naturalist play (separating the audience from the actors, who are seen to operate in a realistic world re-created on stage) engendered apathy in both audience and actor.

There were several productions in which Edith Craig was enlisted by Edward Percy Smith, local Tory MP. In July she directed Tenterden Pageant at Hales Place, Tenterden, to celebrate the King's jubilee. Edith Craig was the Pageant Master [sic], Edward Percy wrote the script and together they devised the pageant. The twelve episodes represent the history of Tenterden from 1150 to 1928. John Drinkwater played the part of Seneschal of the Cinque Ports and Edward Percy Smith the Countryman. In a metatheatrical scene, the Countryman, looking for his sheep, interrupts Seneschal in mid-flow, not realizing the pageant had begun. He is rebuked, 'Can't you see that you're ruining everything? You've spoilt the first scene already! These ladies and gentlemen haven't paid their money to come and see you.' [67]

A production in December 1936 raises questions about Edith Craig's political affiliations. Although she had been involved in the ILP Arts Guild and the Masses' Stage and Film Guild and presumed by her mother to be a Labour voter, Craig became involved with the local Tories. In March 1936 Edward Percy Smith invited Craig to produce a play. Between 2 and 5 December 1936 she directed *The Merry Wives of Windsor* at the County Theatre, Station Road, Ashford, for the Ashford Division of the Conservative and Constitutional Association. The correspondence between Edward Percy Smith and Edith Craig concerns the production and matters such as gardening, rather than politics. The 'brilliantly colourful' production was praised, as so often with Craig's productions, for its 'series of charming pictures'. The use of the theatre was remarkable, in that Craig exploited the centre aisle as an entrance and exit for the actors. Percy Smith played Falstaff, making his 'triumphant exit down the centre of the hall in a buck basket'.[68]

Edward Percy Smith's friendship with Craig survived her death. Her Falstaff wrote an elegy for her. It was 'from an old neighbour', describing her in Franciscan terms similar to those employed by Christopher St John. In addition, Craig appealed to conservative values. He endowed her with a weighty significance in the context of Englishness: she was 'the heart of the place'.[69] That place was very much rooted in the countryside of Kent.

Craig returned to Gloucestershire in January 1937 to give a lecture at the Cheltenham Art Gallery.[70] The chairperson was Miss M. E. Popham, new principal of Cheltenham Ladies' College, making her first public appearance in Cheltenham. The topic of Craig's lecture was the theatre as a building. At the end of the month she directed John Davison's *Wuthering Heights* at the Little Theatre, London, for the New Shop Window Players.[71] Then she was on the road again. As keynote speaker at the Glasgow Women's Citizen's Association dinner on 6 February 1937, she reflected on her contribution to the women's suffrage campaign. Her remarks were self-effacing and diffident.[72] This was the occasion when she told the story from her childhood about urging her frightened brother to be courageous by instructing him to 'be a woman'. Other distinguished women at the dinner were the Reverend Vera M. M. Kenmure, Glasgow's first female minister, and Dr Marion Gilchrist, first female medical graduate of Glasgow University.[73]

The travelling and the responsibility of lectures and productions took their toll. Edith Craig was approaching her seventieth year and it seems that she preferred to ignore her physical limitations. Increasingly frail, Craig found that the rheumatism which had ended her incipient career as a pianist was to affect her mobility. She sometimes used a wheelchair. Her hands appear to have been considerably affected. In February 1937, probably soon after her appearance in Glasgow, she caught pneumonia and very nearly died.[74] She recuperated in Lochearnheard, Perthshire, probably under the care of Vera Holme. Her local newspaper, the *Kent Messenger*, reported towards the end of March that she was recovering.[75] Performances at the Barn Theatre lapsed, indicating the gravity of her illness. This warning of her mortality seems to have precipitated a number of events.

Financial concerns prompted negotiations with the National Trust to take over Smallhythe Place. James Lees-Milne first visited the 'trouts' in May 1938, but it was not until the following year that Craig transferred responsibility for the property to the Trust. Craig's friends were determined to waste no more time and to take action to honour formally her achievements in theatre. To this end Lady Maud Warrender organized a supper at the Savoy in honour of Edith Craig's fifty years on the stage. The committee of the tribute supper numbered seventeen close friends and colleagues.[76] Mary Eversley had been Craig's stage-manager with *Singing Jailbirds*, and Doreen Errol was a costumier. Both women had worked at several Barn Theatre productions, though the illness of Lady Maud's sister prevented her from seeing the final event on 30 October 1938. Sybil Thorndike replaced Lady Maud in the chair. Queen Mary sent a congratulatory telegram. There were ten speakers, concluding with Edith Craig.[77] Edward Knoblock, Herbert Griffith and S. R. Littlewood recalled the Pioneer Players. Cicely Hamilton 'told how Edy thrust her into impossible situations in a pageant, even making her conduct an orchestra when she knew nothing of the ways of orchestra'.[78] Harold Warrender, Lady Maud's son, reported how someone who had worked in a pageant organized by Craig had declared, 'Oh! I *liked* her. She's rude!' Violet Vanbrugh presented Edith Craig with a cheque and a scroll inscribed with the names of 200 friends.

In 1938 other tributes were made. Edith Craig remembered Henry Irving. In March she organized a pilgrimage from her Bedford Street flat of fifty-five former members of the Lyceum Theatre who went to lay a wreath on Irving's tomb in Westminster.[79] The anniversary performance at the Barn Theatre celebrated the memory of Henry Irving as well as Ellen Terry. It marked the centenary of Irving's birth. Reginald Tate read Henry Irving's controversial study of *Macbeth*, reconstructed from a newspaper report on the event of Irving's delivering the lecture to the literary society at Owen's College, Manchester, on December 1894. A miniature exhibition on Irving was set up in a room in Yew Tree Cottage, across the road from the Ellen Terry Memorial.[80] In 1938 Edward Gordon Craig was honoured by the Royal Society for Arts.

Edith Craig was in the local news in September 1938 when she hosted a garden party for the Kent branch of the English Speaking Union at Smallhythe Place.[81] Distinguished guests included Vita Sackville-West, Radclyffe Hall, Lady (Una) Troubridge, Edward Percy, Lady Auckland Geddes and Lady Maud Warrender. In December the national press covered Edith Craig's birthday with a deal of confusion. On her birthday, Craig received her first orchids. It was her sixty-ninth birthday, but many prematurely attributed seventy years to her.

A souvenir play programme for John Gielgud's *Hamlet* at the Lyceum Theatre, 28 June to 1 July 1939, unusually recorded Edith Craig in the role of writer.[82] The performance was suggested by Craig on the event of the Lyceum Theatre's demolition. Macqueen-Pope provided a historical note to the programme on the theatre's history. Craig's essay, entitled 'Ellen Terry and Henry Irving', stresses the fact that the Lyceum Theatre had been destroyed in 1903; Irving's Lyceum had already passed on. She recalled the much larger stage of the earlier Lyceum where Irving had found 'scope for his wonderful use of crowds'. Christopher St John's monograph on Henry Irving is recalled in Craig's allusion to unrealized possibilities: 'We may feel regret at the obliteration of a landmark, and wish that another theatre could have been built on the site.' Gielgud subsequently took the same production of *Hamlet* directly to Kronberg Castle, Elsinore.

Edith Craig's last ventures were local amateur productions. In 1943 she revived *The Shoe* to raise money for a charity which owed its debt to Elizabeth Malleson: the Tenterden and Halden District Nurse Fund. The venue was the town hall, in Tenterden, where Gwen Lally also appeared in scenes from *School for Scandal*, and tableaux of nursing through the ages were staged. In April 1945 Craig took part in a fundraising event 'Forever England', for the Ellen Terry Memorial Museum, coinciding with St George's Day. Held at the White Rock Pavilion, she introduced a parade of Ellen Terry's most famous stage costumes.[83] In January 1946 she stage-managed a programme of events in Tenterden, which included a little-known play by Cicely Hamilton entitled *Dear Edward* and a play by Frankfort Moore, *Kitty Clive*. Later the same year, in July, her swan song in pageantry was the Chilham Pageant.

The script for the Chilham Pageant was written by Somerset de Chair. Following the tradition of the Tenterden Pageant, Edward Percy Smith was the narrator and Edith Craig producer. The performance was given on Friday 5 and Saturday 6 July 1946 in aid of the Kent appeals for the National Association of Boys' Clubs and the Soldiers', Sailors' and Airmen's Families' Association. Tony Atwood was Property Master [*sic*] and Art Director. Craig was one of many episode organizers. She was responsible for episode seven, about Tenterden and featuring Henry VIII and Anne Boleyn. Fearless of the sweep across centuries of history, the pageant began with Julius Caesar and ended with a garden party for Jane Austen.

Edith Craig became an expert in amateur dramatics. The aesthetic of amateur dramatics had been developed through her own experience of the 'free' theatres at the turn of the century and a couple of decades of teaching. Arguing against the use of painted or elaborate scenery in drama festivals, she was increasingly committed to the value of minimal stage furniture and equipment, convinced that this put more of a demand on performers and audience. Everything was straining towards an active experience in the theatre, for actors, director, stage technicians and audience. The passivity of a picture-frame stage was to be rejected. It is in this context that Craig's expertise turned to pageants. The dynamics of the pageant, the difficulty of its vast, untrained cast, the organic acting space which defies containment, all conspired to fuel her addiction to the elusive satisfaction which characterizes play production. Miss La Trobe's furious outbursts at forgotten lines and interruptions have greater provenance. The perfect performance is significant by its absence.

The art of amateur theatre was democratic and subscribed to values which need to be excavated. An analogy for the secrets of amateur dramatics which Craig was determined to pass on to the younger generation is the healing knowledge of the wise woman. Both discourses have become debased, devalued and deposed by a professionalization at once masculine and capitalist, dependent on commodities and individualism. Opposed to the stars of commercial productions, amateur theatre tended towards anonymity. This anonymity is recognizable both in the withdrawal of the artist in Modernism and in the beginnings of British theatre in the church. When Francis Thompson's poem, 'The Hound of Heaven', was performed by an organization called The Grail, the play programme stated that the performers wished to preserve their anonymity.[84] Edith Craig frequently suggested that churches should be used to stage plays, on one occasion briskly claiming that when performing in such an environment, the church took care of two-thirds of the acting. Nevertheless, the acting space became of greater importance to her, particularly with developments in America and Russia where civic theatres were subsidized and new stages were being built. The worst kind of acting spaces, Craig identified, were the village or church halls. Ironically, it is this kind of space which amateur dramatics brings to mind. Bricolage can so easily take on the appearance of bodging.

Chapter 8

DRAMATIC LIVES OR EDITH CRAIG HAD A FAMILY

Edith Craig fulfilled her last ambition: to live long enough to take part in her mother's centenary in 1947. She did not survive to conduct the anniversary performance at the Barn Theatre in July 1947.[1] On 27 March 1947 Edith Craig died at Priest's House, Smallhythe Place. The nineteenth anniversary performance at the Barn Theatre was delayed until 10 August when not one but three women were remembered: Ellen Terry, Edith Craig and Virginia Woolf. Vita Sackville-West read Virginia Woolf's essay on Ellen Terry again. She had read it, shortly after Woolf's death, at the anniversary performance in 1941. Edith Craig missed the Barn Theatre's celebration of her mother's centenary. Recordings were played of America's centenary tribute to Ellen Terry. Margaret Webster organized a broadcast from Columbia Studio on 27 February. Edward Percy Smith read his elegy, 'To Edy from an Old Neighbour', which was to appear in Eleanor Adlard's anthology of essays in memory of Edith Craig.

The recollections of Edith Craig which appeared in print after her death represent a number of different aspects of her life. The dramatic lives of Edith Craig seemed to defy coherence as much after her death as they did when she lived. As her mother's daughter she appeared to Clemence Dane in the shape of the deadly Blanche in *Eighty in the Shade* (1959). Blanche Carroll is, in fact, unlike Edith Craig in one crucial aspect. Blanche is dependent entirely on her mother. She has no independent life, no Chris, Tony or Robinetta. Such a rewriting of Craig's life demands close examination. It fixes Craig within the triad of her first family relationships, with Ellen Terry and Edward Gordon Craig, while denying the triad of her second family, more significant for Dane's narrative for its absence.

Clemence Dane was one of the special number of Barn Thea-tregoers.[2] On 22 July 1956, Dane's *Ellen Terry in the Theatre* was produced at the Barn Theatre for the anniversary performance by Margaret Webster. The following year, Webster combined the Ellen Terry anniversary performance with a memorial to Edith Craig, apparently ending the combined tributes to mother and daughter which had taken the form of lectures from 1949 by a number of famous actors: John Gielgud (1949, 1951); W. J. Macqueen-Pope (1952); Ernest Thesiger (1953); Ernest Milton (1954).

'A Festival for Edy', organized at the Barn Theatre in 1957 by Christopher St John and scripted by Margaret Webster, celebrated the work of Edith Craig.[3] Episodic in form, it was the ultimate pageant of Smallhythe Place, a pageant for Edy. Extracts of the representative plays she had directed were dramatized to a commentary delivered by Webster.

The anniversary performance at the Barn Theatre in 1960 was the first which could not be witnessed by Tony Atwood, Christopher St John or Vera Holme. James Roose-Evans directed the recital of works by Virginia Woolf performed by David March. Roose-Evans was to give Miss La Trobe a prominent place in his book on experimental theatres. The Barn Theatre was about to move into a new phase.[4]

Responsibility for Edith Craig's image was bequeathed to Sybil Thorndike, May Whitty, Margaret Webster and Audrey Cameron. Clemence Dane's interpretation of Craig's family narrative was reductive. The combined tribute to Ellen Terry and Edith Craig, like Craig's work with the anniversary performances at the Barn Theatre, tended to efface memories of her broad and considerable work elsewhere. It lent itself to an automatic attribution of her talents to the Terry inheritance.

The ritual of anniversary performance at the Barn Theatre, the responsibility of memorial lectures, the sharing of memories of Ellen Terry and then Edith Craig became a point of identification for actors, a making of theatre history from within. The memorial was designed to keep Ellen Terry's memory 'evergreen'. On Ellen Terry's eightieth birthday, in response to the numerous tributes to her, she had self-deprecatingly deferred the tribute to Shakespeare and to England. Similarly, Edward Percy Smith had elided Edith Craig with 'the heart of the place', the spirit of the Kentish countryside.[5] Edith Craig had an equivocal attitude to the Barn Theatre. It did not belong to her. The stage of her own was always already her mother's. Her persistent, if often ambivalent, desire for separation from her mother resulted in a confusion of identities. The sharing of her last name with her brother has similarly caused confusion.[6]

Eleanor Adlard's anthology of memoirs was unfortunately denied two of the most interesting perspectives on Edith Craig by the early deaths of Virginia Woolf and Radclyffe Hall. Edward Percy Smith contributed the poem in which Craig was crowned, 'heart of the place'. The warmth and vitality which Smith associates with Craig was recognized by many of those close to her who had benefited from her support. The visual image strikingly combines the agility of thought, the determination and creativity with allusions to her rheumatism and tendency to delegate:

> In your miller's smock halting upon the hill,
> Or in your wheeled chair with your winged mind
> Intent, directing, bent to hunt and find
> Some scrap of gorgeous fabric or the heart
> Of a Shakespeare scene, or someone for a part,
> Or someone else to brew a dish of tea.[7]

The claim for immortality and an imagined reunion with the beloved complete the elegy. Edith Craig is seen to live again and meet her mother once more. The pastoral setting is specifically Kentish, with oast houses and marshes, and ahistorical. A kind of feudalism to which this referred sits uneasily with the democratizing forces of either the BDL or the Masses' Stage and Film Guild. Nevertheless, it was paradoxically appropriate to the power claimed by Craig as guardian of her mother's memory, director of her own theatre at last, active in the promotion of theatre in garden cities and suburbs, in churches and on the backs of lorries, in little theatres and Women's Institutes up and down the country, in the correct pronunciation of the English language through the British Empire Shakespeare Society. Today Edith Craig's old stamping ground is advertised in local tourist information leaflets as 'the jewel of the weald' in '1066 country'.

Her successful long-term relationships with women and possibly her ambiguous social status may have prevented comparisons between Edith Craig and Stephen Gordon in *The Well of Loneliness*. Gordon aspired to be an English country gentleman, like her father. Fiercely patriotic, Hall's lesbian character was convinced of her superiority in social class.[8]

In contrast to Edward Percy Smith, whose metaphor places Edith Craig unequivocally at the centre of Englishnesss, Vita Sackville-West positions Craig subversively on the periphery. Smallhythe

Place is a 'gypsy encampment', of which Edith Craig is its 'Romany matriarch'.[9] The essay, emphatically titled, 'Triptych', foregrounds Craig's life with St John and Atwood. If, as Suzanne Raitt has suggested, Sackville-West and Woolf identified with a 'conservative pastoralism', associating lesbianism with innocence,[10] the Small-hythe 'encampment' signified a different configuration. The essay is, however, ambivalent in its portrayal. It does not idealize this community of women and represents both the power-play and the conflicts. The effect of the representation of Craig, St John and Atwood in racial terms as gypsies is complex. Whereas members of Craig's household and friends were named 'Djinns' within the community, Sackville-West's gypsy encampment is the view of an outsider. As an encampment, its transitory, peripheral status is emphasized: no landowners there. Of course, Sackville-West had been the interloper, or 'snoop' in Radclyffe Hall's terms,[11] when her short-lived affair with Christopher St John had had such a disruptive effect on the women of Priest's House. While 'Triptych' represents the power of these women, it does not empower them.

Virginia Woolf was fascinated by Edith Craig and Ellen Terry during her last years. In her essay on Ellen Terry she seemed preoccupied with the unreality of the actress, the impossibility of being both star of the theatre and wage-earning worker. The materiality of Terry's life as an artist brought together two potent strands of Woolf's thinking, emerging clearly in *Three Guineas*, and less forcefully in *A Room of One's Own*: women's economic independence is necessary for the development of imaginative abilities. For Woolf these were most evident in writers. She was ambivalent about where to place acting in her artistic landscape. As her portrait of Edith Craig working in rehearsal in 1922 as 'a ruddy personage' showed,[12] she seems to have found theatrefolk intellec-tually unimpressive but artistically fascinating. Unlike the so-called 'Bloomsbury Group', it was possible and necessary to apply for membership of the Barn Theatre. In 1933 Woolf wrote to Sackville-West that she intended to write, enclosing a cheque to join the Barn Theatre.[13] There appears to have been some delay. In June 1938 she again wrote to Sackville-West that there was 'No sign from Edie. There's a fate against my joining.'[14]

Virginia Woolf was ambivalent towards Christopher St John, who impinged on Woolf's artistic world more closely through her writings and in her relationship with 'Orlando'. Woolf was caught in the middle. Ethel Smyth attempted to be St John's advocate through Woolf, but Vita Sackville-West was not to be wooed. Over a year after the affair, in January 1934, Woolf wrote to Smyth that St John 'haunts Vita'.[15] In April 1934, St John's 'horrid revelations' were still the subject of Woolf's correspondence with Smyth.[16] As late as March 1935, St John was still a 'complication'.[17]

In a professional context, St John, Sackville-West and Woolf were wary of each other. Christopher St John reviewed Vita Sackville-West's *Saint Joan of Arc* diplomatically in the *New Statesman* in July 1936. In her biography of Ethel Smyth, St John obliquely corrects Virginia Woolf's pronouncements on early music in *A Room of One's Own*. An unidentified article by St John in 1937 met with Woolf's disapproval.[18] Their differences were aesthetic and political. As Hermione Lee has argued, Woolf refused a Sapphist identity.[19] She shared with Vita Sackville-West a disconcerted response to Christopher St John, whom Woolf referred to as 'a mule-faced harridan'.[20]

Ellen Terry's life was particularly attached to Virginia Woolf's imagination. Woolf's play, *Freshwater*, is a surreal comic representation of Ellen Terry leaving first husband, G. F. Watts to elope with a Mr Craig.[21] Woolf began work on the play in July 1923, a year after she had been so moved by her attendance at Craig's rehearsal. *Freshwater* was performed on 18 January 1935 at Vanessa Bell's studio. Ellen Terry appeared mystical. She had been acclaimed an artist in her field, but the dramatic world, particularly that of amateurs, seemed to Woolf to reveal too readily its tarnished secrets. It was the world of amateur dramatics and village pageantry which was to provide the artistic dilemma in her last novel, *Between the Acts*. She had been disappointed that her essay on Ellen Terry had been rejected by *Harper's Bazaar* but cheered by Vita Sackville-West's suggestion on 4 March 1941 that they visit Smallhythe Place.[22] On 28 March 1941 Woolf committed suicide.

Miss La Trobe, Blanche Carroll and Stephen Gordon are unlike Edith Craig in one significant respect. They are all lone, unhappy figures. By contrast, Edith Craig seems to have enjoyed the company of others in her social life. In her work she was often assisted in plays by other people and in her pageants by women, such as Chris, Tony and Jacko. One critic alluded to the female following Craig enjoyed:

I know quite a number of women who would unhesitatingly lay down their lives for Edith Craig. She is not only their friend and teacher, but their very goddess. Edith Craig's influence upon many of the younger artists of the stage is more far-reaching than the public would suppose.[23]

The emphasis in many representations of Craig as a solitary, antisocial individual appears to be grounded in a denial of the lesser-known image of Craig as enigmatic role model to a new generation.

The impact of the war on the possibilities for representation dominates *Between the Acts*. The aeroplane passing overhead, like one of Paul Nash's monstrous beasts, signifies the changes which the war brought. Casting its shadow wide, it brought about an unalterable change in the light. This aspect of Woolf's novel illuminates the patterns of deprivation in Craig's career not attributable to routine prejudice and jealousies. Craig's nickname, Boney, after Napoleon, was fitting. Wars seemed to steal her thunder. With the Pioneer Players her work reached a peak in 1916–18, but the end of the First World War was not a propitious time to seek a permanent post in a theatre. Craig received the accolade of a dinner in her honour in 1938 which publicized her achievements, just before another war began. Christopher St John's remark that Hitler put an end to the Barn Theatre was not entirely true.[24] The memory of Edy entertaining children during air-raids with her charades appears to be a pathetic scene. Yet teaching children the value of theatre had always been a firm belief of both Edith Craig and Ellen Terry. In the end, Edith Craig put into practice the lesson which she had spent a long time learning: that a theatre could be anywhere; it did not depend on a stage, auditorium or elaborate equipment. If she had been given the opportunity of running a major London theatre, her career may have taken a different turn. This was the lost opportunity which her friends found it hard to bear for her. Christopher St John, in particular, took on the role of spokesperson, claiming that Craig had been deprived the Old Vic Theatre for reasons unrelated to her abilities,[25] but there were other reasons which may have placed Edith Craig outside the job market.

In later years, Craig became increasingly frail and immobile. Her rheumatism found her in constant pain, likely to cause irritability or lack of patience. At key points in her career she was unable to work through sickness. At times Craig made use of a wheelchair. Tony Atwood believed that she 'would have found wings very useful'.[26] Yet Craig's later years defy the common assumption that seniority entails contemplation, slowing down. She proves Carolyn Heilbrun's suggestion that it can often prove to be a time 'to take risks, to make noise, to be courageous, to become unpopular'.[27]

Of the three women, Edith Craig was the first to die. St John and Atwood continued to live at Smallhythe Place. Although they are buried in the churchyard next to Priest's House, Craig never joined them. Her ashes were apparently in the possession of Olive Terry who intended one day to scatter them in the churchyard.[28] Obituaries recalled some of her achievements.[29] St John wrote several versions of Ellen Terry's life, biographies of Christine Murrell and Ethel Smyth, but she never published a biography of Edith Craig. Strangely, it was Eleanor Adlard, not the family 'literary henchman' Christopher St John, who edited the collected essays on Edith Craig. Even the occasion of Craig's death was to be ambivalent and equivocal, without official sign or record. In a sense, the fact that Craig ended with no resting place was consistent with her life. It also confirms the failure to recognize her existence, for which Olive Terry was not solely to blame.

In recent years Edith Craig has been remembered in the wave of increased interest in her mother, in women's involvement in theatre and in the women's suffrage movement. She has been rediscovered by lesbian history,[30] appearing in *Lesbian Lists* (1990), *Not a Passing Phase* (1989) and in the chapter 'Edy and the Boys' in Rose Collis's *Portraits to the Wall: Historic Lesbian Lives Unveiled* (1994). Craig was a character actress, a costumier, a director, musician and pageant organizer. She lived a woman-centred life. She identified with Rosa Bonheur and Elizabeth I. She was inspirational in her work and much loved at home. Even Edward Gordon Craig made his peace with her late in life. Perhaps the most radical tribute to Edith Craig would be to recognize each of her achievements, each of her dramatic lives.

NOTES

Introduction

Edith Craig Archive (ECD)

Documents in the Edith Craig Archive (forthcoming publication) are cited by their unique identification number where possible. The type of document is indicated by the following letter code prefixes:

A   letters from Edith Craig (or on her behalf)
B   letters to Edith Craig (or others)
C   pamphlet
D   programme (play or film)
G   press cutting
H   plays
J   journals
K   photographs
M   miscellaneous
N   production document (e.g. lighting plot, cast list, floor plan)
P   playbills and posters

Edith Craig Correspondence File (ECCF)

A number of letters held at the Ellen Terry Memorial Museum were numbered and sorted at an earlier point in the museum's history. These letters are given a unique number in a series with the prefix 3. (e.g. 3.305 ECCF).

1. Jan Montefiore has suggested that, to avoid the 'privatising effect' of biography in the use of women's first names, 'the surname remains the appropriate nomenclature for a writer of either sex'; Jan Montefiore, 'Sylvia Townsend Warner, Authority and the Biographer's Moral

Sense', in David Ellis (ed.), *Imitating Art: Essays in Biography* (London: Pluto Press, 1993), p. 147. My use of 'Craig' rather than 'Edy', the name by which she was known to friends, is therefore strategically awkward.

2. Rosamund Gilder, *Enter the Actress: The First Women in the Theatre* (London: George G. Harrap, 1931) devotes an entire chapter to Hrotsvit, in which St John's translation of Hrotsvit's plays is cited but Craig's historic production is not.

3. Michele Barrett, 'Feminism and the Definition of Cultural Politics', in Rosalind Brunt and Caroline Rowan (eds), *Feminism, Culture and Politics* (London: Lawrence & Wishart, 1982).

4. Christopher St John (ed.), *Ellen Terry and Bernard Shaw: A Correspondence* (London: Constable & Co., 1931), p. 185.

5. Christine Battersby, *Gender and Genius: Towards a Feminist Aesthetics* (London: Women's Press, 1989).

6. I have sorted, categorized and numbered the newspaper cuttings, letters, play programmes and playscripts in the Edith Craig Archive. I am now working on a computerized index and catalogue.

7. 'Lifers: The Rise and Rise of the Literary Biographer', *Bookmark*, BBC2, 9 March 1996.

8. Lesbian History Group, *Not a Passing Phase: Reclaiming Lesbians in History 1840–1985* (London: Women's Press, 1989).

9. Sue Wilkinson and Celia Kitzinger (eds), *Representing the Other* (London: Sage, 1996).

10. Liz Stanley, *The Auto/biographical I: The Theory and Practice of Feminist Auto/biography* (Manchester: Manchester University Press, 1992).

11. Christopher St John, 'Close-up', in Eleanor Adlard (ed.), *Edy: Recollections of Edith Craig* (London: Frederick Muller, 1949), p. 32.

12. Laura Marcus, *Auto/biographical Discourses: Theory, Criticism, Practice* (Manchester: Manchester University Press, 1994).

Chapter 1

1. 'Edith Craig: An Informal Interview', *Yorkshire Post*, 12 March 1923; G174 ECD.

2. Edward Gordon Craig, *On The Art of the Theatre* (Edinburgh and London: T. N. Foulis, 1905).

3. *Glasgow Bulletin*, 6 February 1937; ECD.

4. Ellen Terry, *The Story of My Life* [hereafter *Story*] (London: Hutchinson, 1908), p. x.

5. *Ibid.*

6. *Ibid.*, p. 68. As a child and to friends Edith Craig was known as Edy.

7. *Ibid.*, pp. 63–4.

8. Edith Craig, 'Producing a Play', *Munsey's Magazine*, June 1907, p. 311.

9. Edward Gordon Craig, *Ellen Terry and Her Secret Self* (London: Sampson Low, Marston & Co., 1931), p. vii.

10. *Ibid.*, p. viii.

11. *Ibid.*

12. *Ibid.*

13. Christopher St John, 'Close-Up', in Eleanor Adlard (ed.), *Edy: Recollections of Edith Craig* [hereafter *Edy*] (London: Frederick Muller, 1949), p. 29.

14. Edith Craig and Christopher St John (eds), *Ellen Terry's Memoirs* [hereafter *Memoirs*] (London: Victor Gollancz, 1933), p. xi.

15. *Ibid.*

16. Nina Auerbach, *Ellen Terry: Player in Her Time* (London: Phoenix House, 1987), p. 386.

17. 'The Sad Cat and Why', *Evening News*, 19 February [1923]; G1565 ECD.

18. Sybil Thorndike, 'A Festival for Edy', *Edy*, p. 79.

19. Carolyn Steedman has referred to the attempts to recover that which is lost as 'one of the most powerful rhetorical devices of modern women's history'; *Past Tenses* (London: Rivers Oram Press, 1992), p. 164.

20. Edith Craig is designated Edy Terry by W. Graham-Robertson; *Time Was* (London: Hamish Hamilton, 1931), p. 344.

21. Katharine Cockin, 'New Light on Edith Craig', *Theatre Notebook*, XLV.3, 1991, pp. 132–43.

22. The *British Biographical Index* (1990) includes Edward Gordon Craig under Edward Godwin. The *Concise DNB* (1993) omits Edith Craig and Virginia Woolf alike. The *Missing Persons DNB* (1993) has retrieved Elizabeth Malleson but not Edith Craig.

23. Craig appears in the *Biography and Genealogy Master Index* (2nd edn 1980); *Who's Who on the Stage* (1908); *The Oxford Companion to the Theatre* (1967); *Who Was Who in the Theatre 1912–76* (1976); *Who's Who in Hollywood 1900–1976* (1976); and *Notable Names in the American Theatre* (1976). Feminist reference books such as *The Feminist Companion to Literature in English* (1990) and *Index to Women of the World* (1970) also provide entries on Craig.

24. W. Macqueen-Pope, *Ladies First* (London: Allen), 1952.

25. Jane Marcus, 'Some Sources for *Between the Acts*', *A Virginia Woolf Miscellany*, 6, winter 1977, p. 2.

26. Julie Holledge, *Innocent Flowers: Women in the Edwardian Theatre* (London: Virago, 1981), p. 161.

27. Sandra Gilbert and Susan Gubar, 'Ceremonies of the Alphabet: Female Grandmatologies and the Female Autograph', *The Female Autograph: Theory and Practice of Autobiography from the Tenth to the Twentieth Century*, ed. Domna Stanton (Chicago and London: University of Chicago Press, 1984), p. 39.

28. Quentin Bell, Introduction, *Between the Acts* (London: Hogarth Press, 1992), p. xiii.
29. Virginia Woolf quoted by Quentin Bell, *ibid.*
30. Diana Devlin, *A Speaking Part: Lewis Casson and the Theatre of His Time* (London: Hodder & Stoughton, 1982), p. 236. The prompt copy is held at the Theatre Museum.
31. Clemence Dane, *Eighty in the Shade* (London: Heinemann, 1958), Act II, p. 61.
32. *Ibid.*
33. *Ibid.*, Act I, p. 37.
34. Allan Wade, 'A Thread of Memory', *Edy*, p. 68.
35. Ernest Milton, 'Heart and Hand', *Edy*, p. 89.
36. St John, 'Close-Up', *Edy*, p. 25.
37. The source may have been Cicely Hamilton, who co-authored the history of the Old Vic Theatre with Lilian Baylis.
38. Rosemary Auchmuty, 'By Their Friends Shall We Know Them: The Lives and Networks of Some Women in North Lambeth, 1880–1940', in Lesbian History Group, *Not a Passing Phase: Reclaiming Lesbians in History 1840–1985* (London: The Womens' Press, 1989), p. 59.
39. St John, 'Close-Up', *Edy*, p. 25.
40. On Friday 10 November 1933; Edith Craig seems to have attended the Old Vic annual costume dances.
41. Adlard lived in Winchcombe, Gloucestershire, near Dixton Hall where Craig was educated. Adlard became Curator of the Church Porch Museum, Winchcombe and a local campaigner – against the liberal insurance bill. A member of the WVS, and historian, she was author of an (unpublished) history of Winchcombe; private papers held at Gloucestershire Record Office; Eleanor Adlard, 'Laurels and Rosemary', *Edy*, p. 149.
42. Harcourt Williams, 'Bygones', *Edy*, p. 49.
43. Hugo von Hofmannsthal's *The Great World Theatre* at St Edward's Church, Holbeck, Leeds, in 1924.
44. Christopher St John, 'Well Done Leeds!', *Time & Tide*, 1 February 1924, pp. 106–7; ECD.
45. John Gielgud, quoted in Auerbach, *Ellen Terry*, p. 431.
46. Edith Craig, quoted in 'Women in the Theatre', *Hastings Observer*, 20 May 1933; G171 ECD.
47. *Ibid.*
48. Edith Craig, quoted in 'Miss Edith Craig', *Vote*, 12 March 1910, p. 323.
49. Terry, *Story*, p. 53.
50. *Ibid.*, p. 59.
51. Notably John Fletcher's *The Faithfull Shepherdess*, performed in 1885.
52. Quoted in Joy Melville, *Ellen and Edy* (London: Pandora Press, 1987), p. 73.

53. Edward Gordon Craig was known as Teddy.
54. Daniel Farson, *The Man Who Wrote* Dracula: *A Biography of Bram Stoker* (London: Michael Joseph, 1975).
55. Terry, *Story*, p. 80.
56. *Ibid.*, p. 76.
57. Frederika Blair suggests that Ellen Terry's children were relatively unscathed by the stigma of illegitimacy; *Isadora: Portrait of the Artist as a Woman* (Wellingborough, Northamptonshire: Equation, 1986), p. 154.
58. 'Troubles of the Theatre', *Liverpool Post*, 1 March 1935; G175 ECD.
59. *Picture Post*, 2 December 1944.
60. Graham-Robertson, *Time Was*.
61. Christopher St John (ed.), *Ellen Terry and Bernard Shaw: A Correspondence* [hererafter *Correspondence*] (London: Constable & Co., 1931), p. 250.
62. Edith Craig, quoted in Craig and St John (eds), *Memoirs*, p. 194.
63. Auerbach, *Ellen Terry*, p. 305.
64. Margaret Webster, *The Same Only Different: Five Generations of a Great Theatre Family* (London: Gollancz, 1969), p. 177.
65. Pamphlet, Sunday 11 October 1936; ECD.
66. *Cambridge Daily News*, 30 January [no year]; G158 ECD.
67. Roger Manvell, *Ellen Terry* (London: Heinemann, 1968), p. 305.
68. Holledge, *Innocent Flowers*, p. 120.
69. Florence Locke, 'An American Rehearses with Edy', *Edy*, p. 105.
70. Clare Atwood, 'Edy's Ways', *Edy*, p. 134.
71. Marguerite Steen, *A Pride of Terrys* (London: Longmans, 1962), p. 386.
72. Katharine Cockin, 'The Pioneer Players: Plays of/with Identity', in Gabriele Griffin (ed.), *Difference in View: Women and Modernism* (London: Taylor & Francis, 1994).
73. Chris Baldick, *The Social Mission of English Criticism 1848–1932* (Oxford: Oxford University Press, 1983).
74. Cicely Hamilton, 'Triumphant Women', *Edy*, p. 39.
75. Lisa Tickner, *The Spectacle of Women: Imagery of the Women's Suffrage Movement* (London: Chatto & Windus, 1987), p. 153.
76. Lucy Bland, *Banishing the Beast: English Feminism and Sexual Morality 1885–1914* (Harmondsworth: Penguin, 1995).
77. Sheila Jeffreys, *The Spinster and Her Enemies: Feminism and Sexuality 1880–1930* (London: Pandora Press, 1985).
78. Ellen Terry quoted in Melville, *Ellen and Edy*, p. 195.
79. Webster, *The Same Only Different*, p. 282.
80. Virginia Woolf's view that economic independence was more empowering was widely held by women who, like Cicely Hamilton, felt that enfranchisement was anti-climactic.
81. Edward Percy Smith, *Remember Ellen Terry and Edith Craig* (London: English Theatre Guild, 1948).

82. Liz Stanley, 'Feminist Auto/Biography and Feminist Epistemology', in Jane Aaron and Sylvia Walby (eds), *Out of the Margins: Women's Studies in the Nineties* (London: Falmer Press, 1991), p. 213.

83. Monique Wittig, *The Straight Mind and Other Essays*, trans. Marlene Wildeman (Hemel Hempstead: Harvester Wheatsheaf, 1992).

84. The principle of opposition and difference staged by the male/female, masculine/feminine dyads has been claimed as the philosophical basis of language, which the lesbian appears to challenge; Elizabeth Meese, 'Theorizing Lesbian: Writing-A Love Letter', in Joanne Glasgow and Karla Jay (eds), *Lesbian Texts and Contexts: Radical Revisions* (London: Onlywomen Press, 1992), p. 71.

85. Martha Vicinus (ed.), *Lesbian Subjects: A Feminist Studies Reader* (Bloomington: Indiana University Press, 1996), p. 7.

86. *Ibid.*, p. 4.

87. Stanley, 'Feminist Auto/Biography', p. 215.

88. Whitney Chadwick and Isabelle de Courtivron (eds), *Significant Others: Creativity and Intimate Partnership* (London: Thames & Hudson, 1993), p. 13.

89. St John, 'Close-Up', *Edy*, p. 28.

90. Irene Cooper-Willis, 'The Squares', *Edy*, p. 107

91. St John, 'Close-Up', *Edy*.

92. Vita Sackville-West, 'Triptych', *Edy*, p. 124.

93. In the theatre, playing with roles and identities is commonplace: Ellen Terry's name for a bossy Bram Stoker, acting manager at the Lyceum Theatre, was 'mamma'; Farson, *The Man*, p. 52.

94. James Lees-Milne, *People and Places: Country House Donors and the National Trust* (London: John Murray, 1992), p. 119.

95. Margaret Webster, 'Edy the Magician', *Edy*, p. 56.

96 *Ibid.*, p. 83.

97. *Ibid.*

98. St John, 'Close-Up', *Edy*, p. 18.

99. Terry returned to Florence Stoker a letter from Oscar Wilde which Terry believed had been indirectly intended for Stoker; Farson, *The Man*, p. 61.

100. Unpublished letter from W. F. Casey to Miss Craig, 20 December 1917; 3.131 ECCF.

101. Unpublished letter from H. F. Rubinstein to Miss St John, 4 June 1918; 3.580 ECCF.

102. The Lesbian History Group. St John survived Craig by thirteen years. Atwood died three years after St John. A sale of some items was held at the Ellen Terry Memorial Musuem after their deaths, releasing some objects into private ownership, including two of Craig's scrap albums.

103. Atwood's portraits of Craig include one showing her at work in the Barn Theatre, another of her reading in bed.

104. Melville, *Ellen and Edy*, p. 176.
105. Susan Kingsley Kent, *Sex and Suffrage in Britain 1860–1914* (London: Routledge, 1990), p. 53.
106. Gabriele Griffin, *Heavenly Love? Lesbian Images in Twentieth-Century Women's Writing* (Manchester: Manchester University Press, 1993).
107. St John, 'Close-Up', *Edy*, p. 34.
108. Craig and St John (eds), *Memoirs*, p. viii. See also St John, *Ethel Smyth* (London: Longmans, 1959), p. 58.
109. St John, 'Close-Up', *Edy*, p. 19.
110. Joanne Glasgow, 'What's a Nice Lesbian Like You Doing in the Church of Torquemada? Radclyffe Hall and Other Catholic Converts', in Glasgow and Jay (eds), *Lesbian Texts and Contexts*, pp. 241–54.
111. St John (ed.), *Correspondence*, 4 November 1896, p. 114.
112. *Ibid.*, 27 July 1897, p. 240.
113. St John, 'Close-Up', *Edy*, p. 34.
114. *Ibid.*, p. 32.
115. *Ibid.*
116. Griffin, *Heavenly Love?*, p. 37.
117. Craig and St John (eds), *Memoirs*, p. 305.
118. Atwood, 'Edy's Ways', *Edy*, p. 133.
119. Sandra Gilbert and Susan Gubar, 'Is the Pen a Metaphorical Penis?', in Catherine Belsey and Jane Moore (eds), *The Feminist Reader: Essays in Gender and the Politics of Literary Criticism* (London: Macmillan, 1989).
120. Isadora Duncan, *Isadora: My Life* (London: Sphere Books, 1988), p. 135.
121. Edward Gordon Craig, 'Edy Playing', *Edy*, p. 37.
122. Letter from Vita Sackville-West to Evelyn Irons quoted in Victoria Glendinning, *Vita: The Life of Vita Sackville-West* (Harmondsworth: Penguin, 1984), pp. 250–1.
123. The scenario is intelligible in terms of a butch/femme encounter; Elizabeth Grosz, 'Analysing Perverse Desire: An Interrogation of Teresa de Lauretis's *The Practice of Love*', *differences: a Journal of Feminist Cultural Studies*, vol. 6, nos 2 & 3, 1994, p. 286.
124. Auerbach, *Ellen Terry*, pp. 308, 325.

Chapter 2

1. Edith Craig and Christopher St John (eds), *Ellen Terry's Memoirs* [hereafter *Memoirs*] (London: Victor Gollancz, 1933), p. 296.
2. Gwenllian F. Palgrave, 'Ellen Terry: A Tribute', *Cornhill Magazine*, July 1935, pp. 1–10.
3. Michael Baker, *The Rise of the Victorian Actor* (London: Croom Helm, 1978), p. 89.

4. Frederika Blair, *Isadora: Portrait of the Artist as a Woman* (Wellingborough, Northamptonshire: Equation, 1986), p. 154.

5. Christopher St John, 'Biographical Note', in Eleanor Adlard (ed.), *Edy: Recollections of Edith Craig* [hereafter *Edy*] (London: Frederick Muller, 1949), p. 9.

6. H. F. Rubinstein interviewed in *Evening Standard*, 31 August 1974, p. 13. Other students were Harley Granville Barker and Radclyffe Hall.

7. Ellen Terry, *The Story of My Life* [hereafter *Story*] (London: Hutchinson, 1908), p. 82.

8. Roger Manvell, *Ellen Terry* (London: Heinemann, 1968), p. 80.

9. Terry, *Story*, p. 80.

10. *Glasgow Bulletin*, 8 February 1937; G128 ECD.

11. Manvell, *Ellen Terry*, p. 218.

12. *Ibid.*, p. 220.

13. Laurence Irving, *The Successors* (London: Rupert Hart-Davis, 1967), p. 138.

14. *Ibid.*, p. 160.

15. Daniel Farson, *The Man Who Wrote Dracula: A Biography of Bram Stoker* (London: Michael Joseph, 1975), p. 26.

16. Elizabeth Malleson, *Elizabeth Malleson 1828–1916: Autobiographical Notes and Letters with a Memoir by Hope Malleson* (privately printed, 1926), p. 192.

17. Julie Holledge, *Innocent Flowers: Women in the Edwardian Theatre* (London: Virago, 1981), p. 109; Manvell, *Ellen Terry*, p. 220.

18. Owen Stinchcombe, *Elizabeth Malleson 1828–1916: Pioneer of Rural District Nursing* (Held at Gloucestershire Records Office), 1989, p. 2.

19. Malleson, *Elizabeth Malleson*, p. 212.

20. Ellen Terry, quoted in *ibid.*

21. Malleson, *Elizabeth Malleson*, p. 212.

22. *Ibid.*, p. 100.

23. See Kathryn Gleadle, *The Early Feminists: Radical Unitarians and the Emergence of the Women's Rights Movement 1831–51* (London: Macmillan, 1995).

24. Malleson, *Elizabeth Malleson*, p. 145.

25. June Purvis, *Hard Lessons: The Lives and Education of Working-Class Women in Nineteenth-Century England* (Cambridge: Polity Press, 1989), p. 271.

26. *Ibid.*, p. 204.

27. Play programme; 10–11 April 1885; ECD.

28. Purvis, *Hard Lessons*, p. 205.

29. Malleson, *Elizabeth Malleson*, p. 17.

30. *Ibid.*, p. 50.

31. *Ibid.*, p. 75.

32. *Ibid.*, p. 149.

33. *Ibid.*, p. 142.

34. Ellen Terry, quoted in Nina Auerbach, *Ellen Terry: Player in Her Time* (London: Phoenix House, 1987), p. 375.
35. *Ibid.*, p. 376.
36. Manvell, *Ellen Terry*, p. 222.
37. Craig and St John (eds), *Memoirs*, p. 196.
38. Cicely Hamilton and Lilian Baylis, *The Old Vic* (London: Jonathan Cape, 1926).
39. Christopher St John (ed.), *Ellen Terry and Bernard Shaw: A Correspondence* [hereafter *Correspondence*] (London: Constable & Co., 1931), 4 November 1896, p. 115.
40. St John, 'Close-Up', *Edy*, p. 23.
41. Ellen Terry, quoted in Auerbach, *Ellen Terry*, p. 375.
42. Margaret Webster, *The Same Only Different: Five Generations of a Great Theatre Family* (London: Gollancz, 1969), p. 178.
43. C. B. Cochran, *Showman Looks On* (London: J. M. Dent & Sons, 1945).
44. Craig and St John (eds), *Memoirs*, p. 352.
45. St John, 'Close-Up', *Edy*, p. 21.
46. Atwood's portraits invariably show Craig doing something (*Edy*, facing, p. 113).
47. Terry, *Story*, p. 247.
48. Terry, quoted in Craig and St John (eds), *Memoirs*, p. 194.
49. *Ibid.*, p. 193.
50. St John, 'Close-Up', *Edy*, p. 10.
51. Examination certificate, Senior Division, Local Examination in Music, Trinity College, London, March 1890; ECD.
52. Atwood, 'Edy's Ways', *Edy*, p. 136.
53. M7 ECD.
54. Terry, *Story*, pp. 318–19.
55. *Ibid.*, pp. 10, 194.
56. Programme; P9 ECD.
57. Ella and Nelia Casella co-authored with Gertrude Kingston several books for children. Kingston thus met Ellen Terry; Gertrude Kingston, *Curtesy While You're Thinking* (London: Williams & Norgate, 1937), p. 56.
58. Harcourt Williams, 'Bygones', *Edy*, p. 46.
59. Eleanora Duse, quoted by St John, 'Close-Up', *Edy*, p. 24.
60. Baker, *The Rise of the Victorian Actor*.
61. Edith Craig, quoted in *Evening News*, 25 March 1938; G179 ECD.
62. 'Portraits, Miss Ailsa Craig,' *The Theatre*, 1 October 1895, p. 219; ECD.
63. Williams, 'Bygones', *Edy*, p. 47.
64. Joy Melville, *Ellen and Edy* (London: Pandora Press, 1987), p. 171.
65. May Whitty, 'Edy the Magician', *Edy*, p. 53.
66. St John, 'Close-Up', *Edy*, p. 24.

67. Unidentified cutting, scrap album E.V.6.4. 5/5 ETMM.
68. *Ibid.*
69. Edward Gordon Craig referred to his sister's *Fortnightly Review* column; quoted in Auerbach, *Ellen Terry*, p. 307. A. C. (Edith Craig), 'Notes on the Costume', *The Kensington*, p. 139; G180 ECD.
70. *Ibid.*
71. *Ibid.*
72. Craig and St John (eds), *Memoirs*, p. 256.
73. Yeats remarked that she had done her best; [1 May 1903] John Kelly and Ronald Schuchard (eds), *Letters of W. B. Yeats: Volume 3 1901–1904* (Oxford: Oxford University Press, 1989), p. 353.
74. Craig and St John (eds), *Memoirs*, p. 257.
75. St John (ed.), *Correspondence*, 5 November 1896, p. 119.
76. *Ibid.*
77. *Ibid.*, 11 April 1898, p. 307.
78. Michael Holroyd, *Bernard Shaw Volume 1 The Search for Love* (London: Chatto & Windus, 1988), p. 324.
79. *Ibid.*, p. 380.
80. St John (ed.), *Correspondence*, October 1896, p. 105.
81. *Ibid.*, p. 250.
82. *Candida* in July 1900, *When We Dead Awaken* in January 1903 and *The Good Hope* in April 1903.
83. Stage Society Annual Report 1900-1, p. 8.
84. Unidentified cutting, scrap album E.V.6.4. 5/5 ETMM.
85. *Lady*, 3 May 1900.
86. King Alfred, William the Conqueror, Richard I, Edward I, Henry V, Henry VIII, Charles I and George III.
87. *Lady*, 6 June [no year]; ECD.
88. Mark Girouard, *The Return to Camelot: Chivalry and the English Gentleman* (London: Yale University Press, 1981).
89. Terry, *Story*, p. 215.
90. This collection includes programmes for: Louis N. Parker's Dover Pageant (27 July–1 August 1906); the Oxford Historical Pageant, for which Arthur Quiller-Couch, Walter Raleigh and Laurence Housman wrote episodes (27 June–3 July 1907); the Pageant of London in the Festival of England (May–July 1910); Shakespeare's England organized by Mrs George Cornwallis West at Earl's Court (15 June 1912).
91. St John (ed.), *Correspondence*, 13 April 1898, p. 307.
92. In 1898 her schedule was fairly full but there are periods during which she would have had time to make the long return trip to Africa. She seems to have been free from other work between August and October 1898, January and April and August and November 1899. Julie Holledge quotes a letter from Ellen Terry to Edy in Cairo which appears to be undated; Holledge, *Innocent Flowers*, p. 114. Since Craig

went to Egypt in 1923, it is possible that the letter relates to the later trip.

93. This tour is not listed in the entry for Brown-Potter in *Who Was Who in the Theatre*, but other performances in 1898 are recorded which would leave little time for a journey to Africa. I have not been able to locate Brown-Potter's autobiography, *The Age of Innocence and I* (1933).

94. Alison Roberts, *Hathor Rising: The Serpent Power of Ancient Egypt* (Totnes, Devon: Northgate Publishers, 1995), p. 10.

95. Ayesha in Ryder Haggard's novel *She* (1886).

96. J. P. Wearing states it was first performed at the New Cambridge Theatre. A review cites the original performance at the Parkhurst Theatre, Holloway; *Modern Society*, 20 April 1901, p. 757.

97. *Ibid.*

98. *Ibid.*

99. Play programme; TM.

100. The design of the Lady Macbeth costume has been attributed to Alice Comyns Carr, its construction to Mrs Nettleship; Craig and St John (eds), *Memoirs*, p. 233. One journalist, however, attributed it to Edith Craig; *Liverpool Courier*, 8 December 1929; G1702 ECD.

101. *Modern Society*, 20 April 1901, p. 757.

102. 'Our Captious Critic "Nicandra"', *Illustrated Sporting and Dramatic News*, 20 April 1901, p. 289.

103. Over the cartoon from the *Illustrated Sporting and Dramatic News* is pasted a costume design resembling the description of Nicandra's dress. The design is signed with Pamela Colman Smith's initials, a characteristic C and S intersecting the downstroke of the P, resembling a caduceus.

104. Sheila Jeffreys, *The Spinster and Her Enemies: Feminism and Sexuality 1880–1930* (London: Pandora Press, 1985).

105. *News of the World*, 30 November 1902; G1563 ECD.

106. 'A Married Woman', *Era*, 29 November 1902; G1651 ECD.

107. 'Theatre Metropole', *Pall Mall Gazette*, 25 November 1902; G1650 ECD.

108. *Birmingham Post*, 26 November 1902; G1564 ECD.

109. *Sunday Times*, 30 November 1902; ECD.

110. *Ibid.*

111. [Max Beerbohm], 'A Play in a Suburb', *The Saturday Review*, 29 November 1902, pp. 673–4; ECD.

112. *Ibid.*

113. Terry's reduced financial situation demanded that she move to a flat on the King's Road; Craig and St John (eds), *Memoirs*, p. 306.

114. 'Women in the Theatre', *Hastings Observer*, 20 May 1933; G171 ECD.

115. Farson, *The Man*, p. 163.

116. Two different play programmes and a poster are discussed by Farson, one listing the performance time as 10 a.m., the other at 10.15 a.m., with different cast lists.
117. Craig and St John (eds), *Memoirs*, p. 195.
118. Barbara Belford distinguishes between Lucy and Mina as authentic and inauthentic New Women; *Bram Stoker: A Biography of the Author of* Dracula (London: Weidenfeld & Nicolson, 1996), p. 237.
119. Bram Stoker, *Dracula* (Harmondsworth: Penguin, 1994), p. 449.
120. Farson, *The Man*, p. 164.
121. Stoker, *Dracula*, p. 213.
122. W. Graham-Robertson, *Time Was* (London: Hamish Hamilton, 1931), p. 141.
123. Manvell, *Ellen Terry*, p. 234.
124. Graham-Robertson, *Time Was*, p. 141.
125. *Ibid.*, p. 143.
126. Edward Gordon Craig, *Ellen Terry and Her Secret Self* (London: Sampson Low, Marston & Co., 1931), p. 59.
127. 'Mainly for Women', *Free Lance*, 5 October 1901; ECD.
128. John Berger, *Ways of Seeing* (Harmondsworth: Penguin, 1972), p. 87.

Chapter 3

1. Elaine Showalter, *Sexual Anarchy: Gender and Culture at the Fin de Siècle* (London: Bloomsbury Publishing, 1991).
2. Susan Richards, *The Rise of the English Actress* (London: Macmillan, 1993), p. 118.
3. *The Freewoman*, vol. I, no. 1, 23 November 1911, p. 1.
4. George Bernard Shaw, 'Preface', in Christopher St John (ed.), *Ellen Terry and Bernard Shaw: A Correspondence* [hereafter *Correspondence*] (London: Constable & Co., 1931), p. xiv.
5. *Ibid.*, p. 328.
6. Martha Vicinus, *Independent Women: Work and Community for Single Women 1850–1920* (London: Virago, 1985).
7. Barbara Taylor, *Eve and the New Jerusalem: Socialism and Feminism in the Nineteenth Century* (London: Virago, 1983).
8. Sheila Jeffreys, *The Spinster and Her Enemies: Feminism and Sexuality 1880–1930* (London: Pandora Press, 1985), p. 40.
9. Lucy Bland, *Banishing the Beast: English Feminism and Sexual Morality 1885–1914* (Harmondsworth: Penguin, 1995).
10. Rupert Hart-Davis (ed.), *Letters of Max Beerbohm 1892–1956* (Oxford: Oxford University Press, 1989), p. 6.
11. *Ibid.*
12. Michel Foucault, *The History of Sexuality Volume 1* (Harmondsworth: Penguin, 1990), p. 104.
13. Mrs Penington quoted in Elizabeth Malleson, *Elizabeth Malleson*

1828–1916: Autobiographical Notes and Letters with a Memoir by Hope Malleson (privately printed, 1926), p. 199.

14. Christopher St John, 'Close-Up', in Eleanor Adlard (ed.), *Edy: Recollections of Edith Craig* [hereafter *Edy*] (London: Frederick Muller, 1949), p. 22. St John dates this 1901 in this essay but elsewhere states that Terry bought the property in Michaelmas 1900; St John (ed.), *Correspondence*, p. 387.

15. Photograph reproduced in *Edy*, facing p. 17.

16. Quoted by St John in 'Close-Up', *Edy*, p. 19.

17. Photographs reproduced in press cuttings; G95–G97 ECD.

18. *Cambridge Daily News*, 30 January (no year); G158 ECD.

19. Elizabeth Wilson, *Adorned in Dreams: Fashion and Modernity* (London: Virago, 1985), p. 218.

20. Margaret Webster, *The Same Only Different: Five Generations of a Great Theatre Family* (London: Gollancz, 1969), p. 175.

21. St John (ed.), *Correspondence*, 12 July 1899, p. 331. Sheepshanks lived at 1 Barton Street; Sybil Oldfield, *Spinsters of This Parish: The Life and Times of F. M. Mayor and Mary Sheepshanks* (London: Virago, 1984), p. 95.

22. Vicinus, *Independent Women*.

23. Jerome K. Jerome, *My Life and Times* (New York and London: Harper & Brothers, 1926), p. 120.

24. Vicinus, *Independent Women*, p. 9.

25. Sheila Rowbotham and Jeffrey Weeks, *Socialism and the New Life: The Personal and Sexual Politics of Edward Carpenter and Havelock Ellis* (London: Pluto Press, 1977), p. 85.

26. *Ibid.*, p. 99.

27. Sheila Jeffreys, *Anticlimax: A Feminist Perspective on the Sexual Revolution* (London: The Women's Press, 1990).

28. St John, 'Close-Up', *Edy*, p. 22.

29. Lina Marston is said to have shared rooms with Craig at Smith Square; John Kelly and Ronald Schuchard (eds), *The Collected Letters of W. B. Yeats: Volume 3 1901–1904* (Oxford: Clarendon Press, 1994), p. 329.

30. Harcourt Williams, 'Bygones', *Edy*, p. 49.

31. *The Times*, 25 October 1960.

32. St John quoted in *Correspondence*, p. 441.

33. Steen dates it at 1904; *A Pride of Terrys* (London: Longmans, 1962), p. 250.

34. According to contemporaries Margaret Webster and Marguerite Steen.

35. St John, 'Close-Up', *Edy*, p. 22.

36. Roger Manvell, *Ellen Terry* (London: Heinemann, 1968), p. 305.

37. The League of Arts was established in 1922 at The Guildhouse, Eccleston Square, London SW1.

38. This is explored obliquely in her unpublished play, 'What a Plague is Love!'; ECD.

39. Manvell, *Ellen Terry*, p. 306.
40. Roger Manvell cites the American actor Joe Evans not Sydney Valentine; Manvell, *Ellen Terry*, p. 305.
41. Steen, *A Pride*, p. 250.
42. Ellen Terry's biographers have tended to represent Craig's sexuality in a problematic way. By contrast, Terry appears to have approved of her daughter's relationship with Christopher St John and Tony Atwood.
43. Webster, *The Same Only Different*, p. 175.
44. Griffin, *Heavenly Love? Lesbian Images in Twentieth-Century Women's Writing* (Manchester: Manchester University Press, 1993), p. 37.
45. Jeffner Allen, *Sinuosities: Lesbian Poetic Politics* (Bloomington: Indiana University Press, 1996).
46. Foucault, *History of Sexuality*.
47. Alan Sinfield, *The Wilde Century* (London: Cassell, 1994), p. 3.
48. Eve Sedgwick, *The Epistemology of the Closet* (Berkeley: University of California Press, 1990).
49. Sheila Jeffreys, 'Does it Matter if They Did It?', *Not a Passing Phase: Reclaiming Lesbians in History 1840–1985*, Lesbian History Group (London: Women's Press, 1989), p. 23.
50. *Ibid.*, p. 24.
51. For example, many writers have been preoccupied with sexual intercourse as a defining factor in the relationship between Ellen Terry and Henry Irving; Webster, *The Same Only Different*, p. 191.
52. Manvell, *Ellen Terry*; p. 244; Steen, *A Pride*, p. 327.
53. Edward Gordon Craig, *Ellen Terry and Her Secret Self* (London: Sampson Low, Marston & Co., 1931).
54. St John (ed.), *Correspondence*, p. 115.
55. Gordon Craig, *Ellen Terry and Her Secret Self*, p. 59.
56. Manvell, *Ellen Terry*, p. 309.
57. Steen, *A Pride*, p. 386.
58. Esther Newton, 'The Mythic Mannish Lesbian: Radclyffe Hall and the New Woman', in Martin Duberman, Martha Vicinus and George Chauncey Jr (eds), *Hidden from History: Reclaiming the Gay and Lesbian Past* (Harmondsworth: Penguin, 1991), pp. 281–93.
59. Elizabeth Meese, 'Theorising Lesbian', in Joanne Glasgow and Karla Jay (eds), *Lesbian Texts and Contexts: Radical Revisions* (New York: New York University Press, 1990), p. 78.
60. Jacques Lacan quoted in *ibid.*
61. Webster, *The Same Only Different*, p. 191.
62. James Lees-Milne, *People and Places: Country House Donors and the National Trust* (London: John Murray, 1992), p. 114.
.63. Joanne Glasgow, 'What's a Nice Lesbian Like You Doing in the Church of Torquemeda? Radclyffe Hall and Other Catholic Convents', in

Glasgow and Jay (eds), *Lesbian Texts and Contexts*, p. 251.

64. *Ibid.*

65. Sinfield, *The Wilde Century*, p. 3.

66. Christopher St John, *The Crimson Weed* (London: Duckworth, 1900).

64. Steen mistakenly cites *Hungerheart* as St John's first novel; Steen, *A Pride*, p. 251.

67. Showalter, *Sexual Anarchy*, p. 153.

68. Sinfield, *The Wilde Century*, p. 118.

69. *Ibid.*, p. 143.

70. My copy, number 12,000 of the 1901 reprint, gives the following publication details in the prelims: first edition September, reprinted 4 October and 24 October 1894; May 1895; May 1896; and December 1901.

71. Including Annie E. Holdsworth, *Joanna Traill Spinster*; C. E. Raimond (Elizabeth Robins), *George Mandeville's Husband* and Stephen Crane, *The Red Badge of Courage*.

72. Joy Melville, *Ellen and Edy* (London: Pandora Press, 1987), p. 176.

73. Steen, *A Pride*, p. 250.

74. St John, 'The Golden Book', MS UCLA.

75. Laurie Wolf, 'Suffragettes of the Edwardian Theatre: Edith Craig and the Pioneer Players', Ph.D. thesis, University of California, Los Angeles, 1989, p. 87.

76. Steen, *A Pride*, p. 326.

77. *Ibid.*

78. Nina Auerbach, *Ellen Terry: Player in Her Time* (London: Phoenix House, 1987), p. 294.

79. Gordon Craig, *Ellen Terry and Her Secret Self*, p. 140.

80. *Ibid.*

81. Josephine Guy, *The British Avant-Garde: The Theory and Politics of Tradition* (Hemel Hempstead: Harvester Wheatsheaf, 1991).

82. Ronald Schuchard, 'W. B. Yeats and the London Theatre Societies 1901–1904', *The Review of English Studies*, XXIX, 1978, pp. 415–46.

83. Wayne K. Chapman, 'Yeats's "Theatre of Beauty" and the Masque Tradition', *Yeats: An Annual of Critical and Textual Studies*, VII, 1989, pp. 42–56. Leaflet; ECD.

84. Kelly and Schuchard (eds), *Letters of W. B. Yeats*, 26 December 1902, p. 285.

85. Kelly and Schuchard (eds), *Letters of W. B. Yeats*, 4 December 1902, p. 267.

86. Caricatures; ETMM.

87. Chapman, 'Yeats's "Theatre of Beauty"'.

88. Kelly and Schuchard (eds), *Letters of W. B. Yeats*; Gilbert Murray correspondence, Bodleian Library, and ECCF.

89. Unpublished letter from J. Todhunter to Edith Craig, 5 August 1903; 3.728 ECCF.

90. Kelly and Schuchard (eds), *Letters of W. B. Yeats*, 26 December 1902, p. 285.

91. Unpublished letter from Arthur Symons to Edith Craig, 11 September 1903; 3.672 ECCF.

92. Unpublished letter from Gilbert Murray to the Committee of The Masquers, 27 October 1903; 3.598 ECCF.

93. These included W. B. Yeats and Lady Gregory.

94. Unpublished letter from Gilbert Murray to the Committee of The Masquers, 27 October 1903; 3.598 ECCF.

95. Gilbert Murray feared the influence of 'Miss Craig's poodle'; it has been assumed that this referred to Martin Shaw rather than Christopher St John; quoted in Schuchard 'Yeats and the London Theatre Societies', pp. 440–1.

96. Christopher St John, *Henry Irving* (London: Green Sheaf, 1905), p. 11.

97. *Ibid.*, p. 13.

98. *Ibid.*, p. 18.

99. *Ibid.*, p. 27.

100. A visual allusion links Craig and Irving. The symbolically expiring lantern of the Lyceum has plumes of smoke similar to those issuing from Craig's head in one of Pamela Colman Smith's caricatures; ECD.

101. Stefan Hock, 'Play-Production', *Life and Letters*, summer 1938, pp. 111–19; G6 ECD.

102. Ellen Terry, *The Story of My Life* (London: Hutchinson, 1908), p. 281.

103. Edith Craig and Christopher St John (eds), *Ellen Terry's Memoirs* (London: Victor Gollancz, 1933), p. viii.

104. Letter from Christopher St John to Gabriellino [Gabrielle Enthoven], 3 December 1931; Theatre Museum.

105. Edith Craig, 'Producing a Play', *Munsey's Magazine*, June 1907; Theatre Museum. *The Green Room Book* (1906) provides an entry on Craig and highlights the Terrys in a piece on 'Footlight Families'; pp. 377–85.

106. *Ibid.*

107. *Ibid.*

108. *Ibid.*

109. *Ibid.*

110. *Ibid.*

111. *Ibid.*

112. *Ibid.*

113. *Ibid.*

114. *Ibid.*

115. *Ibid.*

116. *Ibid.*

117. Cooper Willis, 'The Squares', *Edy*, p. 108.

118. 'Ellen Terry "Bossed" by Autocratic Daughter', *Citizen*, 13 February 1907; G178 ECD.

119. *Ibid.*

Chapter 4

1. Unpublished letter from Emmeline Pethick Lawrence to 'My Dear Friends', 25 August 1909; 3.1441 ECCF.

2. Ray Strachey, *The Cause: A Short History of the Women's Movement in Great Britain* (London: Virago, 1978), p. 293.

3. *Ibid.*, p. 294.

4. 'Helpers at the Scottish Exhibition 1. – Miss Edith Craig', *Votes for Women*, 15 April 1910, p. 455.

5. Edward Gordon Craig, *Ellen Terry and Her Secret Self* (London: Sampson Low, Marston & Co., 1932), p. 135.

6. 'Miss Edith Craig', *Vote*, 12 March 1910, p. 233.

7. Sandra Stanley Holton, 'New Directions in Suffrage History'. Conference paper given at the 'Seeing Through Suffrage' Conference, University of Greenwich, April 1996.

8. A. J. R. (ed.), *Suffrage Annual and Women's Who's Who* (London: Stanley Paul & Co., 1913).

9. This play was later to be rewritten in Italian and performed by the Pioneer Players.

10. D16 ECD.

11. Cicely Hamilton, 'Triumphant Women', in Eleanor Adlard (ed.), *Edy: Recollections of Edith Craig* [hereafter *Edy*] (London: Frederick Muller, 1949), pp. 38–9.

12. *Votes for Women*, 15 April 1910, p. 455.

13. *Ibid.*

14. *Ibid.*

15. *Vote*, 12 March 1910, p. 232.

16. 'Miss Edith Craig', *Vote*, 12 March 1910, p. 232.

17. *Votes for Women*, 15 April 1910, p. 455. The Eustace Miles Restaurant was advertised as providing 'the best light and sustaining luncheons for brain-workers'.

18. *Ibid.*

19. *Vote*, 7 May 1910, p. 20.

20. *Vote*, 14 May 1910, p. 32.

21. *Vote*, 16 April 1910.

22. *Vote*, 25 June 1910, p. 100.

23. Lisa Tickner, *The Spectacle of Women: Imagery of the Suffrage Campaign 1907–14* (London: Chatto & Windus, 1987), p. 244.

24. *Ibid.*, pp. 112, 117.

25. *Vote*, 13 July 1912, p. 216.

26. *Vote*, 12 March 1910, p. 240.

27. *Daily Herald*, 15 November 1912, p. 2.

28. *Vote*, 9 July 1910.

29. Margaret Webster, *The Same Only Different: Five Generations of a Great Theatre Family* (London: Gollancz, 1969), p. 248.

30. Unpublished letter from Joseph Pennell to Edith Craig, 21 July 1909; 3.508 ECCF.
31. *Vote*, 8 October 1910, p. 288.
32. *Vote*, 2 April 1910, p. 267.
33. Les Garner, *Stepping Stones to Women's Liberty: Feminist Ideas in the Women's Suffrage Movement* (London: Heinemann Educational, 1984), p. 50.
34. Rosemary Taylor, *In Letters of Gold: The Story of Sylvia Pankhurst and the East London Suffragettes in Bow* (London: Stepney Books, 1993), p. 30.
35. These exist for *A Pageant of Great Women* and *The Pageant of the Stage*; ECD.
36. The Utopia Press printed the *Clarion* newspaper and the *Suffragette*.
37. J. L. Austin, *How One Woman Did It* (London: Utopia Press, nd); ECD.
38. Unpublished letter from Constance Campbell to Edith Craig, 24 July 1914; 3.117 ECCF.
39. Margaret Nilior Meuron, 'The Masque of Women'; H4 ECD.
40. Tickner, *Spectacle of Women*, p. 43.
41. *Votes for Women*, 15 April 1910, p. 455.
42. Tickner, *Spectacle of Women*, p. 85.
43. In this year Beatrice Harraden was a Vice-President, Bessie Hatton Honorary Secretary and Margaret Wynne Nevinson was Honorary Treasurer.
44. Carbon copy letter from Christopher St John to May Whitty, 12 February 1913; ECD.
45. *Ibid.*
46. N11 ECD.
47. *Ibid.*
48. *Votes for Women*, 15 April 1910, p. 455.
49. Margaret Wynne Nevinson, *Fragments of Life* (London: George Allen & Unwin, 1922).
50. Unpublished letter from Ford Madox Hueffer [Ford] to Edith Craig, 24 January 1911; 3.364 ECCF.
51. Tickner *Spectacle of Women*, p. xi.
52. *Ibid.*, p. 30.
53. Rebecca West, 'A Modern Crusader', *The Freewoman*, 23 May 1912, pp. 8–10.
54. Victoria Glendinning, *Rebecca West: A Life* (London: Papermac, 1988), p. 35.
55. West proceeded to criticize Hobson's arguments published elsewhere for the domestic education of working-class women. Hobson, who married J. A. Hobson, liberal economist, in 1885, published poetry and short stories as well as the essays *Ideals True and False* (London: Headley Brothers, 1912).

56. Tickner, *Spectacle of Women*, p. xi.
57. *Vote*, 2 March 1912, p. 226.
58. Tickner, *Spectacle of Women*, p. 20
59. Hamilton, 'Triumphant Women', *Edy*, p. 41.
60. Julie Holledge, *Innocent Flowers: Women in the Edwardian Theatre* (London: Virago, 1981), pp. 122–3.
61. *Ibid.*, p. 63.
62. Unpublished letter from Eva Moore to Edith Craig, nd; 3.593 ECCF.
63. *Era*, 29 October 1910, p. 131.
64. Godfrey Blount, 'Religion and Make-Believe', *The Freewoman*, 15 July 1913, p. 52.
65. 'Well-known Actresses Appear as Famous Women in a Pageant Advocating the Cause of Votes for Women', *Daily Mirror*, 25 May 1911, p. 5; Tickner, *Spectacle of Women*, pp. 170–1.
66. Tickner, *Spectacle of Women*, p. 171.
67. Quoted by Cicely Hamilton, *Vote*, 3 December 1910, p. 63.
68. Billie Melman, *Women's Orients: English Women and the Middle East 1718–1918: Sexuality Religion and Work* (Basingstoke: Macmillan, 1992), p. 267.
69. Quoted by David Glover, 'Introduction', *The Jewel of the Seven Stars* (Oxford: Oxford University Press, 1996, first published by Heinemann, 1903), p. xx.
70. Bram Stoker, *Famous Imposters* (London: Sidgwick & Jackson, 1910).
71. *Vote*, 27 August 1910, p. 206.
72. Julia Swindells, *The Uses of Autobiography* (London: Taylor & Francis, 1995), p. 9.
73. Maud Leyson played Prejudice in Ipswich and Sappho in Swansea.
74. *Vote*, 6 August 1910. Miss Tuke was joint Honorary Secretary of WSPU.
75. N106 ECD.
76. N107 ECD.
77. *Vote*, 10 September 1910, p. 231.
78. At Penarth on 13 December 1909; *Vote*, 9 December 1909, p. 82. See Angela V. John, ' "Run Like Blazes": The Suffragettes and Welshness', *Llanfar: Journal of Welsh Labour History*, 6.3, 1994, pp. 31–2.
79. *Vote*, 19 February 1910, p. 196.
80. Letter from Lillie Langtry to Edith Craig, nd; ECCF.
81. N102 ECD.
82. *Votes for Women*, 15 April 1910, p. 455.
83. G155 ECD.
84. P75 ECD.
85. 'Pageantry. Brilliant Spectacle at the Prince's Theatre. A Didactic Play', Unidentified press cutting, 7 November 1910; Theatre Collection, University of Bristol.
86. Letter from Annie Kenney to Edith Craig; 3.404 ECCF.

87. *Cambridge Chronicle*, 10 October 1910.
88. The meeting was held on 10 October 1910; Cambridge Association for Women's Suffrage Annual Report 1910, Cambridgeshire County Council County Archives.
89. The following accounts indicate the range of costs: Mrs Cleeves, Maesteg, £41.8.11 for Swansea production; Miss Johnson, Ramsay House, Cambridge, £32.16.5 for Cambridge production; and Annie Kenney £46.15.3 for Bristol production.
90. M71
91. N110 ECD.
92. *Ibid.*
93. D182 ECD.
94. *Vote*, 9 December 1909, p. 79.
95. H14 ECD.
96. At the town hall, Sutton Coldfield, 9 March 1911.
97. Charlotte Despard, quoted in 'Pageant of Famous Women. Suffragist Entertainment at Victoria Hall', *Sunderland Echo*, 11 October 1910, G1426 ECD.
98. Tickner, *Spectacle of Women*, p. 189.
99. Elaine Showalter, *Sexual Anarchy: Gender and Culture at the Fin de Siècle* (London: Bloomsbury Publishing, 1991), p. 128.
100. Nina Auerbach, *Ellen Terry: Player in Her Time* (London: Phoenix House, 1987), p. 12.
101. Tracy Davis, *Actresses as Working Women: Their Social Identity in Victorian Culture* (London: Routledge, 1991), p. 124.
102. The early Victorian maiden, the ideal woman or domesticated matron, the suffragette, the objector.
103. 'Woman in History. Beautiful Pageant at Cambridge', *Cambridge Daily* [illegible]; G1424 ECD.
104. 19 April 1911; M70 ECD.
105. Katharine Cockin, 'New Light on Edith Craig', *Theatre Notebook*, XLV.3, 1991, p. 142.
106. Lis Whitelaw, *The Life and Rebellious Times of Cicely Hamilton* (London: Women's Press, 1990), p. 126.
107. N101; N102 ECD.
108. Rosemary Cullen Owens, *Smashing Times: A History of the Irish Women's Suffrage Movement 1889–1992* (Dublin: Attic Press, 1995), pp. 66, 80.
109. Unpublished letter from Iska Teleki; B93 ECD.
110. *Ibid.*
111. *Ibid.*
112. *Ibid.*
113. Unpublished letter from Cicely Hamilton to Iska Teleki; A20 ECD.
114. *Ibid.*
115. *Ibid.*

116. Rosika Schwimmer (1877–1948) was Vice-President of the Women's International League for Peace and Freedom and in 1918–19 Hungarian minister to Switzerland; B95 ECD.

117. Arncliffe Sennett Collection, British Library.

118. It is not clear what stance on women's suffrage was taken by the film.

119. N. Schoonderwoerd, *J. T. Grein Ambassador of the Theatre 1862– 1935: A Study in Anglo-Continental Theatrical Relations* (Assen: Von Gorcum, 1963), p. 124. 'Michael Field' was the pen name of Katherine Bradley (1846–1914) and Edith Cooper (1862–1913).

120. Unpublished letter from Iska Teleki and others to 'Dear Madam' [Ellen Terry], 25 February 1913; B94 ECD.

121. Christopher St John (ed.), *Ellen Terry and Bernard Shaw: A Correspondence* (London: Constable & Co., 1931), p. 445.

122. Cicely Hamilton, *A Pageant of Great Women* (London: Marian Lawson, 1948), p. 15.

123. Cicely Hamilton quoted in Holledge, *Innocent Flowers*, p. 94.

124. D162 ECD.

125. C71, M72; ECD.

126. Letter from May Sinclair to Edith Craig, 11 July 1914; ECCF.

127. Hamilton, *A Pageant*, p. 14.

128. Unpublished letter from Beatrice Harraden, 16 November; 3.320 ECCF.

129. Hamilton, *A Pageant*, 1948, opp. p. 10.

130. 'Suffrage Atelier At Home', *Vote*, 5 October 1912, p. 401.

131. Emmanuel Cooper, *The Sexual Perspective: Homosexuality and Art in the Last 100 Years in the West* (London: Routledge & Kegan Paul, 1994), p. 47.

132. *Ibid.*

133. Rose Collis, *Portraits to the Wall: Historic Lesbian Lives Unveiled* (London: Cassell, 1994), pp. 73–85.

134. Virginia Woolf, 'Character in Fiction', *The Essays of Virginia Woolf, Volume III 1919–1924*, ed. Andrew McNellie (London: Hogarth Press, 1988), p. 421.

135. Christabel Pankhurst, *Unshackled* (London: Century Hutchinson, 1987), p. 148.

136. Edith Craig quoted in *Glasgow Herald*, 8 February 1937. See Ann Escott, 'True Valour', in Kevin McCarra and Hamish Whyte (eds) *A Glasgow Collection: Essays in Honour of Joe Fisher* (Glasgow: Glasgow Libraries, 1990).

137. This is suggested by the representations of the movement in autobiographies by those who took part in it.

138. Hamilton, 'Triumphant Women', *Edy*, p. 39.

139. D164 ECD.

140. *Vote*, 1 April 1911, p. 272.

141. Nevinson, *Fragments of Life*, p. 229.

142. *Votes for Women*, 10 November 1911.

Chapter 5

1. AFL Annual Report, 1909–10, p. 3; Fawcett Library.
2. Margaret Webster, *The Same Only Different: Five Generations of a Great Theatre Family* (London: Gollancz, 1969), p. 249.
3. Pioneer Players' Annual Reports, 1911–12, p. 3, [PPAR] ECD.
4. Elaine Aston, *An Introduction to Feminism and Theatre* (London: Routledge, 1995), p. 31.
5. PPAR ECD.
6. Gabrielle Enthoven (1868–1950), dramatist and theatre historian, donated her collection of theatrical memorabilia to the V&A in 1924, now held by the Theatre Museum where the research room is named in her memory. In 1948 she was the first president of the Society for Theatre Research.
7. Olive Terry was Edith Craig's cousin.
8. Ellen Terry played the Abbess in Hrotsvit's *Paphnutius*.
9. Christopher St John, 'Close-Up', in Eleanor Adlard (ed.), *Edy: Recollections of Edith Craig* [hereafter *Edy*] (London: Frederick Muller, 1949), p. 26.
10. For a discussion of Edith Ellis's work, see Jill Davis, ' "This Be different": The Lesbian Drama of Mrs Havelock Ellis', *Woman: A Cultural Review*, 2.2, summer 1991, pp. 134–48.
11. Christopher St John, *Ethel Smyth* (London: Longmans, Green and Co., 1959), p. xv.
12. C67 ECD.
13. The men involved in women's suffrage have only recently received attention. See Angela V. John and Claire Eustance (eds), *The Men's Share? Masculinities, Male Support and Women's Suffrage in Britain 1890–1920* (London: Routledge, 1997).
14. Lena Connell's photographic studio; Rosabel Watson's Ladies' Orchestra.
15. My thanks to Angela V. John for this information.
16. Dorothy Knowles, *The Censor, the Drama and the Film 1900–1934* (London: George Allen & Unwin, 1934); Richard Findlater, *Banned! A Review of Theatrical Censorship in Britain* (London: MacGibbon & Kee, 1967).
17. 'Little Interviews: Miss Edith Craig at the Pioneer Players', *Pall Mall Gazette*, 13 April 1912, p. 12.
18. Margaret O. Kennedy wrote for the *Vote* and was a member of the Pioneer Players when the *Pall Mall Gazette* interviewed Craig.
19. Charles Thursby frequently played Prejudice in *A Pageant of Great Women*, a role otherwise performed by Leonard Craske and on one occasion by Nigel Playfair.

20. Virginia Woolf, 'The Diary of a Lady in Waiting', *Times Literary Supplement*, 23 July 1908.
21. Leonora Davidoff and Catherine Hall, *Family Fortunes: Men and Women of the English Middle Class 1780–1850* (London: Hutchinson, 1987).
22. Flora Fraser, *The Unruly Queen: The Life of Queen Caroline* (London: Macmillan, 1996).
23. Findlater, *Banned!*, p. 118.
24. Julie Holledge, *Innocent Flowers: Women in the Edwardian Theatre* (London: Virago, 1981), p. 128.
25. Holledge incorrectly cites this author as Richard; *Innocent Flowers*, p. 132.
26. Susan Kingsley Kent, *Sex and Suffrage in Britain 1860–1914* (London: Routledge, 1990), p. 155. *Common Cause*, 6 March 1914.
27. Jess Dorynne, *The Surprise of His Life*; MS ECD.
28. Florence Edgar Hobson, *A Modern Crusader* (London: A. C. Fifield, 1912).
29. *The Times*, 9 May 1911, p. 13.
30. Lady Cynthia Asquith, *The Diaries of Lady Cynthia Asquith 1915–18* (London: Century Hutchinson, 1987), p. 411.
31. H. M. Harwood (1874–1959) known as Tottie, was the husband of F. Tennyson Jesse (1889–1958). Harwood was an ordinary member of the Pioneer Players (1912–13 and 1916–20) and a member of the Executive (1916–20).
32. *Daily Herald*, 17 December 1912.
33. *Vote*, 8 November 1912.
34. Elizabeth Howe, *The First English Actresses* (Cambridge: Cambridge University Press, 1992), p. 19. Howe states that the identity of the woman who played Desdemona is unknown. Photographs of Nancy Price as Margaret Hughes and other performers in costume are held in the Pioneer Players' Scrapbook, Theatre Museum.
35. Christopher St John and Laurence Alma-Tadema campaigned for Poland.
36. Phyllis Hartnoll, *Oxford Companion* (Oxford: Oxford University Press, 1972) cites a translation by H. M. Tillyard, 1923, and the 1914 production by Edith Craig of St John's translation but not St John's published translation.
37. See also Katharine M. Wilson (ed.), *Medieval Women Writers* (Athens, GA: University of Georgia Press, 1984).
38. Leon Bakst (1866–1924) was designer with the Ballets Russes.
39. 'The Pioneer Players' mi-careme Ball', *Tatler*, 25 March 1914, p. 329.
40. The society held two 'mi-careme' costume balls in 1912–13 and in March 1914.
41. *Vote*, 26 March 1910.
42. Cicely Hamilton and Christopher St John photographed in costume in Cicely Hamilton, *Life Errant* (London: J. M. Deutsch, 1935).

43. Gwen John, *Bookman*, June 1917. Gwen John, the author of *Luck of War*, was a prolific dramatist and not the artist as Julie Holledge states (*Innocent Flowers*, p. 137).

44. Unpublished letter from Basil Rathbone to Edith Craig, 13 November 1919; 3.551 ECCF.

45. ADA, 3 April 1914; D146 ECD.

46. Lis Whitelaw, *The Life and Rebellious Times of Cicely Hamilton* (London: The Women's Press, 1990), p. 139. The Pioneer Players did not, as Whitelaw asserts, fold at the outbreak of the First World War (p. 137).

47. PPAR 1914–15, pp. 8–9.

48. Mary Sheepshanks (1872–1958) was editor of the internationalist women's suffrage newspaper, *Ius Suffragii*. Irene Cooper-Willis was a member of the No Conscription Fellowship. Florence Edgar Hobson and Miles Malleson (1888–1969) published pacifist writings.

49. Geoffrey Whitworth, *The Making of a National Theatre* (London: Faber & Faber, 1961), p. 114.

50. *Ibid.*, p. 113.

51. D174 ECD.

52. G113 ECD.

53. W. Bridges-Adams (1889–1965) had been a member of OUDS, the Marlowe Society and later author of *The Irresistible Theatre* (1957).

54. Programme; ECD.

55. Christopher St John, *Christine Murrell MD: Her Life and Work* (London: Williams & Norgate, 1935), p. 58.

56. Play programme; ECD.

57. SSAR 1916–17, p. 10.

58. Marek Kohn, *Dope Girls: The Birth of the British Drug Underground* (London: Lawrence & Wishart, 1992), p. 37.

59. Edward Knoblock (Knoblauch; 1874–1945) was a successful dramatist. He and his sister, the sculptor Gertrude Knoblock, lent their Paris flat to Vita Sackville-West. Knoblock had worked at the Kingsway Theatre until his dismissal for disloyalty to Lena Ashwell.

60. Marie Potapenko was the model for Anton Chekhov's Irina Arkadin in *The Seagull*; Ronald Hingley, *A Life of Chekhov* (Oxford: Oxford University Press, 1989), pp. 192–5.

61. Margaret Morris (1891–1980) had her own theatre in London, which was used on one occasion for the Pioneer Players' AGM. She developed a system of dancing and notation of dance movement on which she published several books.

62. A Camargo Society was founded to promote classical ballet until the Sadler's Wells Ballet was formed.

63. See Katharine Cockin, 'The Pioneer Players: Plays of/with Identity', in Gabriele Griffin (ed.), *Difference in View: Women and Modernism* (London: Taylor & Francis, 1994); and Margaret Morris, *My*

Galsworthy Story (London: Peter Owen, 1967).

64. Unpublished letter from W. F. Casey to Edith Craig, 20 December 1917; 3.131 ECCF.

65. Christopher St John, trans. *The Plays of Roswitha* (London: Chatto & Windus, 1923), p. xiv.

66. Marjorie Patterson's play was published in America. In an interview she appears to have resented being categorized as an American actress. She may have been involved in one of Craig's later experimental theatres, the York Everyman Theatre, where a Margery W. Patterson was a member of the committee.

67. Cockin, 'The Pioneer Players'.

68. See *Stage*, 14 June 1917, p. 7; *Sketch*, 20 June 1917.

69. Saint-Georges de Bouhélier, 'Edith Craig', *Edy*, p. 59.

70. *Ibid.*

71. *Ibid.*, p. 61.

72. Christopher Innes, *Avant-Garde Theatre 1892–1992* (London: Routledge, 1993), p. 101.

73. *Ibid.*, p. 100.

74. 'Death and the Lady', as arranged by Lucy E. Broadwood, had been produced for Jean Sterling Mackinlay's matinee on 17 February 1917 at the Aeolian Hall. It may have been brought to the Pioneer Players' attention by Mackinlay or her husband Harcourt Williams.

75. Jessica Douglas-Home, *Violet: The Life and Loves of Violet Gordon Woodhouse* (London: Harvill Press, 1996).

76. Sybil Thorndike, 'The Festival', *Edy*, p. 79.

77. Djuna Barnes appeared as an extra in the Provincetown Players' production of Paul Claudel's *L'annonce faite à Marie*; Andrew Field, *Djuna: The Life and Times of Djuna Barnes* (New York: G. P. Putnam & Sons, 1983).

78. F. Goddard, 'The Pioneer Players', *The Future*, March 1918, pp. 104–105; G986 ECD.

79. Atwood was a member of the Pioneer Players' Executive Committee, 1917–20.

80. Clare Atwood, 'Edy's Ways', *Edy*, p. 134.

81. PPAR 1917–18, p. 9.

82. Lena Ashwell, *Modern Troubadours: A Record of the Concerts at the Front* (London: Gyldenhall, 1922), p. 189.

83. *Evening News*, 25 March 1938; ECD.

84. Letter from J. T. Grein to Edith Craig, 27 March 1918; 3.305 ECCF.

85. *Ibid.*, 10 April 1918; 3.306 ECCF.

86. Letter from Torahiko Kori to Edith Craig, 19 December 1917; 3.405 ECCF.

87. *Pall Mall Gazette*, 13 April 1912, p. 12.

88. Michael Orme, *J. T. Grein: The Story of a Pioneer 1862–1935* (London: John Murray, 1936), p. 224.

89. *On the East Side* was set in New York. St John had spent two years in Italy, some time before 1911.

90. C33 ECD.

91. Philip Dodd, 'Englishness and the National Culture', in Robert Colls and Philip Dodd (eds), *Englishness: Politics and Culture 1880–1920* (London: Croom Helm, 1986).

92. Orme, *J. T. Grein*, p. 262.

93. Elaine Showalter, *Sexual Anarchy: Gender and Culture at the Fin de Siècle* (London: Bloomsbury Publishing, 1991), p. 162. Showalter notes that while performances by Ida Rubinstein of Salome had been permitted, the decapitated head could not be openly displayed.

94. N. Schoonderwoerd, *J. T. Grein Ambassador of the Theatre 1862– 1935: A Study in Anglo-Continental Theatrical Relations* (Assen: Von Gorcum, 1963), pp. 189–92.

95. Kohn, *Dope Girls*, p. 4.

96. Julie Wheelwright, *The Fatal Lover: Mata Hari and the Myth of Women in Espionage* (London: Collins & Brown, 1992), p. 34.

97. Asquith, *Diaries*, p. 411.

98. Louys's work was used in Natalie Barney's private performances in the 1920s; Sue-Ellen Case, *Feminism and Theatre* (London: Macmillan, 1988), p. 52.

99. *Observer*, 20 December 1914; G1602 ECD.

100. Gwen Lally was a lesbian actress whose Protean act involved male impersonation; Cathleen Nesbitt, *A Little Love and Good Company* (London: Faber & Faber, 1975), p. 75. Gwen Lally's play *Pierrot Philanders* was directed by Craig in aid of prisoners of war of the Scottish regiments on 29 May 1917 at the Strand Theatre; D173 ECD.

101. D103 ECD.

102. E. K. Chambers (1866–1956), a civil servant and Medieval literature specialist, was first president of the Malone Society founded in 1906 to reprint early English plays.

103. D22 ECD.

104. 'Nativity Play at Rye', *Sussex Express*, 17 January 1919. Rye Monastery is now the premises of a pottery business.

105. K86 ECD.

106. *Sussex Express*, 17 January 1919.

107. G1568 ECD.

108. The Plough was not, as I originally thought, a periodical but a subscription theatre society; Katharine Cockin, 'New Light on Edith Craig', *Theatre Notebook*, XLV.3, 1991, pp. 132–43.

109. D153 ECD. The cast of twelve included one Executive member and one ex-member of the Pioneer Players.

110. In 1917 Baroness D'Erlanger's donation to a fund-raising tombola was a piece of land in the Chiltern Hills; Ashwell, *Modern Troubadours*, p. 116. She was the subject of a portrait by artist Romaine Brooks.

111. Goddard, 'The Pioneer Players'.
112. C37 ECD.
113. 22 August 1919; M77 ECD.
114. 22 August 1919; G212 ECD.
115. *Daily Telegraph*, 22 August 1919; G216 ECD.
116. *Ibid.*
117. *Ibid.*
118. Cockin, 'New Light', p. 140.
119. *Morning Post*, 23 May [year unknown]; G173 ECD.
120. In the year of Craig's death, 1947, the first British university drama department was set up at Bristol university.
121. St John, 'Close-Up', *Edy*, p. 28.
122. Unpublished letter from H. F. Rubinstein to Miss St John, 4 June 1918; 3.580 ECCF.

Chapter 6

1. J. C. Trewin and Wendy Trewin, *The Arts Theatre, London* (London Society for Theatre Research, 1986), p. 1.
2. 'Edith Craig. An Informal Interview', *Yorkshire Post*, 12 March [192?]; G174 ECD.
3. *Bolton Evening News*, 21 December 1932; G138 ECD.
4. The Pioneer Players had performed Constance Holme's rural drama, *The Home of Vision*. Craig was later to direct *The Child Born at the Plough* by Sheila Kaye-Smith and a dramatization by Moira Shedden of Vita Sackville-West's prize-winning poem, *The Land*.
5. The Pioneer Players advertised several women's businesses, such as the Alston Weaving Studio, the Honourable Gabriele Borthwick's ladies' automobile workshops and school of driving, Miss E. M. Stear's typing and Mrs Wood-Smith, dispensing chemists.
6. Prospectus, Everyman Theatre; C73 ECD.
7. *Ibid.*
8. *Ibid.*
9. Edward Rollinson, *Sydney Valentine 1865–1919: An Actor's Actor* (Harefield, Middlesex: Sarratt Publishers, 1996), pp. 6–7.
10. Norman MacDermott, *Everymania: The History of the Everyman Theatre, Hampstead 1920–26* (London: Society for Theatre Research, 1975), p. 30. A contract for her direction of *Man and Superman* is extant; 3.460 ECCF.
11. *Ibid.*
12. Alison Light, *Forever England: Femininity, Literature and Conservatism Between the Wars* (London: Routledge, 1991), pp. 9, 216.
13. Chris Baldick, *The Social Mission of English Criticism 1848–1932* (Oxford: Oxford University Press, 1983).

14. Light, *Forever England*, p. 75.
15. St John's collection of recordings of music which she reviewed are held at the Ellen Terry Memorial Museum.
16. Virginia Woolf, *The Diary of Virginia Woolf Volume II: 1920–24* (London: Hogarth Press, 1978), p. 174.
17. Craig produced *The Shoe*, on 16 January 1923 for the same charity. Sybil Thorndike and her children Mary and Ann took part; P107 ECD.
18. D137 ECD.
19. F. H. Harris, *The Gentleman Dancing Master*. Wearing records this production but not *The Shoe*.
20. D168, C23, P70 ECD.
21. C23 ECD.
22. B118 ECD.
23. D8 ECD.
24. P15, C23 ECD.
25. B20 ECD.
26. B127 ECD.
27. B121 ECD.
28. B128 ECD.
29. B21 ECD.
30. B23 ECD.
31. 'More Egyptian Discoveries', *Sunday Express*, 1 February 1923; G1581 ECD.
32. 'British Generals See Film Dervish Charge', G1573 ECD.
33. 'More Egyptian Discoveries', *Sunday Express*, 1 February 1923; G1581 ECD.
34. 'Her Racing Camel: Miss Ellen Terry's Daughter Back From Egypt'; G1589 ECD.
35. G1565 ECD.
36. G1579 ECD.
37. Charles F. Smith gave Donald Sinden his first job in the theatre and acted as mentor for many years; *Laughter in the Second Act* (London: Hodder & Stoughton, 1985), p. 165.
38. B84 ECD. The press cuttings refer to St Edward's Church, Holbeck, whereas the LAT prospectus cites St Thomas's Church, Holbeck as the venue. See also Tom Steele, *Alfred Orage and the Leeds Arts Club 1893–1923* (Aldershot, Hampshire: Scolar Press, 1990), p. 247.
39. 27 October 1923; B85 ECD. Railton had played the Old Man in *Thirty Minutes in a Street*.
40. 30 October 1925; B79 ECD.
41. 16 November 1923; G1387 ECD.
42. B83 ECD.
43. B82 ECD.
44. A19 ECD.
45. G1364 ECD.

46. B91 ECD.
47. G1370 ECD.
48. *Yorkshire Post*, 10 March [1922]; G1391 ECD.
49. G1367, G1389 ECD.
50. C73 ECD.
51. *The Times*, 4 August 1924; G1372 ECD.
52. 25 November 1924; B88 ECD.
53. This fourth season is not mentioned by Steele; *Alfred Orage*, p. 249.
54. C22 ECD.
55. 'Everyman Theatre. Miss Edith Craig as the Inspirer. Her Coming Work at York', *Yorkshire Post*, 20 September [1924]; G1376 ECD.
56. D91 ECD.
57. D207 ECD.
58. *Ibid.*
59. Steele, *Alfred Orage*, p. 208.
60. C83 ECD
61. 2 December 1924; B144 ECD.
62. Pearn sent a copy of the script as originally produced by Craig at the Everyman Theatre to the New York Theatre Guild, 15 December 1924; B162 ECD.
63. Quoted by Beatrice Ensor, 20 November 1924; B145 ECD.
64. 3.535 ECCF.
65. 4 November 1924; B147 ECD.
66. B163 ECD.
67. B152 ECD.
68. B158 ECD.
69. N207 ECD.
70. Lesley Ferris, *Acting Women: Images of Women in Theatre* (London: Macmillan, 1990), p. 58.
71. *Stage*, 11 December; G1431 ECD.
72. *Referee*, 11 January [1925]; G1435 ECD.
73. *The Death of Torahiko Kori*, directed by Anne Woods, written by Takenary Maeda, London International Film School, 1989.
74. M84 ECD.
75. D268 ECD.
76. M81 ECD.
77. C83 ECD.
78. 3.608 ECCF.
79. Elaine Aston, *An Introduction to Feminist Theatre* (London: Routledge, 1994), p. 116.
80. Review; ECD.
81. *Observer*, 18 October [1925]; G1670 ECD.
82. Programme; ECD.
83. *Bath Chronicle*, 15 December 1925; G1466 ECD.
84. Edith Kinney Doten, *A Chronicle Play of Mary the Mother Our Lord*,

and Grace Winifred McGavran, *The Shepherd Who Could Not Go*; D75 ECD.

85. *Star*, 14 January 1927; G1470 ECD.
86. D59 ECD.
87. C25 ECD.
88. D155 ECD.
89. Light, *Forever England*, p. 215.
90. Angela V. John, *Elizabeth Robins: Staging a Life 1862–1952* (London: Routledge, 1995), p. 95.
91. Gwen Lally had a special 'crow's nest' built at the top of the grandstand when she was organizing a pageant; 'Gwen Lally Producing a Pageant', *Morning Post*, 22 May 1935; G187 ECD.
92. E. Sylvia Pankhurst, *The Suffragette Movement: An Intimate Account of Persons and Ideals* (London: Longmans, Green & Co., 1931), p. 225.
93. G41 ECD.
94. G37 ECD.
95. 9 September 1927; B14 ECD.
96. B81 ECD.
97. M44 ECD.
98. Trewin and Trewin, *The Arts Theatre*, p. 2.
99. Vera Brittain, *Radclyffe Hall: A Case of Obscenity* (London: Femina Press, 1968), pp. 94–5. See also Jeffrey Weeks, *Coming Out: Homosexual Politics in Britain from the Nineteenth Century to the Present* (London: Quartet Books, 1977), p. 87.
100. Michael Baker, *Our Three Selves: The Life of Radclyffe Hall* (London: Hamish Hamilton, 1985), p. 283.
101. Brittain, *Radclyffe Hall*, p. 42.
102. *Ibid.*, p. 106.
103. *Ibid.*, p. 126.
104. Baker, *Our Three Selves*, p. 283.

Chapter 7

1. Press cuttings from *Kent Messenger*; Barn Theatre scrapbook, ETMM.
2. *Kentish Express*, 24 August 1929; ETMM.
3. She was manager for Jean Sterling Mackinlay, the Glastonbury Players and the Film Society in London.
4. *Kent Messenger*, 24 July 1953; ETMM.
5. *Kent Messenger*, 29 July 1939; ETMM.
6. *Kent Messenger*, 30 July 1938; ETMM.
7. The extant speeches were short, handwritten on the reverse of the play programme; ECD.
8. D299 ECD.

9. B175 ECD.
10. A27 ECD.
11. B184 ECD.
12. J. E. Sewell, 'Singing Jailbirds', *New Statesman*, 1 March 1930, p. 666; G1690 ECD.
13. G1694 ECD.
14. *Ibid.*
15. *Ibid.*
16. *Queen*, 10 November 1938; G176 ECD.
17. Michael Baker, *Our Three Selves: The Life of Radclyffe Hall* (London: Hamish Hamilton, 1985).
18. April 1931, quoted in *ibid.*, p. 271.
19. 1934; ECD.
20. Tom Steele, *Alfred Orage and the Leeds Art Club 1893–1923* (Aldershot, Hampshire: Scolar Press, 1990), p. 249.
21. *Ibid.*, p. 250.
22. *New Era*, March 1931, p. 80.
23. G1407 ECD.
24. C36 ECD.
25. G1397 ECD.
26. Shakespeare Society, Cheltenham, scrapbook; D5434 4/1, Gloucestershire Records Office.
27. *Nottingham Evening Post*, 22 March 1932; G1659 ECD.
28. *Yorkshire Telegraph*, 29 March 1932; ECD.
29. 9 December 1934; G1410 ECD.
30. *Glasgow Bulletin*, 9 February 1937; G119 ECD.
31. *Yorkshire Observer*, 29 October 1934; G1660 ECD.
32. G174 ECD.
33. It was her contribution to the fundraising event in aid of Tenterden and Halden District Nurse Fund at Tenterden Town Hall on 17–18 August 1943. Other performances in the event were a pageant of nursing through the ages and Gwen Lally in scenes from *A School for Scandal*.
34. D21 ECD.
35. *Daily News*, 15 October 1931.
36. *Daily Gleaner*, Kingston Jamaica, 26 January 1932; G106 ECD.
37. *Newcastle Evening Chronicle*, 11 September 1931; G169 ECD.
38. *Yorkshire Observer*, 7 December 1934; G105 ECD.
39. G116 ECD.
40. *Glasgow Bulletin*, 9 February 1937; G119 ECD.
41. May 1933.
42. *Leicester Mercury*, 25 April 1932; G123 ECD.
43. D12 ECD.
44. Baker, *Our Three Selves*, p. 286.
45. St John quoted in Victoria Glendinning, *Vita: The Life of Vita Sackville-West* (Harmondsworth: Penguin, 1984), p. 253.

46. Edith Craig's will includes a codicil to her 'adopted daughter'; ETMM.
47. ECD.
48. Spring term school report, lower-fourth form, St Joan of Arc's Convent, Rickmansworth, Hertfordshire, 1935; ECD.
49. 'Miss Edith Craig, Actress and Producer', *Vote*, 31 March 1933, J3 ECD.
50. The late Gwen Watford was one of Edith Craig's many students. Another, Elizabeth Blake, founded the New Zealand Drama League; *Hawkes Bay Herald*, 4 September 1933; G1654 ECD.
51. 'Make-Up Secrets for Amateurs', G115 ECD.
52. D169 ECD.
53. The hostels were located at 27 Upper East Smithfield and 9 De Crespigny Park, Camberwell.
54. 'Debutantes of 1933', *Birmingham Mail*, 8 March 1933; G1622 ECD.
55. 3.535 ECCF.
56. *Gloucester Citizen*, 15 June 1937; G100 ECD.
57. C24 ECD.
58. The other nine were Sir Philip Ben Greet, Clifford Bax, John Gielgud, Amner Hall, Sir Barry Jackson, Theodor Komisarjedsky [*sic*], Gertrude Kingston, Gwen Ffrangcon Davies and Hubert Griffith; C24 ECD.
59. 'Women in the Theatre', *Hastings Observer*, 20 May 1933; G171 ECD.
60. On another occasion, Craig gave a lunch-time lecture on 'Women and the Stage' at the British Commonwealth League in London on Thursday 1 February; D44 ECD.
61. M8 ECD.
62. M5 ECD.
63. M3 ECD.
64. M4 ECD.
65. *Times Educational Supplement*, 16 June 1934; G103 ECD.
66. 'Troubles of the Theatre', *Liverpool Post*, 1 March 1935; G175 ECD.
67. D220 ECD.
68. Press cuttings; ECD.
69. Edward Percy Smith, 'To Edy', in Eleanor Adlard, *Edy: Recollections of Edith Craig* (London: Frederick Muller, 1949).
70. 'Theatres – Good and Bad', *Gloucestershire Echo*, 12 January 1937; G170 ECD.
71. G1643 ECD.
72. *Glasgow Herald*, 8 February 1937; ECD.
73. 'Diary of a "Times" Woman', *Glasgow Evening Times*, 20 January 1937; ECD.
74. Atwood, 'Edy's Ways', *Edy*, p. 143.
75. 'Chatter from the Weald: Recovery', *Kent Messenger*, 27 March 1937; G159 ECD.
76. Clare Atwood, Maisie Britton, Doreen Errol, Mary Eversley, John Gielgud, Edward Knoblock, Sir John Martin Harvey, Lady Martin

Harvey, Julia Nielson-Terry, John Parker, Christopher St John, George Skillan, Reginald Tate, Dame Sybil Thorndike DBE, Violet Vanbrugh, Dame May Whitty DBE and Harcourt Williams.

77. Cicely Hamilton, Violet Vanbrugh, Vita Sackville-West, Dame May Whitty, Edward Knoblock, John Gielgud, Herbert Griffith, Sybil Thorndike and Mr S. R. Littlewood paid tribute to her.

78. *Queen*, 10 November 1938; G176 ECD.

79. 'Edith Craig Tells of Being Sacked on Stage', *Evening News*, 25 March 1938; G179 ECD.

80. *Kent Express*, 11 February 1938.

81. G130 ECD.

82. D60 ECD.

83. D164 ECD.

84. C55 ECD.

Chapter 8

1. Documents at the Ellen Terry Memorial Museum relating to the Barn Theatre have yet to be sorted and numbered. These include several scrapbooks of newspaper cuttings.

2. The names of performers in the annual memorial production would be burned into the wooden timbers inside the theatre. A small sum would buy a named seat in the theatre. Some of these seats have survived and the National Trust is now reviving the idea of named seats to raise funds to support the property.

3. Margaret Webster, 'A Festival for Edy', MS ECD.

4. Anthony Thomas directed plays at the Barn Theatre from 1961–88. Anthony Thomas has written a booklet detailing his productions at the Barn Theatre; *The Story of the Barn Theatre 1929–1989* (Stone-in-Oxney, Anthony Thomas, 1989). The present director of plays for the Barn Theatre Society is Anthony Weare.

5. Edward Percy Smith, 'To Edy from an Old Neighbour', in Eleanor Adlard (ed.), *Edy: Recollections of Edith Craig* [hereafter *Edy*] (London: Frederick Muller, 1949), p. 13.

6. It has been assumed that 'E. Craig', co-editor with C. St John of *Ellen Terry's Memoirs*, was Edward Gordon Craig; Virginia Woolf, *Killing the Angel in the House* (Harmondsworth: Penguin, 1995), pp. 88–9. Craig's date of birth has been incorrectly cited as 1864 (Virginia Woolf, *The Diary of Virginia Woolf Volume II 1920–1924* (London: Hogarth Press, 1978, p. 174) and 1870 (Susan Richards, *The Rise of the English Actress* (London: Macmillan, 1993), p. 131).

7. Percy Smith, 'To Edy', *Edy*, p. 14.

8. Jonathan Dollimore, *Sexual Dissidence: Augustine to Wilde, Freud to Foucault* (Oxford: Clarendon Press, 1991).

9. Vita Sackville-West, 'Triptych', *Edy*, p. 118.

10. Suzanne Raitt, *Vita and Virginia: The Work and Friendship of V. Sackville-West and V. Woolf* (Oxford: Clarendon Press, 1993), p. 12.
11. Michael Baker, *Our Three Selves: The Life of Radclyffe Hall* (London: Hamish Hamilton, 1985), p. 286.
12. Woolf, *Diary Volume II*, p. 174.
13. Virginia Woolf, *The Sickle Side of the Moon. The Letters of Virginia Woolf Volume V: 1932–1935*, ed. Nigel Nicholson (London: Hogarth Press, 1979), p. 225.
14. *Ibid.*, p. 232.
15. *Ibid.*, p. 272.
16. *Ibid.*, p. 289.
17. *Ibid.*, p. 379.
18. Virginia Woolf, *Leave the Letters Till We're Dead. The Letters of Virginia Woolf Volume VI: 1936–1941*, ed. Nigel Nicholson (London: Hogarth Press, 1980), p. 136.
19. Hermione Lee, *Virginia Woolf* (London: Chatto & Windus, 1996), p. 490.
20. Victoria Glendinning, *Vita: The Life of Vita Sackville-West* (Harmondsworth: Penguin, 1984), p. 271.
21. Virginia Woolf, *Freshwater*, ed. Lucio P. Ruotolo (London: Hogarth Press, 1976).
22. 4 March [1941], Woolf, *Letters Volume VI*, p. 476.
23. ECD.
24. St John, 'Close-Up', *Edy*, p. 27.
25. *Ibid.*, p. 25.
26. Clare Atwood, 'Edy's Ways', *Edy*, p. 139.
27. Carolyn Heilbrun, *Writing a Woman's Life* (New York: Ballantine Books, 1988).
28. Donald Sinden, *Laughter in the Second Act* (London: Hodder & Stoughton, 1985), p. 57. Olive Terry was apparently similarly careless with the ashes of James Carew.
29. *Daily Mail*, 28 March 1947; *The Times*, 28 and 29 March 1947; *Observer*, 30 March 1947. None of these refer to Tony Atwood, citing only St John as her 'housemate'.
30. The Lesbian History Group, *Not a Passing Phase: Reclaiming Lesbians in History 1840–1985* (London: The Women's Press, 1989); Dell Richards, *Lesbian Lists* (London: Alysom, 1990); Rose Collis, *Portraits to the Wall: Historic Lesbian Lives Unveiled* (London: Cassell, 1994).

APPENDIX:
Chronology and Selected Dates of Performance

Key:
ACT	acted		DIR	directed	
COST	responsible for costumes		ORG	organized	
COSTD	designed costumes		PP	for the Pioneer Players	
COSTM	made costumes		SCDES	designed scenery	
			STAGE	stage-managed	

		Work Events	Life Events
1869	9 Dec		Edith Craig born
1872			Edward Gordon Craig born
1874			Ellen Terry returns to stage
1877			Ellen Terry marries Charles Wardell
1878		ACT (debut) *Olivia*, Court Theatre	
1882	30 Dec	Attends Gilbert and Sullivan, *Princess Ida*	
1883		Boarder at Mrs Cole's school, Earls Court, London	
1886			Edward William Godwin dies
1887–90		Studies music with Alexis Hollander, Berlin	
1888		ACT (debut) New York	
1888		Member of the Mummers Society (London); Ellen Terry is President	
1890		Attends Royal Academy of Music	
1890	Mar	Passes piano exam, Trinity College, London	
1890		ACT (Polly Flamborough) *Olivia*, Grand Theatre, Islington	
1891	4 May	Attends Ibsen, *Hedda Gabler*, Vaudeville Theatre	
1892			Sarah Terry, Craig's grandmother, dies

		Work Events	Life Events
1893–7			Edward Gordon Craig married to May Gibson
1893	18 Mar	Attends Ibsen, *A Doll's House*, Royalty Theatre	
1895	May–June	ACT (Maid) A. W. Pinero, *Bygones* (noticed by George Bernard Shaw)	
1895	June	ACT (Jessica) *The Merchant of Venice*, Lyceum Theatre	
1895	June	ACT (Sozel) *The Bells*, Lyceum	
1895	July	ACT (Niece) *The Lyons Mail*, Lyceum (praised by Eleanora Duse)	
1895	July	ACT (Donalbain) *Macbeth*, Lyceum	
1895	31 Aug	Sails with Ellen Terry for America; Lyceum tour	
1895			Craig's relationship with Sydney Valentine is terminated
1895	1 Oct	Biographical portrait of Ailsa Craig published in *The Theatre*	
1895			Henry Irving is knighted
1896			Christopher St John meets Edith Craig for the first time
1896		Stage name changed from Ailsa to Edith Craig	
1897	18 May	ACT (reads?) (Mina Harker) Bram Stoker, *Dracula*, Lyceum	
1897		ACT Independent Theatre's tour of *A Doll's House* and *Candida*	
1898			George Bernard Shaw marries
1898	June–July	ACT (Servant) with Stella (Mrs Patrick) Campbell in Maurice Maeterlinck, *Pelleas and Melisande*, Prince of Wales Theatre	
1898		Craig is sent to Paris to make prompt book of *Cyrano de Bergerac*	
1898			Holiday with Ellen Terry in Boulogne
1898		Craig possibly toured Africa with Cora Brown-Potter	
1899	Apr–July	ACT, COST (Mme de Lavergne) *Robespierre*, Lyceum	
1899	Autumn		Craig and St John live together at 7 Smith Square, London
1899	Dec	COSTM, *The Snow Man*, Lyceum	

	Work Events	Life Events
1900		Christopher St John publishes *The Crimson Weed*
1900 [Feb]	COSTD tableaux, 'The New Beauties' for Boer War charity	
1900 Mar–June	COSTD, COSTM Laurence Irving, *Bonnie Dundee*, Adelphi Theatre	
1900 May	COSTD, COSTM Miss Terry's dresses as Rosalind	
1900 1 July	ACT (Proserpine Garnett) George Bernard Shaw, *Candida*, Stage Society, Strand Theatre	
1900-5	Member, Council of Management, Stage Society	
1900 June–July	COST W. G. Wills, *Olivia*, Lyceum	
1900 Sept	COSTD, COSTM *Sweet Nell of Old Drury*, Haymarket Theatre	
[1901?]		Craig and St John cycle to Smallhythe Place to investigate property
1901 Apr	COST Cora Brown-Potter's dress *Nicandra*, Avenue Theatre	
1901 May–June	COST *The Sacrament of Judas*, Comedy Theatre	
1901 June	COST *Madame Sans Gene*, Lyceum	
1901 5 Oct	Article about Craig in the *Free Lance*	
1902 Jan	COST Paul Kester, *Mademoiselle Mars*, Imperial Theatre	
1902 Mar	COST John Gay, *Acis and Galatea*, Great Queen Street; Henry Purcell, *The Masque of Love*	
1902 Aug	COST Kendal celebration	
1902–3	SCDES with Pamela Colman Smith, W. B. Yeats, *Where There Is Nothing* and Synge's *The Well of the Saints*	
1902 Nov	ACT (Lady Muriel) Frederick Fenn, *A Married Woman*, Metropole Theatre, Camberwell	
1902		Edward Gordon Craig elopes with Elena Meo
1903 Jan	ACT Ibsen, *When We Dead Awaken*, Imperial Theatre, Stage Society	
1903	STAGE, ACT, COST (inc. *The Good Hope, The Vikings*) for Ellen Terry's productions at the Imperial Theatre	

		Work Events	Life Events
1903	Mar–Oct	The Masquers society is formed and disbanded without giving a performance	
1903–4 [?]			Relationship with Martin Shaw
1903-4	Dec–Jan	COST Philip Carr, *Snowdrop and Seven Little Men* and *Brer Rabbit and Brer Fox*, Royal Court	
1904			Edward Gordon Craig lives abroad; relationship with Isadora Duncan
1904			G. F. Watts dies
1905			Henry Irving dies
1905	Mar–May	COST Jean Richepin, *Du Barri*, trans. C. St John, Savoy Theatre	
1906	12 June	Ellen Terry jubilee matinee, Drury Lane	
1906	5 July	COST, Alix Egerton, *The Masque of the Princess*, Stafford House	
1907	15 Feb	Brooklyn newspaper story about Craig fining Terry for forgetting lines	
1907	June	Publishes article in *Munsey's Magazine*	
1907–9			Ellen Terry married to James Carew
1908	May–July	ACT George Bernard Shaw's *Getting Married*, Haymarket Theatre	
1908	July	DIR Christopher St John, *On the East Side*, Royal Court	
1908	Autumn	AFL formed	
1908			Ellen Terry, *The Story of My Life*, is published
1909	28 Mar	DIR Maurice Maeterlinck, *Sister Beatrice*, Royal Court	
1909	13 Apr	DIR Cicely Hamilton and Christopher St John, *How the Vote Was Won*, Royalty Theatre	
1909	15–17 Apr	SCDES & DIR Tableaux of Famous Women for WFL's Green White and Gold Fair, Caxton Hall	
1909	25 Oct	DIR *How the Vote Was Won*, Corn Exchange, Stratford-upon-Avon	
1909	12 Nov	DIR *A Pageant of Great Women*, Scala Theatre	
1909	11 Dec	DIR *A Pageant of Great Women*, Royal Albert Hall	

		Work Events	Life Events
		ACT (Mrs Brewster) *The Pot and the Kettle*	
1909	14 Dec	DIR Christopher St John, *The Wilson Trial*, Royal Court	
1910		DIR nationwide productions of *A Pageant of Great Women*	
1910	12 Mar	Interviewed by the *Vote*	
1910	June	DIR George Bernard Shaw, *Press Cuttings*, Rehearsal Theatre, Maiden Lane	
1911	8 May	DIR The Pioneer Players' first subscription performances: St John, *The First Actress*, Hamilton, *Jack and Jill and a Friend* and Nevinson, *In the Workhouse* (PP)	
1911	11 June	Ellen Terry performs Shakespeare's Triumphant Women, Garrick Theatre (PP)	
1911	26 Nov	DIR with the author, Laurence Housman, *Pains and Penalties*, Savoy Theatre (PP)	
1911	Nov		Appears in court as a witness in case against Sime Seruya for obstruction
1912	11 June	DIR Christopher St John, *The Pageant of the Stage*	
1912	3 Nov	DIR Herman Heijermans, *The Good Hope*, King's Hall, Covent Garden (PP)	
1912	13 & 15 Nov	DIR Charlotte Perkins Gilman, *Three Women*	
1912	29 Nov	DIR Christopher St John, *The First Actress*, Lyceum Theatre for AFL	
1913	Feb–Mar	Correspondence with Rosika Schwimmer, Seventh International Woman Suffrage Congress	
1913			Drowning of Edward Gordon Craig's child, Deirdre
1913			Death of housekeeper Boo Rumball
1913	Dec		Woman's Theatre opens at Coronet Theatre
1914	11–12 Jan	DIR Hrotsvit's *Paphnutius*, Savoy Theatre (PP)	
1914	Mar	ORG Pioneer Players' 'Mi-careme' ball	

		Work Events	Life Events
1914	29 June	COST Costume Dinner, Hotel Cecil for AFL and WWSL	
1914	Nov		AFL forms Women's Theatre Camps Entertainment
1915			Christopher St John's novel *Hungerheart* published anonymously
1915	5–8 Jan	DIR Father Cuthbert, *The Shepherds*, Westminster Cathedral Hall	
1915	7 Mar	DIR Nikolai Evreinov, *The Theatre of the Soul*, Little Theatre (PP)	
1915	2 May	DIR Paul Claudel, *Exchange*, Little Theatre (PP)	
1915	3 Dec	DIR Nikolai Evreinov, *The Theatre of the Soul*, Shaftesbury Theatre	
1916	6 Feb	DIR Marjorie Patterson, *Pan in Ambush*; Delphine Gray, *The Conference*, Royalty Theatre (PP)	
1916	2 Apr	DIR Gabrielle Enthoven and Edmund Goulding, *Ellen Young*, Savoy Theatre (PP); Radclyffe Hall, Mabel Batten and Una Troubridge attend	
1916	21 Apr	DIR Shakespeare Evening Entertainment at Shakespeare Hut	
1916	May/ June	DIR A Shakespeare Pageant, Drury Lane	
1916			Atwood moves in with St John and Craig
1916			Martin Shaw marries Jean Cobbold
1916		ACT with Ellen Terry in film, *Her Greatest Performance*	
1917	May	STAGE Chekhov, *The Wedding*, Grafton Galleries	
1917	13 May	DIR Gwen John, *Luck of War*, Kingsway Theatre (PP)	
1917	29 May	DIR Gwen Lally, *Pierrot Philanders*, Strand Theatre	
1917	10 June	DIR, SCDES Paul Claudel, *The Tidings Brought to Mary*, Strand Theatre (PP)	
1917	19 June	ACT Madame Clara Butt's Matinee for War Seal Foundation, Chiswick Empire	
1917	16 Dec	DIR with the author, Torahiko Kori, *Kanawa*	

		Work Events	Life Events
		DIR W. F. Casey, *Insurrection*, and George Bernard Shaw, *The Inca of Perusalem*, Criterion Theatre (PP)	
1918	6 Feb	Representation of the People Act extended to some women	
1918	17 Feb	DIR Pierre Louys and Pierre Frondaie, *The Girl and the Puppet*, Princes Theatre (PP)	
1918		ACT (Mary Rowntree) [STAGE?] in *The National Film* (aka *Victory and Peace* or *The Invasion of Britain*)	
1918	7–13 May	COST Louis N. Parker, *The Pageant of Freedom*, Queen's Hall, Langham Place	
1918	9 June	Attends a performance by The Plough society	
1918	July		J. T. Grein's production of Oscar Wilde's *Salome* in which Maud Allan appeared
1918	10 July	[DIR?] Charles Latour, *The Purple Mask*, Lyceum	
1919	13–14 Jan	STAGE *An Early English Nativity Play*, Rye Monastery	
1919	9 Feb	DIR Constance Holme, *The Home of Vision*, Miles Malleson, *The Artist*, Christopher St John, *Nell'Est*, and Susan Glaspell, *Trifles*, King's Hall, Covent Garden (PP)	
1919	23 Mar	DIR Paul Claudel, *The Hostage*, Scala Theatre (PP)	
1919	Aug	ORG Exhibition of Scenic Models, Stratford	British Drama League founded
1919	24 Nov	DIR Christopher St John and A. L. Ellis, *Just A Wife Or Two*, Brighton	
1919	23 Dec		Sydney Valentine dies
1919	Dec–Jan	DIR *Through the Crack*, Everyman Theatre, Hampstead	
1920		DIR several productions at the Everyman Theatre, Hampstead	
1920	25 Jan	DIR Chekhov, *The Wedding* and *On the High Road* St Martin's Theatre (PP)	
1920	11 Apr	DIR M. E. M. Young, *The Higher Court*, Strand Theatre (PP). Virginia Woolf reviews this for the *New Statesman*	

		Work Events	Life Events
1920	20 June	DIR Saint-Georges de Bouhélier, *The Children's Carnival*, Kingsway Theatre (PP)	
1920	25 Oct	Ninth Annual General Meeting of the Pioneer Players – resolution passed that the society should cease to exist	
1920	16 Nov	Craig is a member of the Ladies' Committee of the Sydney Valentine Memorial Matinee, Alhambra Theatre	
1920	Dec	DIR *An Old English Nativity Play*, Everyman Theatre	
1920	Dec–Jan	DIR *Through the Crack*, Everyman Theatre	
1921	Jan–Aug	DIR George Bernard Shaw plays at Everyman Theatre, Hampstead	
1921		ACT in film, *God in the Garden*	
1922	19–20 Mar	DIR John Dryden, *All for Love*, Shaftesbury Theatre for Phoenix Society	
1922	2 Apr	DIR Beatrice Mayor, *Thirty Minutes in a Street*, Kingsway Theatre	
1922	27 June	DIR her play, *The Shoe*, Palace Theatre	
1922	3–21 Oct	DIR Torahiko Kori, *The Toils of Yoshitomo*, Little Theatre	
1922	18–26 Dec	DIR *Through the Crack*, Apollo Theatre	
1923–4		DIR plays for the Everyman Theatre York and St Christopher's Theatre, Letchworth	
1923	18–20 Jan	DIR *York Nativity Play*, Guildhouse, London, League of Arts	
1923	8 Feb– 11 Apr	ACT in film, *Fires of Fate*, shot in Egypt and directed by Tom Terriss	
1923	24–5 June	DIR John Fletcher, *The Faithfull Shepherdess*, Shaftesbury Theatre for Phoenix Society	
1923	1 Sep– 16 Nov	DIR Arthur Richman, *Ambush*, Garrick Theatre for Theatre Guild London	
1924	7–26 Jan	DIR Hugo von Hofmannsthal, *The Great World Theatre*, St Edward's Church, Holbeck, Leeds for Leeds Art Theatre	
1924	24 Mar	DIR Arthur Richman, *Ambush*, Theatre Royal, Leeds	

		Work Events	Life Events
1924	29 Apr	DIR burlesque of *Ambush* and *Marion's Crime*, Leeds Art Theatre At Home, Scala Picture House, Leeds	
1924	19 June	DIR, ACT (policeman) entertainments, Castle Hall, Chilham, *Pan in Pimlico*	
1924–5		DIR for the St Christopher's Theatre, Letchworth (*Through the Crack, Mirandolina, The Fog on the Moor, The Young Person in Pink*)	
1925	5 Jan	DIR *An Old English Nativity Play*, Guildhall York for York Everyman Theatre	
1925	29 Mar	The Pioneer Players revived to perform Susan Glaspell's *The Verge*, Regent Theatre	
1925			Ellen Terry is made a DBE
1925	Oct	DIR John Webster, *The White Devil*, Scala Theatre for Renaissance Theatre Society	
1925	15 Dec	DIR ACT (First Monk) *An Old English Nativity Play*, Daly's Theatre	
1925	Dec–Jan	DIR Cicely Hamilton, *The Beggar Prince*, Q Theatre	
1927	24–6 Jan	DIR *Old English Nativity Play*, St Paul's Church, Covent Garden	
1927	30 Jan	DIR Mordaunt Shairp, *The Bend in the Road*, Apollo Theatre	
1927	1 Feb	DIR BESS show	
1927	7 Mar	DIR Ansky, *The Dybbuk*, Leeds	
1927	Mar–Nov	Adjudication work for BESS and BDL	
1927	1–3 Sep	DIR Lady Bell, *The History of the Carthusian Monks*, Mount Grace Priory Pageant, Northallerton	
1928	Jan	DIR *Marion's Crime*, Cave of Harmony	
1928	Apr-Sep	Works for the BDL at various day schools	
1928	21 July		Ellen Terry dies
1928	Nov		Radclyffe Hall's novel, *The Well of Loneliness*, prosecuted for obscene libel
1929	23 Apr		ORG matinee at Palace Theatre for Ellen Terry Memorial

		Work Events	Life Events
1929	21 July	DIR Ellen Terry Memorial performance, Barn Theatre	
1929	Dec		Recuperating in Swanage
1930	9 Feb	DIR Upton Sinclair, *Singing Jailbirds*, Apollo Theatre for Masses' Stage and Film Guild	
1930	May	DIR *Back to Methuselah* for Leeds Civic Playhouse	
1930		DIR *St Paul*, St Aidan's Church for Leeds Civic Playhouse	
1930			Vita Sackville-West lives at Sissinghurst, Kent
1930			Radclyffe Hall and Una Troubridge move to Rye, Kent
1930	Aug		Hall and Troubridge take tea at Smallhythe Place
1930	4 Dec	Lecture on Drama in Churches for Leeds Luncheon Club	
1931	5 Feb	DIR Jane Moorland, *The Other Side*, for Moorland Players, Church House, Wrexham	
1931	Mar	Interview with the *Vote*	
1931	8 Jun	Lays wreath at Mrs Siddons's centenary for BDL	
1931			Christopher St John edits *Correspondence*
1931			Edward Gordon Craig publishes *Ellen Terry and Her Secret Self*
1931	14 Oct	Craig places rosemary on Henry Irving's grave	
1931	26 Oct	Attends Colette, *Cheri*, first night, Prince of Wales Theatre	
1931	Oct	Craig attends the opening of the Eyebrow Club, Leeds Civic Playhouse	
1931			Christmas spent with Hall and Troubridge at Smallhythe Place and the Black Boy, Rye
1932	20 Jan	Craig attends reception in honour of Susan Glaspell at American Woman's Club, London	
1932	Feb–Apr	Adjudicator for BDL and BESS	
1932	Apr		Robinetta, Craig's adopted daughter, acts in school plays

		Work Events	Life Events
1932	Apr	Craig lectures on The Drama in Relation to Villages, Kent WI	
1932			Christmas at Bedford Street with Hall and Troubridge
1932–Oct 1933			St John's affair with Sackville-West
1933/5		Christopher St John and Edith Craig publish *Ellen Terry's Memoirs* (revised version of *The Story of My Life*)	
1933	Feb	British Theatrical Exhibition, Dudley House	
1933	28 Feb	Craig attends Forum Club luncheon in honour of Terry family	
1933	13 Mar	DIR H. A. Jones, *The Liars*, Garrick Theatre for charity	
1933	Mar	Adjudicator for WI	
1933	May	Lecture for WFL on Women's Work in the Theatre	
1933	May	Presents death mask and cast of Ellen Terry's hands at Shakespeare Memorial Library, Stratford	
1933	July–Aug	Patron, with Virginia Woolf and others, of the Commonwealth Theatre, Oxford which produced Fletcher, *The Faithfull Shepherdess*, Oxford Playhouse	
1934	Apr	Speaks at opening of The Players' Theatre Club, 43 King St, Covent Garden	
1934	Apr	Appointed as one of four Shute Lecturers for University of Liverpool	
1934	17 June	Invited to syllabub party by Elizabeth Robins and Octavia Wilberforce, Backsettown	
1934	June	Teaches amateurs at Cambridge Summer meeting	
1934	Nov	Adjudicator for WI	
1934	Dec	Presents prizes for BESS, Haymarket Theatre	
1934	Dec		Charles F. Smith directed *The Great World Theatre*, St Edward's Church, Holbeck, Leeds
1935	27 Feb	Speaks at Ellen Terry Festival Week, Civic Reception, Coventry	

		Work Events	Life Events
1935	28 Feb	Shute Lecture on The Performance of Plays, University of Liverpool	
1935	20 Apr	Adjudicator, South Wales finals, BDL one-act play festival, Mardy	
1935	3–4 July	DIR Tenterden Jubilee Pageant, Hales Place, Tenterden	
1935	July	DIR episodes from Tenterden Jubilee Pageant, garden fete, Great Maytham, Rolvenden	
1936	3 Mar	Lends costumes for RADA production, *The Good Hope*, Theatre Royal Haymarket	
1936	19 Apr	DIR Laurence Housman plays, Atwood makes props, Barn Theatre	
1936	11 Oct	Attends Drama Section Dinner, The Clans of the Theatre, Forum Club	
1936	2–5 Dec	DIR *The Merry Wives of Windsor*, County Theatre, Station Road, Ashford for Ashford Division, Conservative & Constitutional Association	
1937		President of the Servers of the Blind League	
1937	11 Jan	Lecture, Theatres Good and Bad, Cheltenham Art Gallery	
1937	31 Jan	DIR John Davison, *Wuthering Heights*, Little Theatre for New Shop Window Players	
1937	6 Feb	Speaks at the Glasgow Women's Citizen's Association dinner	
1937	Feb		On holiday, Lochearnhead recovering from (near-fatal) pneumonia
1937	9 Feb	Interview *Glasgow Bulletin*	
1937		ACT (Bennett's Secretary) in film, *Behind the Headlines*	
1937	June	ACT in film, *Heredity and Eugenics*, made by Gaumont-British Instructional Films and the Eugenics Society	
1938	May		James Lees-Milne for the National Trust visits Smallhythe Place
1938	14 Sep	Holds garden party for Kent Branch of English Speaking Union at Smallhythe Place	

		Work Events	Life Events
1938	30 Oct	Honoured by celebration dinner at the Savoy Theatre	
1938	Dec	Invited to AFL 30th birthday tea party at Grosvenor House	
1938	Dec	Press coverage of Craig's birthday	
1939			Gives Smallhythe Place to the National Trust
1939		Writes short piece for play programme, John Gielgud's production of *Hamlet*, Lyceum Theatre	
1940	Apr	Makes a codicil to her will	
1941			Virginia Woolf's suicide; posthumous publication of *Between the Acts*
1943	17–18 Aug	DIR *The Shoe* for charity at the town hall, Tenterden	
1944	27 May	Makes codicil to her will	
1945	Apr	Introduces parade of Ellen Terry's most famous stage costumes at Forever England production for St George's Day at White Rock Pavilion for Ellen Terry Memorial Museum	
1946	30 [Jan]	STAGE several plays inc. Cicely Hamilton, *Dear Edward*, Tenterden	
1946	5–6 July	DIR Chilham Pageant	
1947	27 Mar	Edith Craig dies at Priest's House, Smallhythe Place, Tenterden, Kent	
1948	June	Ellen Terry Fellowship founded	
1957	July	*A Festival for Edy*, Barn Theatre, Smallhythe Place, Tenterden, Kent	
1957		Edward Gordon Craig publishes *Index to the Story of My Days*	
1959		Christopher St John publishes her biography of Ethel Smyth	
1960		Christopher St John dies	
1963		Tony Atwood dies	
1966		Edward Gordon Craig dies	

Edith Craig's Productions of *A Pageant of Great Women*

1909	12 Nov	Scala Theatre
1909	11 Dec	Royal Albert Hall, for WFL
1910	5 May	Albert Hall, Swansea
1910	2–3 June	Devonshire Park Theatre, Eastbourne
1910	24 Sep	Public Hall, Beckenham
1910	10 Oct	Victoria Hall, Sunderland
1910	15 Oct	Albert Hall, Sheffield
1910	20 Oct	Public Hall, Ipswich for WFL
1910	26 Oct	Guildhall, Cambridge
1910	5 Nov	Prince's Theatre, Bristol for WSPU
1910	18 Nov	Aldwych, for AFL and WWSL
1911	4 May	Mechanics Large Hall, Nottingham (PP)
1912	2 Feb	Philharmonic Hall, Liverpool

Edith Craig's production of nativity plays

1915	5, 7–8 Jan	Westminster Cathedral Hall in aid of the Franciscan Hop Fields Mission (*The Shepherds* by Father Cuthbert)
[1918]	13–15 Feb	Wigmore Hall in aid of Women War Workers (*Early English Nativity Play*)
1919	13–14 Jan	Rye Monastery in aid of Borough Nursing Fund (*Early English Nativity Play*)
1920		Everyman Theatre, Hampstead (*Old English Nativity Play*)
1923	18–20 Jan	Guildhouse, League of Arts (*York Nativity Play*)
1924	3 & 5 Dec	Florence Etlinger Dramatic School (*York Nativity Play*)
1925	5 Jan	Guildhall, York (*An Old Nativity Play*)
1925	16 Dec	Daly's Theatre in aid of the Children's Country Holidays' Fund (*Old English Nativity Play*)
1927	Jan	St Paul's Church, Covent Garden (*Old English Nativity Play*)

Edith Craig's productions of *The Shoe*

[1922]	27 June	Palace Theatre for the Women's League of Service for Motherhood in aid of the Infant Welfare Centres
1923	16 Jan	King George's Hall, for the Women's League of Service for Motherhood
1932	27 July	Old Vicarage, Smallhythe Place, in aid of the repair of the school and for the general purposes' committee
1943	17–18 Aug	Town hall, Tenterden, in aid of the Tenterden and Halden District Nurse Fund

Edith Craig's pageant productions

1927	1–3 Sep	Mount Grace Pageant, Mount Grace Priory, Northallerton, Yorkshire
1935	3–4 July	Tenterden Jubilee Pageant, Hales Place, Tenterden (devised by Edith Craig and Edward Percy; written by Edward Percy)
1935	26 July	Scenes from Tenterden Pageant, Great Maytham, Rolvenden, for Church Restoration Fund
1946	5–6 July	Chilham Pageant (written by Somerset de Chair)

Edith Craig's film credits (date of release)

1916   *Her Greatest Performance* (The dresser)
1918   *The National Film/Invasion of Britain* (Mary Rowntree)
1921   *God in the Garden*
1924   *Fires of Fate* (Miss Adams)
1937   *Behind the Headlines* (Bennett's secretary)

Edith Craig's adjudication at drama festivals

BDL: British Drama League; WI: Women's Institute; BESS: British Empire Shakespeare Society

1924		London, for BESS
1924	8 Feb	Huddersfield
1925	9 July	Albert Hall, London
1927	12 & 14 Mar	Edinburgh and Glasgow for BESS
1927	Jun	Lewis
1927	15 Nov	BDL
1928	5–29 June	WI, Kent
1928	13 Aug	Summer School, Battle
1928	30 Aug	Shrewsbury School
1928	7–15 Sep	Newcastle School
1929	21 Jan	Southampton Musical Festival
1929	1 Aug	Fairlight School
1929	11 Oct	BDL
1932	19 Feb	Edinburgh Elocution Competition for BESS
1933	Feb	Cambridgeshire Rural Community Council for WI
1933	Mar	Sudbury Drama Festival, West Suffolk County for WI
1934	28 Nov	Folkestone, for East Kent Federation of WI
1934	29 Nov	Ashford for East Kent Federation of WI
1934	30 Nov	Canterbury for East Kent Federation of WI
1934	Dec	Prize Giving, for BESS, Haymarket Theatre, London

BIBLIOGRAPHY
A listing of all works cited
and selected further reading

Key: ECD = Edith Craig Archive.
  LCP = Lord Chamberlain's Play Collection, British Library.

Archives and Public Record Offices

Arncliffe Sennett Collection, British Library.
British Empire Shakespeare Society Records, Gloucestershire Record Office.
British Film Institute.
County Records, East Sussex County Council.
Cumbria Records Office.
Edith Craig Archive, Ellen Terry Memorial Museum, Tenterden, Kent.
Eleanor Adlard Papers, Gloucestershire Record Office.
Fawcett Library, London.
Gilbert Murray Papers, Bodleian Library, Oxford.
Lord Chamberlain's Play Collection, Manuscripts Dept., British Library.
Mander and Mitchenson Theatre Collection.
National Museums and Galleries on Merseyside.
Newspaper Library, Colindale, London.
Theatre Museum, London.

Unpublished Theses

Cockin, Katharine, 'The Pioneer Players (1911–25): A Cultural History', Ph.D. thesis, Department of English, Leicester University, 1994.
Gandolfi, Roberta, 'La Prima Regista: Le sfide di Edith Craig nel temp del suffragismo e della nuova arte scennica', Dipartimento di Musica e Spettacolo, Universita degli Studi di Bologna, 1995.
Heath, Mary T. 'A Crisis in the Life of the Actress: Ibsen in England', Ph.D. thesis, University of Massachusetts, 1986.
Holledge, Julie M., 'Women's Theatres – Women's Rights', Ph.D. thesis, Bristol University, 1985.
Marcus, Jane Connor, 'Elizabeth Robins', Ph.D. thesis, Northwestern University, 1973.
Watson, Mary Jane, 'The Independent Theatre in London 1891–1914', M.Litt. dissertation, University of Bristol, 1970.

Wolf, Laurie Jayne, 'Suffragettes of the Edwardian Theatre: Edith Craig and the Pioneer Players', Ph.D. thesis, University of California, Los Angeles, 1989.

Unpublished Documents

St John, Christopher, 'The Golden Book', MS University of California Los Angeles.
Edith Craig Scrapbooks, Ellen Terry Memorial Museum, Kent.
Pioneer Players' Scrapbook 1911–14, Theatre Museum, London.
Pioneer Players' Scrapbook 1914–18, privately owned.

Articles by Edith Craig

'The Progress of Stage Costume'; M13 ECD.
'Notes on the Costumes', *The Kensington*, nd, p. 139; G180 ECD.
'Producing a Play', *Munsey's Magazine*, June 1907, pp. 311–14.
'Make-up Secrets for Amateurs'; G115 ECD.

Interviews with Edith Craig

'The Making of Beautiful Dress: A Chat with Miss Edith Craig', unidentified, scrap album, E.V.6.4.5/5 ETMM.
'Miss Ellen Terry's Costumes in the New Play', *Morning Leader*, 14 April 1903.
Vote, 12 March 1910.
Votes for Women, 15 April 1910, p. 455.
'Little Interview: Miss Edith Craig at the Pioneer Players', *Pall Mall Gazette*, 13 April 1912, pp. 5, 12.
'Edith Craig – An Informal Interview', *Yorkshire Post*, 12 March; G174 ECD.
'Edith Craig on Amateur Dramatics', *New Era*, March 1931, pp. 78–80.
Vote, 31 March 1933; G109 ECD.
'Edith Craig Tells of Being Sacked on Stage', *Evening News*, 25 March 1938; G179 ECD.
'Her First Orchids', *Daily Sketch*, 10 December 1938; G161 ECD.

Primary Published Sources

Adlard, Eleanor (ed.), *Edy: Recollections of Edith Craig* (London: Frederick Muller, 1949).
Auerbach, Nina, *Ellen Terry: Player in Her Time* (London: Phoenix House, 1987).
Baker, Michael, *Our Three Selves: The Life of Radclyffe Hall* (London: Hamish Hamilton, 1985).
Cockin, Katharine, 'New Light on Edith Craig', *Theatre Notebook*, XLV.3, 1991, pp. 132–43.
Cockin, Katharine, 'The Good Hope', *International Dictionary of Theatre: Plays Volume 1* (Chicago and London: St James' Press, 1992), pp. 296–7.
Cockin, Katharine, 'The Pioneer Players: Plays of/with Identity', in Gabriele Griffin (ed.), Difference in View: Women and Modernism (London: Taylor & Francis, 1994), pp. 142–54.

Cockin, Katharine, 'Cicely Hamilton', in Pamela Kester-Shelton (ed.), *Feminist Writers* (London: St James's Press, 1996), pp. 218–20.

Cockin, Katharine, 'Women's Suffrage Drama', in Maroula Joannou and June Purvis (eds), *New Feminist Essays in Women's Suffrage* (Manchester: Manchester University Press, 1997), pp. 110–22.

Cockin, Katharine, *The Pioneer Players: From Women's Suffrage to Art Theatre* (Basingstoke: Macmillan, forthcoming).

Collis, Rose, *Portraits to the Wall: Historic Lesbian Lives Unveiled* (London: Cassell, 1994).

Craig, Edith and Christopher St John (eds), *Ellen Terry's Memoirs* (London: Gollancz, 1933).

Craig, Edward Gordon, *Ellen Terry and Her Secret Self* (London: Sampson Low, Marston & Co., 1931).

Craig, Edward Gordon, *Index to the Story of My Days* (London: Hulton Press, 1957).

Craig, Edward Gordon, *On the Art of the Theatre* (Edinburgh and London: T. N. Foulis, 1905).

Despard, Charlotte, *Woman in the New Era* (London: Suffrage Shop, 1910).

Dymkowski, Christine, 'Entertaining Ideas: Edy Craig and the Pioneer Players', in Viv Gardner and Susan Rutherford (eds), *The New Woman and Her Sisters: Feminism and Theatre 1850–1914* (Hemel Hempstead: Harvester Wheatsheaf, 1992).

Elliman, Michael and Frederick Roll, *Pink Plaque Guide to London* (London: GMP, 1986).

Gielgud, Kate Terry, *An Autobiography* (London: Max Reinhardt, 1953).

Graham-Robertson, W., *Time Was* (London: Hamish Hamilton, 1931).

Hamilton, Cicely, *Marriage as a Trade* (London: Chapman & Hall, 1909).

Holledge, Julie, *Innocent Flowers: Women in the Edwardian Theatre* (London: Virago, 1981).

Lees-Milne, James, *People and Places: Country House Donors and the National Trust* (London: John Murray, 1992).

Manvell, Roger, *Ellen Terry* (London: Heinemann, 1968).

Marcus, Jane, 'Some Sources for *Between the Acts*', *A Virginia Woolf Miscellany*, 6, winter 1977, pp. 1–3.

Melville, Joy, *Ellen and Edy* (London: Pandora Press, 1987).

Richards, Dell, *Lesbian Lists* (London: Alysom, 1990).

Sinden, Donald, *A Touch of the Memoirs* (London: Hodder & Stoughton, 1982).

Sinden, Donald, *Laughter in the Second Act* (London: Hodder & Stoughton, 1985).

Smith, Edward Percy, *Remember Ellen Terry and Edith Craig* (London: English Theatre Guild, 1948).

St John, Christopher, *Henry Irving* (London: Green Sheaf, 1905).

St John, Christopher, *Ellen Terry* (London: John Lane, 1907).

St John, Christopher, 'Mrs Despard: An Impression' in *Charlotte Despard, Woman in the New Era* (London: Suffrage Shop, 1910).

[St John, Christopher], *Hungerheart* (London: Methuen, 1915) (published anonymously).

St John, Christopher, *Ellen Terry: A Short Biography* (London: The Pelican Press, 1947).

St John, Christopher (ed.), *Ellen Terry and Bernard Shaw: A Correspondence* (London: Constable & Co., 1931).

St John, Christopher, (ed.), *Ellen Terry: Four Lectures on Shakespeare* (London: Martin Hopkinson, 1932).

Steen, Marguerite, *A Pride of Terrys* (London: Longmans, 1962).

Terry, Ellen, *The Story of My Life* (London: Hutchinson, 1908).

Thomas, Anthony, *The Story of the Barn Theatre 1929–1989* (Stone-in-Oxney: Anthony Thomas, 1989).

Webster, Margaret, *The Same Only Different: Five Generations of a Great Theatre Family* (London: Gollancz, 1969).

Woolf, Virginia, 'Ellen Terry', in Rachel Bowlby (ed.), *The Crowded Dance of Modern Life* (Harmondsworth: Penguin, 1993).

Woolf, Virginia, *The Essays of Virginia Woolf Volume I 1904–1918*, ed. Andrew McNeillie (London: Hogarth Press, 1995).

Woolf, Virginia, *The Essays of Virginia Woolf Volume III 1919–1924*, ed. Andrew McNeillie (London: Hogarth Press, 1988).

Fiction

Hall, Radclyffe, *The Unlit Lamp*, 1924 (London: Virago Press, 1986).

Hall, Radclyffe, *The Well of Loneliness*, 1928 (London: Virago, 1987).

Hichens, Robert, *The Green Carnation*, 1894 (London: William Heinemann, 1901).

Smith, Pamela Colman, *Annancy Stories* (New York: R. H. Russell, 1899).

Smith, Pamela Colman, *The Golden Vanity and the Green Bed* (New York: Doubleday and McClure, 1899).

Smith, Pamela Colman, *Widdicombe Fair* (New York: Doubleday and McClure, 1899).

St John, Christopher, *The Crimson Weed* (London: Duckworth, 1900).

Stoker, Bram, *Dracula*, 1897 (Harmondsworth: Penguin, 1994).

Stoker, Bram, *The Jewel of the Seven Stars*, 1903 (Oxford: Oxford University Press, 1996).

Woolf, Virginia, *Between the Acts*, 1941 (London: Hogarth Press, 1992).

Drama

Unpublished Plays

Claudel, Paul, 'Exchange', prompt copy; ECD.

Claudel, Paul, 'The Tidings Brought to Mary', prompt copy; ECD.

De Bouhélier, Saint-Georges, 'The Children's Carnival', prompt copy; ECD.

Fenn, Frederick, 'A Married Woman'; LCP ADD MSS J.53691.

Gilman, Charlotte Perkins, 'Three Women'; prompt copy; ECD.

Gray, Delphine, 'The Conference'; prompt copy; ECD.

Meuron, Margaret Nilior, 'The Masque of Women'; H4 ECD.

St John, Christopher, 'Erikson's Wife'; LCP ADD MSS 1904/20.

St John, Christopher, 'Her Will'; LCP ADD MSS 1914/14.

St John, Christopher, 'Macrena'; ECD.

St John, Christopher, 'What a Plague Is Love'; ECD.

St John, Christopher, 'The Wilson Trial'; LCP ADD MSS 1909.

Vaun, Russell, 'Nicandra'; LCP ADD MSS F.53662.

Webster, Margaret, 'A Festival for Edy'; ECD.

Published Plays

Dane, Clemence, *Eighty in the Shade* (London: Heinemann, 1959).

Evreinov, Nikolai, *The Theatre of the Soul: A Monodrama in One Act*, trans. Marie Potapenko and Christopher St John (London: Hendersons, 1915).

Fitzsimmons, Linda and Viv Gardner (eds), *New Woman Plays* (London: Methuen, 1991).

Gardner, Viv (ed.), *Sketches from the Actresses' Franchise League* (Nottingham: Nottingham Drama Texts, 1985).

Glaspell, Susan, *Trifles* (New York: Frank Shay, 1916).

Glaspell, Susan, *The Verge* (Boston: Small Mayward, 1922).

Hamilton, Cicely, *A Pageant of Great Women* (London: The Suffrage Shop, 1910).

Hamilton, Cicely, *Jack and Jill and a Friend* (London: Lacy's Acting Edition, 1911).

Heijermans, Herman, *The Good Hope: A Play in Four Acts*, trans. Christopher St John (London: Hendersons, 1921).

Hobson, Florence Edgar, *A Modern Crusader* (London: A. C. Fifield, 1912).

Holme, Constance, *The Home of Vision*, in *Four One-Act Plays* (London: Kirkby Lonsdale, 1932).

Housman, Laurence, *Bethlehem* (London: Macmillan, 1902).

Housman, Laurence, *Pains and Penalties* (London: Sidgwick & Jackson, 1911).

Hrotsvit, *Paphnutius*, in *The Plays of Roswitha*, trans. Christopher St John (London: Chatto & Windus, 1923).

John, Gwen, *Luck of War* (London and Glasgow: Repertory Plays, 1922).

Kori, Torahiko, *The Toils of Yoshitomo: A Tragedy of Ancient Japan* (London: Selwyn & Blount, 1922).

Kori, Torahiko, *Kanawa: The Incantation*, in *Fifty One-Act Plays*, ed. Constance M. Martin (London: Gollancz, 1934).

Nevinson, Margaret Wynne, *In the Workhouse* (London: International Suffrage Shop, 1911).

Patterson, Marjorie, *Pan in Ambush* (Baltimore: Norman Remington, 1921).

Spender, Dale and Carol Hayman (eds), *How the Vote Was Won and Other Suffragette Plays* (London and New York: Methuen, 1985).

St John, Christopher, *The First Actress* (London: Utopia Press, nd).

Woolf, Virginia, *Freshwater*, ed. Lucio P. Ruotolo (London: Hogarth Press, 1976).

Yeats, W. B. *Where There is Nothing: Being Volume One of Plays for an Irish Theatre* (London: A. H. Bullen, 1903).

Young, M. E. M., *The Higher Court* (London: Burns Oates & Wishbourne, 1931).

Selective Secondary Reading

Autobiographies of Edith Craig's Contemporaries

Ashwell, Lena, *Modern Troubadours: A Record of the Concerts at the Front* (London: Gyldenhall, 1922).

Ashwell, Lena, *Myself a Player* (London: Michael Joseph, 1936).

Asquith, Lady Cynthia, *The Diaries of Lady Cynthia Asquith 1915–18* (London: Century Hutchinson, 1987).

Carpenter, Edward, *My Days and Dreams: Being Autobiographical Notes* (London: George Allen & Unwin, 1918).

Cochran, C. B., *Showman Looks On* (London: J. M. Dent & Sons, 1945).

Duncan, Isadora, *Isadora: My Life*, 1928 (London: Sphere Books, 1988).

Fyfe, H. Hamilton, *My Seven Selves* (London: George Allen & Unwin, 1935).

Hamilton, Cicely, *Life Errant* (London: J. M. Deutsch, 1935).

Housman, Laurence, *The Unexpected Years* (London: Jonathan Cape, 1937).

Jerome, Jerome K. *My Life and Times* (New York and London: Harper and Brothers Publishers, 1926).

Kingston, Gertrude, *Curtesy While You're Thinking* (London: Williams & Norgate, 1937).

Knoblock, Edward, *Around the Room: An Autobiography* (London: Chapman & Hall, 1939).

Lanchester, Elsa, *Charles Laughton and I* (London: Faber & Faber, 1938).

Malleson, Elizabeth, *Elizabeth Malleson 1828–1916: Autobiographical Notes and Letters with a Memoir by Hope Malleson* (privately printed, 1926).

Moore, Eva, *Exits and Entrances* (London: Chapman & Hall, 1923).

Morris, Margaret, *Margaret Morris Dancing* (London: Kegan Paul, Trench, Trubner & Co., 1925).

Morris, Margaret, *My Galsworthy Story* (London: Peter Owen, 1967).

Nesbitt, Cathleen, *A Little Love and Good Company* (London: Faber & Faber, 1975).

Nevinson, Margaret Wynne, *Fragments of Life* (London: George Allen & Unwin, 1922).

Nevinson, Margaret Wynne, *Life's Fitful Fever: A Volume of Memories* (London: A & C Black, 1926).

Rhondda, Viscountess, *This Was My World* (London: Macmillan, 1933).

Shaw, Martin, *Up To Now* (London: Oxford University Press, 1929).

Warrender, Lady Maud, *My First Sixty Years* (London: Cassell, 1933).

Wilberforce, Octavia, *Octavia Wilberforce: The Autobiography of a Pioneer Woman Doctor*, ed. Pat Jalland (London: Cassell, 1989).

Woolf, Virginia, *The Diary of Virginia Woolf: Volume I 1915–1919* (London: Hogarth Press, 1977).

Woolf, Virginia, *The Diary of Virginia Woolf Volume II 1920–1924* (London: Hogarth Press, 1978).

Woolf, Virginia, *The Diary of Virginia Woolf Volume IV 1931–1935* (London: Hogarth Press, 1982).

Letters

Craig, Edward, (ed.), *Edward Gordon Craig: The Last Eight Years 1958–1966 Letters from Ellen Gordon Craig* (Andoversford, Glos.: The Whittington Press, 1983).

Hart-Davis, Rupert (ed.), *Letters of Max Beerbohm 1892–1956* (Oxford: Oxford University Press, 1989).

Kelly, John and Ronald Schuchard (eds), *The Collected Letters of W. B. Yeats: Volume 3 1901-1904* (Oxford: Clarendon Press, 1994).

Nicholson, Nigel (ed.), *The Sickle Side of the Moon. The Letters of Virginia Woolf Volume V: 1932–1935* (London: Hogarth Press, 1979).

Nicholson, Nigel (ed.), *Leave the Letters Till We're Dead. The Letters of Virginia Woolf Volume VI: 1936–1941* (London: Hogarth Press, 1980).

Biographies of/by Edith Craig's Contemporaries

Albanesi, E. M., *Meggi Albanesi* (London: Hodder & Stoughton, nd).

Belford, Barbara, *Bram Stoker: A Biography of the Author of* Dracula (London: Weidenfeld & Nicolson, 1996).

Blair, Frederika, *Isadora: Portrait of the Artist as a Woman* (Wellingborough, Northamptonshire: Equation, 1986).

Blunt, Wilfrid, *Lady Muriel* (London: Methuen, 1962).

Casson, John, *Lewis and Sybil: A Memoir* (London: Collins, 1972).

Cline, Sally, *Radclyffe Hall: A Woman Called John* (London: John Murray, 1997).

Collenbrander, Joanna, *A Portrait of Fryn: A Portrait of F. Tennyson Jesse* (London: Andre Deutsch, 1984).

Devlin, Diana, *A Speaking Part: Lewis Casson and the Theatre of His Time* (London: Hodder & Stoughton, 1982).

Douglas-Home, Jessica, *Violet: The Life and Loves of Violet Gordon Woodhouse* (London: Harvill Press, 1996).

Engen, Rodney, *Laurence Housman* (Stroud, Gloucestershire: Catalpa Press, 1983).

Farson, Daniel, *The Man Who Wrote* Dracula: *A Biography of Bram Stoker* (London: Michael Joseph, 1975).

Field, Andrew, *Djuna: The Life and Times of Djuna Barnes* (New York: G. P. Putnam & Sons, 1983).

Glendinning, Victoria, *Vita: The Life of Vita Sackville-West* (Harmondsworth: Penguin, 1984).

Glendinning, Victoria, *Rebecca West: A Life* (London: Papermac, 1988).

Harwood, Ronald, *Sir Donald Wolfit: His Life and Work in the Unfashionable Theatre* (Oxford: Amber Lane Press, 1983).

Hingley, Ronald, *A Life of Chekhov* (Oxford: Oxford University Press, 1989).

Holmes, Marion, 'Concerning Muriel Matters', *Vote*, 19 February 1910, p. 196.

Holroyd, Michael, *Bernard Shaw Volumes 1–3* (London: Chatto & Windus, 1988, 1989, 1990).

Irving, Laurence, *The Successors* (London: Rupert Hart-Davis, 1967).

John, Angela V., *Elizabeth Robins: Staging a Life 1862–1952* (London: Routledge, 1995).

Lee, Hermione, *Virginia Woolf* (London: Chatto & Windus, 1996).

Morley, Ann and Lis Stanley (eds), *The Life and Death of Emily Wilding Davison: A Biographical Detective Story* (London: Women's Press, 1988).

Mulvihill, Margaret, *Charlotte Despard: A Biography* (London: Pandora Press, 1989).

Oldfield, Sybil, *Spinsters of This Parish: The Life and Times of F.M. Mayor and Mary Sheepshanks* (London: Virago, 1984).

Orme, Michael, *J. T. Grein: The Story of a Pioneer 1862–1935* (London: John Murray, 1936).

Pethick Lawrence, Emmeline, *My Part in a Changing World* (London: Gollancz, 1938).

Price, Nancy, *Into an Hour Glass* (London: Museum Press, 1953).

Rollinson, Edward, *Sydney Valentine (1865–1919): An Actor's Actor* (Harefield, Middlesex: Sarratt Publishers, 1996).

St John, Christopher, *Christine Murrell, MD: Her Life and Work* (London: Williams & Norgate, 1935).

Stinchcombe, Owen, *Elizabeth Malleson 1828–1916: Pioneer of Rural District Nursing*, 1989 (Held at Gloucestershire Records Office).

Stokes, John, Michael Booth and Susan Bassnett, *Bernhardt, Terry, Duse: The Actress in Her Time* (Cambridge: Cambridge University Press, 1988).
Whitelaw, Lis, *The Life and Rebellious Times of Cicely Hamilton* (London: Women's Press, 1990).

Theatre—History

Ashwell, Lena, *Modern Troubadours: A Record of the Concerts at the Front* (London: Gyldenhall, 1922).
Baker, Michael, *The Rise of the Victorian Actor* (London: Croom Helm, 1978).
Chapman, Wayne K., 'Yeats's "Theatre of Beauty" and the Masque Tradition', *Yeats: An Annual of Critical and Textual Studies*, VII, 1989, pp. 42–56.
Clark, Ian, *Edwardian Drama: A Critical Study* (London: Faber & Faber, 1989).
Davies, Andrew, *Other Theatres: The Development of Alternative Experimental Theatre in Britain* (London: Macmillan, 1987).
De Jongh, Nicholas, *Not in Front of the Audience: Homosexuality on Stage* (London: Routledge, 1992).
Findlater, Richard, *Banned! A Review of Theatrical Censorship in Britain* (London: MacGibbon & Kee, 1967).
Guy, Josephine M. *The British Avant-Garde: The Theory and Politics of Tradition* (Hemel Hempstead: Harvester Wheatsheaf, 1991).
Hamilton, Cicely and Lilian Baylis, *The Old Vic* (London: Jonathan Cape, 1926).
Innes, Christopher, *Modern British Drama 1890–1990* (Cambridge: Cambridge University Press, 1992).
Innes, Christopher, *Avant-Garde Theatre 1892–1992* (London: Routledge, 1993).
Knowles, Dorothy, *The Censor, the Drama and the Film 1900–1934* (London: George Allen & Unwin 1934).
MacDermott, Norman, *Everymania: The History of the Everyman Theatre, Hampstead 1920–26* (London: Society for Theatre Research, 1975).
Macleod, Joseph, *The Actor's Right to Act* (London: Lawrence & Wishart, 1981).
Marshall, Norman, *The Other Theatre* (London: John Lehmann, 1947).
McDonald, Jan, *The 'New Drama' 1900–1914* (London: Macmillan, 1986).
Payne, Ben Iden, *A Life in a Wooden O: Memoirs of the Theatre* (New Haven and London: Yale University Press, 1977).
Pogson, Rex, *Miss Horniman and the Gaiety Theatre* (Manchester and London: Rockliff, 1952).
Roose-Evans, James, *Experimental Theatre from Stanislavsky to Peter Brook* (London: Routledge & Kegan Paul, 1989).
Samuel, Raphael, Ewan MacColl and Stuart Cosgrove, *Theatres of the Left 1880–1935: Workers' Theatre Movements in Britain and America* (London: Routledge & Kegan Paul, 1985).
Schoonderwoerd, N. J. T. *Grein Ambassador of the Theatre 1862–1935: A Study in Anglo-Continental Theatrical Relations* (Assen: Von Gorcum, 1963).
Schuchard, Ronald, 'W. B. Yeats and the London Theatre Societies 1901–1904', *Review of English Studies*, XXIX, 1978, pp. 415–46.
Steele, Tom, *Alfred Orage and the Leeds Art Club 1893–1923* (Aldershot, Hampshire: Scolar Press, 1990).
Stokes, John, *Resistible Theatres: Enterprise and Experiment in the Late Nineteenth Century* (London: Paul Elk Books, 1972).

Trewin, J. C. and Wendy Trewin, *The Arts Theatre, London* (London: Society for Theatre Research, 1986).

Wade, Allan, *Memories of the London Theatre 1900–1914*, (ed.) Alan Andrews (London: Society for Theatre Research, 1983).

Wearing, J. P., *The London Stage [1890 Onwards]* (Metuchen, NJ and London: The Scarecrow Press).

Whitworth, Geoffrey, *The Making of a National Theatre* (London: Faber & Faber, 1961).

Woodfield, James, *English Theatre in Transition 1881–1914* (London: Croom Helm, 1984).

Wyckham, Glynn, *A History of the Theatre* (Oxford: Phaidon, 1985).

Women–Feminism–Theatre

Ashwell, Lena, *Reflections from Shakespeare*, ed. Roger Pocock (London: Hutchinson, nd).

Aston, Elaine, *An Introduction to Feminism and Theatre* (London: Routledge, 1995).

Case, Sue-Ellen, *Feminism and Theatre* (London: Macmillan, 1988).

Cockin, Katharine, *The Pioneer Players: From Women's Suffrage to Art Theatre*, forthcoming (Basingstoke: Macmillan, 1998).

Davis, Tracy, *Actresses as Working Women: Their Social Identity in Victorian Culture* (London: Routledge, 1991).

[Dorynne, Jess], *The True Ophelia: And Other Studies of Shakespeare's Women* (London: Sidgwick & Jackson, 1913) (published anonymously).

Ferris, Lesley, *Acting Women: Images of Women in the Theatre* (London: Macmillan, 1990).

Gardner, Viv and Susan Rutherford (eds), *The New Woman and Her Sisters: Feminism and Theatre 1850–1914* (Hemel Hempstead: Harvester Wheatsheaf, 1992).

Gilder, Rosamund, *Enter the Actress: The First Women in the Theatre* (London: George G. Harrap, 1931).

Goodman, Lizbeth, *Contemporary Feminist Theatres: To Each Her Own* (London: Routledge, 1993).

Howe, Elizabeth, *The First English Actresses 1660–1700* (Cambridge: Cambridge University Press, 1992).

Keyssar, Helene, *Feminist Theatre: An Introduction To Plays of Contemporary British and American Women* (London: Macmillan, 1984).

Macqueen-Pope, Walter, *Ladies First* (London: Allen, 1952).

Morris, Margaret, *The Notation of Movement: Text, Drawings and Annotations* (London: Kegan Paul, Trench, Trubner & Co., 1928).

Phelan, Peggy, *Unmarked: The Politics of Performance* (London: Routledge, 1993).

Richards, Susan, *The Rise of the English Actress* (London: Macmillan, 1993).

Stowell, Sheila, *A Stage of Their Own: Feminist Playwrights of the Suffrage Era* (Ann Arbor: University of Michigan Press, 1992).

Terry, Ellen, *Four Lectures on Shakespeare*, ed. Christopher St John (London: Martin Hopkinson, 1932).

Wandor, Michelene, *Understudies: Theatre and Sexual Politics* (London: Eyre Methuen, 1981).

Women–History–Suffrage

A. J. R. (ed.), *The Suffrage Annual and Women's Who's Who* (London: Stanley Paul & Co., 1913).

Bock, Gisela and Susan James (eds), *Beyond Equality and Difference* (London: Routledge, 1992).

Brown-Potter, Cora, *The Love of the Incas* (London: The Orient Press Service, nd).

Davidoff, Leonora and Catherine Hall, *Family Fortunes: Men and Women of the English Middle Class 1780–1850* (London: Macmillan, 1996).

Dobbie, B. Wilmott, *A Nest of Suffragettes in Somerset* (Batheaston, Avon: The Batheaston Society, 1979).

Dodd, Kathryn (ed.), *The Sylvia Pankhurst Reader* (Manchester: Manchester University Press, 1993).

Fraser, Flora, *The Unruly Queen: The Life of Queen Caroline* (London: Macmillan, 1996).

Garner, Les, *Stepping Stones to Women's Liberty: Feminist Ideas in the Women's Suffrage Movement* (London: Heinemann Educational, 1984).

Hirschfield, Claire, 'The Actresses' Franchise League and the Campaign for Women's Suffrage', *Theatre Research International*, 10.2, 1985, pp. 129–53.

Holton, Sandra Stanley, *Suffrage Days* (London: Routledge, 1996).

Joannou, Maroula and June Purvis (eds), *New Feminist Essays on Women's Suffrage* (Manchester: Manchester University Press, 1997).

John, Angela V. and Claire Eustance (eds), *The Men's Share? Masculinities, Male Support and Women's Suffrage in Britain 1890–1920* (London: Routledge, 1997).

Kent, Susan Kingsley, *Sex and Suffrage in Britain 1860–1914* (London: Routledge, 1990).

Kohn, Marek, *Dope Girls: The Birth of the British Drug Underground* (London: Lawrence & Wishart, 1992).

Lesbian History Group, *Not a Passing Phase: Reclaiming Lesbians in History 1840–1985* (London: The Women's Press, 1989).

Liddington, Jill and Jill Norris, *One Hand Tied Behind Us: The Rise of the Women's Suffrage Movement* (London: Virago Press, 1984).

Malleson, Mrs Frank (Elizabeth), *Notes on the Early Training of Children* (London: W. Swan Sonnenschein & Co., 1854).

Melman, Billie, *Women and the Popular Imagination in the Twenties: Flappers and Nymphs* (London: Macmillan, 1988).

Owen, Alex, *The Darkened Room: Women, Power and Spiritualism in Late Victorian England* (London: Virago, 1989).

Owens, Rosemary Cullen, *Smashing Times: A History of the Irish Women's Suffrage Movement 1889–1992* (Dublin: Attic Press, 1984, reprint 1995).

Pankhurst, E. Sylvia, *The Suffragette Movement: An Intimate Account of Persons and Ideals* (London: Longman, Green & Co., 1931).

Parsons, Melinda Boyd, 'Mysticism in London: The "Golden Dawn": Synaesthesia and "Psychic Automatism" in the Art of Pamela Colman Smith', in Kathleen J. Regier (ed.), *The Spiritual Image in Modern Art* (London: The Theosophical Publishing House, 1987).

Purvis, June, *Hard Lessons: The Lives and Education of Working-Class Women in Nineteenth-Century England* (Cambridge: Polity Press, 1989).

Rubinstein, David, *Before the Suffragettes: Women's Emancipation in the 1890s* (Sussex: Harvester, 1986).

St John, Christopher, *A Little Book of Polish Saints* (London: Burns & Oates, 1918).

Stoker, Bram, *Famous Imposters* (London: Sidgwick & Jackson, 1910).

Strachey, Ray, *The Cause: A Short History of the Women's Movement in Great Britain* (London: Virago, 1978).

Taylor, Barbara, *Eve and the New Jerusalem: Socialism and Feminism in the Nineteenth Century* (London:Virago, 1983).

Taylor, Rosemary, *In Letters of Gold: The Story of Sylvia Pankhurst and the East London Suffragettes in Bow* (London: Stepney Books, 1993).

Thompson, Paul, *The Edwardians: The Remaking of British Society* (London:Weidenfeld & Nicolson, 1975).

Tickner, Lisa, *The Spectacle of Women: Imagery of the Suffrage Campagin 1907–14* (London: Chatto & Windus, 1987).

Vicinus, Martha, *A Widening Sphere: Changing Roles of Victorian Women* (Bloomington and London: Indiana University Press, 1977).

Vicinus, Martha, *Independent Women: Work and Community for Single Women 1850–1920* (London: Virago, 1985).

Wheelwright, Julie, *Amazons and Military Maids: Women Who Dressed as Men in Pursuit of Life, Liberty and Happiness* (London: Pandora Press, 1989).

Wheelwright, Julie, *The Fatal Lover: Mata Hari and the Myth of Women in Espionage* (London: Collins & Brown, 1992).

Williams, Raymond, *The Country and the City* (London: Hogarth Press, 1973, 1993).

Gender–Culture–Modernism

Baldick, Chris, *The Social Mission of English Criticism 1848–1932* (Oxford: Oxford University Press, 1983).

Battersby, Christine, *Gender and Genius: Towards a Feminist Aesthetics* (London: Women's Press, 1989).

Bradbury, Malcolm and James McFarlane (eds), *Modernism: A Guide to European Literature 1890-1930* (Harmondsworth: Penguin, 1991).

Clark, Suzanne, *Sentimental Modernism:Women Writers and the Revolution of the World* (Indiana: Indiana University Press, 1991).

Colls, Robert and Philip Dodd (eds), *Englishness: Politics and Culture 1880–1920* (London: Croom Helm, 1986).

Gilbert, Sandra and Susan Gubar, *No Man's Land Volume 1–2* (New Haven and London: Yale University Press, 1984, 1988).

Gillespie, Diane T. 'Virginia Woolf's Last Struggle Against Masculine Values', *Women and Literature*, 5, 1977, pp. 38–46.

Girouard, Mark, *The Return to Camelot: Chivalry and the English Gentleman* (London: Yale University Press, 1981).

Griffin, Gabriele, (ed.), *Difference in View: Women and Modernism* (London: Taylor & Francis, 1994).

Hennessy, Rosemary, *Materialist Feminism and the Politics of Discourse* (London: Routledge, 1993).

Humm, Maggie, *Border Traffic: Strategies of Contemporary Women Writers* (Manchester: Manchester University Press, 1991).

Joannou, Maroula, *'Ladies, Please Don't Smash These Windows': Women's Writing, Feminist Consciousness and Social Change 1918–38* (Oxford and Providence, RI: Berg, 1995).

Light, Alison, *Forever England: Femininity, Literature and Conservatism Between the Wars* (London: Routledge, 1991).

Melman, Billie, *Women's Orients: English Women and the Middle East 1718–1918: Sexuality, Religion and Work* (London: Macmillan, 1992).

Miller, Jane Eldridge, *Rebel Women: Feminism, Modernism and the Edwardian Novel* (London: Virago, 1994).

Raitt, Suzanne, *Vita and Virginia: The Work and Friendship of V. Sackville-West and V. Woolf* (Oxford: Clarendon Press, 1993).

Roberts, Alison, *Hathor Rising: The Serpent Power of Ancient Egypt* (Totnes, Devon: Northgate Publishers, 1995).

Robins, Gay, *Women in Ancient Egypt* (London: British Museum Press, 1993).

Rowbotham, Sheila, *Hidden from History: 300 Years of Women's Oppression and the Fight Against It* (London: Pluto Press, 1973).

Showalter, Elaine, *Sexual Anarchy: Gender and Culture at the Fin de Siècle* (London: Bloomsbury Publishing, 1991).

Williams, Raymond, *Culture* (London: Fontana, 1983).

Williams, Raymond, 'The Bloomsbury Fraction', in *Problems in Materialism and Culture: Selected Essays* (London: Verso, 1989).

Wilson, Elizabeth, *Adorned in Dreams: Fashion and Modernity* (London: Virago, 1985).

Wolff, Janet, *Feminine Sentences: Essays on Women and Culture* (Cambridge: Polity Press, 1990).

Auto/biography and Representation

Auchmuty, Rosemary, 'By Their Friends Shall We Know Them: The Lives and Networks of Some Women in North Lambeth, 1880–1940', in Lesbian History Group, *Not a Passing Phase: Reclaiming Lesbians in History 1840–1985* (London: The Women's Press, 1989).

Barrett, Michele, 'Feminism and the Definition of Cultural Politics', in Rosalind Brunt and Caroline Rowan (eds), *Feminism, Culture and Politics* (London: Lawrence & Wishart, 1982).

Batchelor, John (ed.), *The Art of Literary Biography* (Oxford: Oxford University Press, 1995).

Berger, John, *Ways of Seeing* (Harmondsworth: Penguin, 1972).

Chadwick, Whitney and Isabelle de Courtivron (eds), *Significant Others: Creativity and Intimate Partnership* (London: Thames & Hudson, 1993).

Gilbert, Sandra and Susan Gubar, 'Is the Pen a Metaphorical Penis?', in Catherine Belsey and Jane Moore (eds), *The Feminist Reader: Essays in Gender and the Politics of Literary Criticism* (London: Macmillan, 1989).

Heilbrun, Carolyn, *Writing a Woman's Life* (New York: Ballantine Books, 1988).

Kitzinger, Celia and Sue Wilkinson (eds), *Representing the Other* (London: Sage 1996).

Marcus, Laura, *Auto/biographical Discourses: Theory, Criticism, Practice* (Manchester: Manchester University Press, 1994).

Montefiore, Jan, 'Sylvia Townsend Warner, Authority and the Biographer's Moral Sense', in David Ellis (ed.), *Imitating Art: Essays in Biography* (London: Pluto Press, 1993).

Stanley, Liz, *The Auto/biographical I: The Theory and Practice of Feminist Auto/biography* (Manchester: Manchester University Press, 1992).

Stanley, Liz, 'Feminist Auto/biography and Feminist Epistemology', in Jane Aaron and Sylvia Walby (eds), *Out of the Margins: Women's Studies in the Nineties* (London: Falmer Press, 1991).

Stanton, Domna (ed.), *The Female Autograph: Theory and Practice of Autobiography from the Tenth to theTwentieth Century* (Chicago and London: University of Chicago Press, 1984).

Steedman, Carole, *Past Tenses* (London: Rivers Oram Press, 1992).

Swindells, Julia (ed.), *The Uses of Autobiography* (London: Taylor & Francis, 1995).

Woolf, Virginia, 'The New Biography', *Collected Essays Volume IV*, ed. Leonard Woolf (London: Chatto and Windus, 1967).

Sexuality–Politics

Allen, Jeffner, *Sinuosities: Lesbian Poetic Politics* (Bloomington: Indiana University Press, 1996).

Bland, Lucy, *Banishing the Beast: English Feminism and Sexual Morality 1885–1914* (Harmondsworth: Penguin, 1995).

Brittain, Vera, *Radclyffe Hall: A Case of Obscenity* (London: Femina Press, 1968).

Cooper, Emmanuel, *The Sexual Perspective: Homosexuality and Art in the Last 100 Years in the West* (London: Routledge & Kegan Paul, 1994).

Davis, Jill, ' "This Be Different": The Lesbian Drama of Mrs Havelock Ellis', *Women: A Cultural Review*, 2.2, summer 1991, pp. 134–88.

Dollimore, Jonathan, *Sexual Dissidence: Augustine to Wilde, Freud to Foucault* (Oxford: Clarendon Press, 1991).

Duberman, Martin, Martha Vicinus and George Chauncey Jr (eds), *Hidden from History: Reclaiming the Gay and Lesbian Past* (Harmondsworth: Penguin, 1991).

Foucault, Michel, *The History of Sexuality Volume I*, 1976 (Harmondsworth: Penguin, 1990).

Glasgow, Joanne and Karla Jay (eds), *Lesbian Texts and Contexts: Radical Revisions*, 1990 (London: Onlywomen Press, 1992).

Griffin, Gabriele, *Heavenly Love? Lesbian Images in Twentieth-Century Women's Writing* (Manchester: Manchester University Press, 1993).

Jeffreys, Sheila, *The Spinster and Her Enemies: Feminism and Sexuality 1880–1930* (London: Pandora Press, 1985).

Jeffreys, Sheila, *Anti-Climax: A Feminist Perspective on the Sexual Revolution* (London: Women's Press, 1990).

Meese, Elizabeth, 'Theorising Lesbian', in Karla Jay and Joanne Glasgow (eds), *Lesbian Texts and Contexts: Radical Revisions* (New York: New York University Press, 1990).

Newton, Esther, 'The Mythic Mannish Lesbian: Radclyffe Hall and the New Woman', in Martin Duberman, *Hidden from History: Reclaiming the Gay and Lesbian Past* (Harmondsworth: Penguin, 1991), pp. 281–93.

Rowbotham, Sheila and Jeffrey Weeks, *Socialism and the New Life: The Personal and Sexual Politics of Edward Carpenter and Havelock Ellis* (London: Pluto Press, 1977).

Schor, Naomi and Elizabeth Weed (eds), *Differences: More Gender Trouble; Feminism Meets Queer Theory*, summer–fall, 1994.

Sinfield, Alan, *The Wilde Century* (London: Cassell, 1994).

Vicinus, Martha (ed.), *Lesbian Subjects: A Feminist Studies Reader* (Bloomington: Indiana University Press, 1996).

Weeks, Jeffrey, *Coming Out: Homosexual Politics in Britain from the Nineteenth Century to the Present* (London: Quartet Books, 1977).

INDEX

'EC' denotes Edith Craig.